# ADVANCE PRAISE FOR
## *THIS WAY DAYBREAK COMES*

*"The planet is in danger, but few know what to do. Here is the inspiring story of some individual women who do know what to do."*
Gerald Barney, Director,
Global 2000 Report to the President

*"The remarkable thing about* This Way Daybreak Comes *is its zeal, which is no small feat in itself. Cheatham and Powell have set a precedent!*

*"It is not easy putting together a new enterprise, be it a TV sitcom, marketing concept or a book, but when there is a special love of labor and a cast of thousands, it can be accomplished—only because everyone cooperated. Therefore, probably no decision was as important as the selection of the women involved. In my opinion, this inspiring book is a MUST!"*
Michaela Walsh, President,
Women's World Banking

*"This work culminates four years of dedication and love toward a task borne of the individual and collective vision of women across this country. No one interested in the future should fail to pay close attention to the insight and challenge presented by Annie Cheatham and Mary Clare Powell."*
Senator Albert Gore,
United State Senate

*"Many books and articles accurately report the hardships under which women live and these writings are necessary to the process of righting the wrongs in United States society. But* This Way Daybreak Comes *does something more. Women are not waiting until injustices are corrected to create "life-giving futures." Mary Clare Powell and Annie Cheatham affirm the efforts of a thousand women who are involved in changing the ways they relate to each other, who are creating the physical spaces they need; and who pursue world peace, because they feel nuclear weapons are the greatest threat to our future. The descriptions of the extensive work* ⋯ *to improve the quality of life in their neighborhood* ⋯ *will cause many women to say, 'I ca* ⋯ *The sun is rising!' "*

THIS WAY
DAYBREAK
COMES

**new society publishers**
philadelphia, pa

ANNIE CHEATHAM & MARY CLARE POWELL

# THIS WAY DAYBREAK COMES:

## Women's Values and the Future

Afterword by Gloria Anzaldúa

Inquiries regarding request to republish all or part of *This Way Daybreak Comes: Women's Values and the Future* should be addressed to:

New Society Publishers
4722 Baltimore Avenue
Philadelphia, PA 19143

ISBN: 0-86571-069-4 Paperback
0-86571-070-8 Hardcover
Printed in the United States.
Front Cover Design by Mara Loft

New Society Publishers is a project of the New Society Educational Foundation and a collective of Movement for a New Society. New Society Educational Foundation is a non-profit, tax-exempt public foundation. Movement for a New Society is a network of small groups and individuals working for fundamental social change through non-violent action. To learn more about MNS, write: Movement for a New Society, 4722 Baltimore Avenue, Philadelphia PA 19143. Opinions expressed in this book do not necessarily represent positions of either the New Society Educational Foundation or Movement for a New Society.

# FOR WINNIE MANDELA

Black South African activist who, in spite of over twenty years of police harassment, imprisonment, and banning, has resisted, organized, and stood for life in one of the world's most repressive countries.

We salute your courage to withstand oppression and to work for a free and just society. Even though your window on the world is restricted, your vision for a future safe for all people is broad. We and all your sisters join you in your determination to live.

FOR WINNIE MANDELA

# CONTENTS

# ACKNOWLEDGMENTS

Now we understand why many acknowledgments begin, "Hundreds of people helped produce this book." It is true. Four and a half years ago when we began, we had only a vague idea about where the Future is Female Project would lead. Today, we sit in our office in Northampton, Massachusetts and marvel at the boxes of correspondence, file cards, photographs, computer diskettes, and manuscript drafts that represent the women who have filled our minds and hearts.

This book project had two parts—research and writing—and each part had particular needs which were always met by generous and loving people. To those who participated in the two years of research, we are grateful.

To our Washington, D.C. friends who met with us in the spring of 1981, and helped us define the project's purpose:

Norrie Huddle, Vera Pierce, Verna Dozier, Laurel Schneider, Linda Donald, Sonya Dyer, Emily Benson, Karen Rosenblum, Ronnie Fiet, Juanita Weaver, Rita Goldman, Sarna Marcus, Tina Lunson, Jane Leiper, Marilyn Gadzuk, Scarlet Cheng, Maxine Thornton-Denham, Joyce Angell, Eileen Harrington, Mary Carol Dragoo, Janice Sanchez.

To the women artists who contributed their work for our traveling art exhibit:

Deborah Vanko, Austin, Texas; Roberta Ain, Washington, D.C.; Joan E. Biren, Washington, D.C.; Scarlet Cheng, Arlington, Virginia; Diane Ayott, Cambridge, Massachusetts; Rosanne Colvard, Crofton, Maryland; Nancy Cusick, Falls Church, Virginia; Kyrie Dragoo, Bethesda, Maryland; Ann Gibson, Hatfield, Massachusetts; Dana Gordon, New York, New York; Pat Helsing, Washington, D.C.; Arlette Jassell, Bethesda, Maryland; Ann Langdon, New Haven, Connecticut; Sarna Marcus, Takoma Park, Maryland; Jana Morgana, Falls Church, Virginia; Margaret Paris, Bethesda, Maryland; Leslie Phillips, McLean, Virginia; Gail Rebhan, Washington, D.C.; Jean Rutka, Washington, D.C.; Daphne Shuttleworth, Washington, D.C.; Alice Sims, Falls Church, Virginia; Menucha, Rockville, Maryland; Lyndia Terre, Alexandria, Virginia; Rosie Thompson, Hillsborough, North Carolina; Elizabeth Vail, Bethesda, Maryland; Claudia Vess, Washington, D.C.; Noreen Wells, Takoma Park, Maryland; Jo Wright Whitten, Rochester, New York; Alison Days, New Haven, Connecticut.

To the women who arranged group meetings as we traveled, during which we looked at art and talked about women's images, or simply shared information about different projects and life decisions:

Colleen Sterling and Laura Catanzaro, Cambridge, Massachusetts; Anne Wiseman, Cambridge, Massachusetts; Ann Brown, Marblehead, Massachusetts; Vicki Hovde, Amherst, Massachusetts; Roz Payne, Burlington, Vermont; Ann Gibson, Hatfield, Massachusetts; Betsy Feick, Northampton, Massachusetts; Elizabeth Vail, Washington, D.C.; Ann Langdon, New Haven, Connecticut; Nona Diamond and Elin Menzies, Palenville, New York; Meg Walker, Burlington, Vermont; Janet Braun-Reinitz, Ithaca, New York; Arleen Hartman, Cleveland, Ohio; Kit Dorsey and Mary Zuiderveen, Grand Rapids, Michigan; Becky Neely, Champaign, Illinois; Gail Riordan, Milwaukee, Wisconsin; Lorene Senesac and Nan Parsons, Basin, Montana; Joan Tucker, Seattle, Washington; Faedra Kosh and Hollis Giammatteo, Seattle, Washington; Louise Grout, Issaquah, Washington; Yolanda Retter, Los Angeles, California; Janet Burdick, Claremont, California; Joanne Kerr, San Diego, California; Skip and Judy Spensley, Boulder, Colorado; Helen Redman, Denver, Colorado; Elaine Langerman, Denver, Colorado; Peggy Feerick, Albuquerque, New Mexico; Dorothy Austin, Austin, Texas; Ginger Bloomer, Austin, Texas; Lavender and Barbara, St. Augustine, Florida; Sue Fisher and Peggy Myers, Knoxville, Tennessee; Carol Crystal and the Dykes of Hoboken, Hoboken, New Jersey; Robin Moulds, Louisa, Virginia.

Research is impossible without money, shelter, food, and clothing. We financed the project ourselves, but many people made donations. We are grateful to all the giftgivers.

To those who gave us money, and especially to Cathy Fort, Robert Sargent, Barbara Peck, and Sr. Marian McAvoy of the Sisters of Loretto who gave us low-interest loans. And to all the others who made contributions or gave other gifts—rolls of stamps, freshly baked cinnamon rolls, clothes, pots and pans, massages, haircuts:

Arleen Hartman, Cleveland, Ohio; Margaret Honton, Columbus, Ohio; Tess and Susan Wiseheart, Grand Rapids, Michigan; Linda Smith, Grand Rapids, Michigan; Jenna Weston, Grand Rapids, Michigan; Pam Armour and Hildy White, Concord, Massachusetts; Christine Hahn, Iowa City, Iowa; Jimmie Reams, Jacksonville, Florida; Kay Pulliam, Elkhart, Indiana; Anjie Hoogterp, Grand Rapids, Michigan; Becky Neely, Champaign, Illinois; Jane Boyer, Chicago, Illinois; Candis Ahrendt, Milwaukee, Wisconsin; Meg Walker and the Vermont Women's Caucus for Art, Burlington, Vermont; Olivia Edmonson, Smithfield, North Carolina; Ben and Tillie Hovde, Del Rapids, South Dakota; Wilma Needham, Banff, Alberta, Canada; Nancy Mathieson, Helena, Montana; Jane Holding, Smithfield, North Carolina; Virginia Harris, Smithfield, North Carolina; Ann Langdon, New Haven, Connecticut; Rhandi Rachlis, Basin, Montana; Susan Graetz, Ithaca, New York; Sister Jane Richardson, Nerinx, Kentucky; Jay (Wattles) Goldspinner, Worcester, Massachusetts; Linda Schierman, Seattle, Washington; Nan Day, Seattle, Washington; Louise Grout, Issaquah, Washington; Gail Fairfield and Kay Ries, Seattle, Washington; Miriam Handler, Eugene, Oregon; Elizabeth Wright Ingraham, Colorado Springs, Colorado; Estelle Chacon, San Diego, California; Gwenyth Lewis, Albuquerque, New Mexico; Jennifer Thompson and Kathleen Coyne, Austin, Texas; Sue Williams ("Rainbow"), Winter Park Florida; Julia Jordan, Washington, D.C.; Lenora Trussell, Washington, D.C.; Marilyn Gadzuk, Gaithersburg, Maryland; The Seekers Faith Community, Church of the Savior, Washington, D.C.; Bread and Roses Church, Washington, D.C.; Owen and Priscilla Goldfarb, Troy, New York; Sandra de Sylvia, Greenfield, Massachusetts; Elizabeth Knowlton, Atlanta, Georgia; Rebecca Harrington, Washington, D.C.; Maureen Newton, Roanoke, Virginia; Caroline Krebs, Brooklyn, New York; Pat Christy, Santa Fe, New Mexico; Carol Bruce, Oakton, Virginia; Sidney Oliver, Washington, D.C.; Virginia, Ken, Staci, and Shani Cooley, Front Royal, Virginia; Chris Herdell and Anne Plunkett, Luray, Virginia; Clara Lopez, Vicky Opperman, Robin Moulds, Lisa Fusco, Lisa Gershuny, and Tammy Reid—our housemates in Northampton, Massachusetts; Emma Missouri and Butterfly Arts, Northampton, Massachusetts;

Mary Hunt, Diane Neu, and WATER, Silver Spring, Maryland;
Mary Kenny, Northampton, Massachusetts; Christine Ratzel,
Amherst, Massachusetts; Sandy Lovejoy and Barbara Reinhold,
Easthampton, Massachusetts.

Throughout this project, we have relied on others for shelter. We
especially thank Sisters Jean, Letitia, and Dorcas of the Dekoven
Foundation for sheltering us in Racine, Wisconsin after our van was
stolen in Chicago. We stayed with them for nine days while our van
and spirits were repaired. When we left, they outfitted us with many
items that had been stolen. Charlotte Bunch gave us her Front Royal,
Virginia house to live in while we wrote the book. It was our first home
in three years. For all of you who gave us places to stay, we offer thanks:

Colleen Sterling and Laura Catanzaro, Cambridge, Massachu-
setts; Ann Gibson and Melissa Tefft, Hatfield, Massachusetts;
Lois Foley, Essex Junction, Vermont; Carol Fitch, Bethesda,
Maryland; Lenora Trussell, Washington, D.C.; Ann Langdon and
Drew, Alison, and Elizabeth Days; Joan Sprague, Newport,
Rhode Island; Nona Diamond and Elin Menzies, Palenville, New
York; Ellie and Ned Pattison, West Sand Lake, New York; Janet
Braun-Reinitz, Ithaca, New York; Phillipa Proudfoot and
Autumn W. Craft, Rochester, New York; Bev and Gordon
Rodrigue, Toronto, Ontario, Canada; Nora Cline, Pittsburgh,
Pennsylvania; Arleen Hartman, Cleveland, Ohio; Margaret
Honton, Columbus, Ohio; Jenna Weston and Jo Olszewska,
Grand Rapids, Michigan; Kit Dorsey and Mary Zuiderveen,
Grand Rapids, Michigan; Mary Appelhoff and Mary Frances
Fenton, Kalamazoo, Michigan; Kay and Mike Pulliam, Elkhart,
Indiana; Jane Boyer, Chicago, Illinois; Yolanda Tarango,
Chicago, Illinois; Martha Boesing and Phyllis Rose, Minneapolis,
Minnesota; Tom and Ming Bedell, Spirit Lake, Iowa; Ben and
Tillie Hovde, Del Rapids, South Dakota; Rhandi Rachlis, Basin,
Montana; Lorene Senesac and Nan Parsons, Basin, Montana;
Diane Sands and Sally, Missoula, Montana; Richard Dunnough,
Missoula, Montana; Don and Lillian Kocher, Vancouver, British
Columbia, Canada; Faedra Kosh and Hollis Giammatteo, Seattle,
Washington; Louise Grout, Issaquah, Washington; Mary Lee
Nicholson and Barb Nachman, Eagle River, Alaska; Miriam
Handler, Eugene, Oregon; Ruth and Jean Mountaingrove, Wolf
Creek, Oregon; Jeff, Sarah, and Heather Wentworth, South Lake
Tahoe, California; Jean and Dave McKeen, Yuba City,
California; Winnie Tang, Al Wong, and Serena, San Francisco,
California; Betsy and Keith Smith, Derek and Cameron, Fresno,
California; Sister Elizabeth Thoman, Los Angeles, California;
Janet Burdick and Scott Miller, Claremont, California; Jan Aust-
Schminke, Costa Mesa, California; Anne Ewing, San Diego,
California; Anne Wilson Schaef and Diane Fassel, Boulder,
Colorado; Sister Lydia Peña, Denver, Colorado; Peggy Feerick,

Albuquerque, New Mexico; Sister Anne Greenslade and Sisters of Loretto, El Paso, Texas; Jennifer Thompson and Kathleen Coyne, Austin, Texas; Elana Freedom and Elizabeth Freeman, Durham, North Carolina; Rosemary Curb, Winter Park, Florida; Women of the Pagoda (especially Barbara, Lavender, Edith, and Alethia), St. Augustine, Florida; Agnes Davey, Tallahassee, Florida; Hazel Henderson, Gainesville, Florida; Women of the ALFA House, Atlanta, Georgia; Eleanor McCallie and Mel Cooper, Chattanooga, Tennessee; Sue Fisher and Peggy Myers, Knoxville, Tennessee; Maureen Newton, Roanoke, Virginia; Sister Paulette Peterson, New York, New York.

To the one thousand women who talked into our tape recorder, who told their stories by showing their art, who came to group sessions, who walked us around their land or houses or sidewalks and said who they were. Many of the women we met aren't even in this book but their voices inform it. To all of you, we express enormous appreciation for your willingness to stop and talk with us, for your life and work.

After we finished interviewing and traveling, it took us two more years to write the book. Another group of people entered our lives to help us complete it. We are grateful to these people:

To William Zinsser, author of *On Writing Well*, for lessons on how to build simple, clear sentences. We were novice writers, and Zinsser, without knowing it, became our teacher. We thank him for his well-written book about writing well.

To Kathe McCleave, our Illinois editor, who was the first person to see the whole book. She saw discontinuities when we saw none, unclear sentences when we fully understood, and mismatched chapters when we thought we had one whole. Her good eye and sensible, Midwestern mind kept us honest and true to the task.

To Taylor and others at the Twin Oaks Community in Louisa, Virginia, who contributed the Index; to Susan Moore, the calligrapher who so painstakingly lettered the title; and especially to Mara Loft who labored over the cover design, taking time to design it *with* us.

To Nina Huizinga of New Society Publishers who visited us in Virginia mid-way through the writing and helped us take a needed break, extend our unrealistic deadline, and move to Massachusetts where we had a larger support system. At a critical time, she urged us to break through a logjam, and move on.

As in any project of this magnitude, several people were our core supporters. Their love and friendship sustained us when we were homeless, exhausted, and broke. To these people, we offer special thanks:

To Lois and Kenny Stewart who gave Mary Clare a place to heal after a particularly painful period with Annie. To Ursula Ording and Trina

McCormick who later gave her a home on the rocky coast of Massachusetts. Judy McLamb and Jean Stabell offered Annie solace and love while she recovered from burn-out in New Salem, Massachusetts. Sandra de Sylvia, Lydia Savasten, Carol Fitch, Margaret Kierstein, and Martha Ayers gave hours of therapy sessions and helped us move through one crisis after another. All of these people helped us restore perspective about our individual lives and our relationship, appreciate the difficulty of our task, and continue to do it.

To Anne Wilson, Annie's mother, who died half way through the project. From her death came the money to complete the book and to live for two years without income. We thank her and Annie's father, James, ordinary people and not wealthy, for the years of saving for their children's future. Little did they know that they would help fund a book about women and the future.

To Mary Clare's mother, Ruth, for her quiet support and acceptance throughout this four-year project. Many times she made room in her house and life for one or both of us to crash, to cry, to rest from the road or from each other. She stored many of our possessions and always graciously moved over to let us in.

To Ann Gibson, who has been involved in this project from the beginning. She was our road manager during the trip—home base, telephone number, contact person. Our mothers called her to find out where we were. She was bookkeeper, card file organizer, graphics designer, and the coordinator who assembled and mailed three thousand "Future is Female" newsletters. When we stopped traveling and started writing, she read drafts fresh from the computer, gave feedback, massages, sent colorful cards and banners for encouragement. She has been our most constant and present supporter.

And finally, we thank each other. I, Annie, thank you, Mary Clare, for your energy and enthusiasm, for teaching me about feminism and women's issues. Thank you for telling me over and over the meaning of a concept, for digging around in secondary sources, for your love of interviewing and insistence that we stay with each woman until some "meeting" happened. Your instincts and wisdom have deepened and enriched this book beyond measure.

I, Mary Clare, am grateful to you, Annie, for generating the underlying idea for the whole project, for holding the vision, for perseverance in spite of exhaustion, and for your futures perspective. Thank you for keeping us organized—our van home, our files, the writing of chapters—and for being such a bridge builder, insisting that we send newsletters and updates to women in our network. I'm grateful for your commitment to the women we met, your respect for them and their material. Thanks for pushing me to write clearly, for your willingness to write twenty drafts when I would have been content with two, for your wonderful, clear writing style, and your deep commitment to communicating.

Our gratitude is boundless. Even though we initiated the project without institutional support or financial backing, even though we used our own resources throughout, we have not been alone. Hundreds of you have shared our vision and believed in us. We offer this book as our expression of thanks.

# Introduction

**W**omen are creating a new society. We are using intellect, intuition, politics, magic, and art to restructure existing institutions and invent new ones. We are working quietly, persistently, vigorously. Most of us don't understand the consequences of our efforts. Many feel alone. This book is intended to introduce us to each other so we can grasp the magnitude of the changes we are fashioning in the present and comprehend the significance of those changes for the future.

Women are intimately involved with life—birth, death, peacemaking, governing, gardening, artmaking. We are harvesters, teachers, scientists, witches, and mediators. We invent, nurse, counsel, cook, design, and administer. Life-loving values, socialized as "female," are not exclusive to women. Many men exhibit them, and some women don't. But the traits relegated to women as unnecessary or unworthy of men—e.g., flexibility, receptivity, nurturing, reverence for life, cooperativeness— are turning out to be the very qualities necessary for sustenance of life on this planet. Therefore, if we are going to have a future world different from the one we have now—i.e., a world safe to live in— women are the best hope for getting us there.

In 1981, we left our home, friends, jobs, and dog, and traveled for two years across 30,000 miles of Canada and the United States to search for women who are leading us along paths to this new society. We called our project "The Future is Female."

Before we began, Annie was Director of the Congressional Clearinghouse on the Future in the U.S. Congress, and Mary Clare was a feminist artist and teacher. As bridge builders and creators, both generalists, we sought a broad sample of women, so we mailed press releases to six hundred publications—new age, women's, arts, futures. Hundreds of women responded or were recommended by others, and as we traveled we collected more names—three thousand in all. Over a two year period, we interviewed, individually or in groups, approximately one thousand women. In spite of our project's scope, this book represents only a small number of women who are creating a new society.

We aren't scholars, so our journey was not an academic research project. We relied on an intuitive, inductive interview method. We had no prepared list of questions, no outline for a book. If a woman nominated herself or was suggested by someone else, we wondered why and stayed with her until we knew. We were looking for examples of innovative organizations, creative ideas, and positive life choices, and we followed leads as they were given. In the end, being non-academics was a blessing and a curse. It was a curse because we wasted a lot of time figuring out what we were doing. It was a blessing because we didn't exclude anyone because they didn't fit our thesis.

We met all kinds of women—inner city dwellers and farmers, church ministers and psychics, leaders of radical grassroots organizations and Congresswomen, scientists and steelworkers. We also met over two hundred artists. Unlike other women, they often work nonverbally to convey their visions for a new society. Their vital images are revealed through dance, song, theater, and mime as well as in drawings, paintings, and sculpture. In every medium, women artists are demonstrating an incredible fertility of mind, heart, and spirit and an absolute devotion to the creative process and to its ability to heal and transform. This book is illustrated by over fifty of their images.

Throughout the project, we looked for the good news. Some critics will say our decision to write a book devoid of breakdowns was naive, but we are not unconscious. We know the troubles. We know that relationships, building projects, coalitions, and peace initiatives fail. We know that racism eats away at everyone's freedom, that class, educational privilege, and physical ability divide us. We know the intolerance and splits in women's communities—divisions between lesbians and non-lesbians, between radical feminists and non-feminists, between anti-pornography groups and women who advocate total sexual freedom.

Women are not perfect, ideal. We distrust and criticize each other, compete, fear change. We don't always reach beyond what is known and comfortable. We label each other with polarizing definitions. Still, we all experience oppression and a longing for life. And most of us, in one form or another, are working for the same goal—a future safe for ourselves, our children, our companions, and all other life forms on the planet.

In the book, we talk about women as though we speak for all women. Of course, we can't. We are limited by who we are and what we have experienced. Since we are both white, middle-aged, middle-class, United States lesbians, we see the world differently from black, Hispanic, Asian, native American, Jewish, older, poor, widowed, differently abled, and married women. Yet, in every chapter, we have written, "Women are."

We do not mean that all women share the same mind, heart, culture, history, or vision. We imagine no melting pot called "women." On the contrary, we celebrate the diversity of women's paths. But we acknowledge the oneness of womankind, not only in our common oppression, but in our yearning for life. Therefore, when we say "Women are," we affirm our bond with other women, and assert our belief that women, as a group, are the planet's best hope for survival.

We believe this because the innovative and brave individuals we met base most of their decisions on two fundamental assumptions. First, *women take the "self" as their major reference point*. Everywhere, they are questioning authority—of governments and social service agencies failing to serve; of religions and holy books that demean women; of the customs, mores, practices, and assumptions about women in a misogynic culture. They are silencing internalized messages that insinuate, "You are inferior and weak, inadequate for public life, powerless," and listening, instead, to their deepest, inner voices. By paying attention to images and impulses, and naming their reality, women are taking utterly seriously their own wisdom.

The second assumption builds on the first: *the "self" is the major reference point only in the context of connectedness*. Women we interviewed don't apply for membership in the "cult of narcissism." Taking the "self" as authority does not lead them to "me first" or "me only" attitudes. It leads to an acknowledgement of profound relatedness—to oneself, to nature, and to others. They want planetary resources to be shared; they respect ecological interdependence; they know that what happens to one affects all. Women take the "self" as the major reference point, but they affirm that the "self" is inextricably bound to, and one with, all of life.

We drove thousands of miles to meet women who are regularly ignored by the Associated Press and United Press International. Their stories are rarely, if ever, reported; "PM Magazine" doesn't know they exist. But anonymity doesn't stop them. They launch new ventures every day. It was all we could do to keep up.

• A New Hampshire woman arranges face-to-face meetings between Americans and Russians so they can know each other directly. *Women are bringing about world peace through international understanding.*

• A formerly homeless, alcoholic woman helps low-income families stay together by finding housing for them in Washington, D.C. *Women are*

*working on the local level, in towns and neighborhoods, because they believe the center is there.*
• A worm farmer in Michigan teaches others the chemistry of recycling garbage at home. *Women are restoring the balance between humans and all other planetary life.*
• A U.S. Congresswoman, in the minority, builds coalitions with majority Members to ensure that items on the women's agenda are debated in the nation's policy making chambers. *Women are altering the processes of government.*
• A Massachusetts architect and urban planner converts abandoned buildings into low-income housing with built-in employment opportunities and child care facilities. *Women are restructuring the built environment.*
• A Vancouver woman's family includes the thirty-odd members of her community collective. *Women are creating families with people other than blood kin. In the process, they are redefining family.*
• A Virginia woman teaches Head Start children, elders, prisoners, and families in crisis to analyze their dreams for healing and transformation. *Women are focusing on their most interior voices—dreams, hunches, psychic voices—and teaching others to listen.*
• Seven Florida women form a collective in which each woman's role is based on her gifts and inclinations. One woman is the "dreamer" for the group. *Women are working together efficiently and respectfully.*
• A New York City artist plans to convert New York's Bryant Park into "A Living Library" where the interconnections between plants, animals, and humans can be celebrated. *Women are creating art and displaying it everywhere—in streets, on sides of buildings, from the air—and it is changing minds and hearts.*

Evidence is clear, available, and abundant that women are creating a new society. We are reshaping every facet of life—international relations, family, work, politics, culture. We are shedding malignant sexist, racist, and classist attitudes and reestablishing our connection with plants, animals, and all other human beings on the planet. We are moving out of restrictive "women's arenas" and into every arena, redefining social structures, inventing alternatives, and changing the rules of every game.

And not a minute too soon. Women understand that our planet is in danger. Disruptions abound. Unions are broken, babies beaten, killers killed. The gap between rich and poor widens while nuclear weapons, poised to destroy everything, hide in underground silos and submarines. The international economy hovers near chaos, with most world governments financed by deficit spending. Technological breakthroughs continue unabated and without comment while legal pundits define life—when it starts, when it ends, what it's worth. Lives of factory workers seem interchangeable as machine parts, and lives of starving millions don't seem worth much at all. Toxic wastes seep into ground-water systems, and burgeoning populations in the Third

World denude forests for firewood. Animal species vanish while scientific geniuses manufacture and patent new life forms.

Everything seems upside down. The future mixes with the present—high-tech inventions co-exist with abject poverty. Extremists have a heyday; suspicion runs rampant; worse-case scenarios sound entirely plausible. Competition for limited resources; environmental abuse; attitudes of racial, gender, class, national, or religious superiority; and angry, nuclear posturing are getting us nowhere fast. Many of us stand, confused and paralyzed, with one foot mired in yesterday and the other straining toward tomorrow.

We ask experts for help—prophets, seers who name the trends. Every era has them. Our own busy bunch does its best to satisfy, publishing books, magazines, and newsletters. We hang onto every word. When Alvin Toffler said we suffered from "future shock," we examined ourselves for symptoms. When Fritjof Capra plotted a "turning point," we rushed to see where we fitted on the curve. And when John Naisbitt pointed to ten "megatrends" shaping society, we kept his book on the bestseller list for sixty-three weeks.

But descriptions about the future don't help us live differently day-to-day. Hadley Smith, currently doing research in human systems design, uses a cafeteria metaphor to describe what's needed. "The culture is set up for us to go down the line with our trays," she said, "and pick out what we want on the basis of impulse and instant appeal. 'I love brussels sprouts.' 'Give me three of those.' 'I think I'll have a salad.' We're encouraged to pick and choose, to be consumers, dependent on products and status for our sense of self-worth. But we must teach ourselves to jump over to the other side of the cafeteria line where all the goodies are made. There, we become creators and providers of new options for ourselves and others. It's more complicated to live on that side, and we don't get immediate satisfaction, but it sure is a lot more fun."

This book is about the future but there are no experts here—only women struggling to live their lives congruent with their values. Standing on the creative side of the cafeteria line, they know that daily decisions create the future. If they want peace in the world, they learn to resolve conflict in their neighborhoods. If they want shared leadership, they share power. If they want to end racism, they acknowledge their own. If they want a renewable energy future, they dry their clothes in the sun. They know the year 2010 isn't "out there," fully formed. Science fiction is fiction, and the future isn't going to "happen" to them. Rather, the future is a result of choices they make every single day.

We undertook the Future is Female Project because we wanted to meet inventive women who are creating new options for us all. Their vibrant voices and art images have filled our lives for over four years now. Their lively and courageous stories fill every page of this book. No task is too challenging for them, no assignment too difficult. They know how to listen to themselves and to others; they know how to resolve conflicts; they know how to govern their love for life, and their persistent demands that it go on, are the propelling forces for the future. Their experiments, musings, and courage defy any doubter's mumblings that women don't know how to change the world. They have taught us, again and again, that there is *nothing* we cannot do.

Annie Cheatham
Mary Clare Powell
Northampton, Massachusetts
June, 1985

# PART I:
## WOMEN RELATE

# 1

# THE WISE WOMAN INSIDE

From every direction, we are told who we are and who we should be. Advertising geniuses on Madison Avenue spend their creative energy convincing us to buy home computers, fast food, and toothpaste. Religious leaders, sex therapists, diet experts, and popular psychologists appear on television talk shows to give directions for living. Articles in monthly magazines quiz readers about preferences, attitudes, and fetishes. The *New York Times* bestseller list is topped by one "how to" book after another.

Labels are tossed around like confetti—yuppies, neo-conservatives, baby boomers, seniors. We file into appropriate slots and do what is expected. We work out, slim down, and jog our bodies into shape. We read book reviews because we don't have time to read books, and we dutifully answer questionnaires, apply self-help theories, follow fashions. Problem is, we forget who we are in Calvin Klein jeans. We become who Calvin Klein wants us to be.

When we forget, we are vulnerable—to merchants and presidents waiting to exploit us. We pursue false goals, feel lonely, get sick. We no longer notice clouds. Our ears can't hear our hearts beat. Our noses can't smell our own scents. We may have arrived in "modern times," and technological wizardry may make all our dreams come true, but we are standing here profoundly alienated from ourselves.

3

"We have all been taught to distrust our own feelings and doubt our ability to deal with our lives," said **Anne Wilson Schaef**, Colorado lecturer, therapist, and author of *Women's Reality*. "Most of us were taught as children not to know what we know, not to feel what we feel, not to see what we see. Maybe our fathers told us we weren't hurt when we lay crying with a skinned knee. Or told us to get up and play when we wanted to feel the hurt. Or our mothers kissed it and said it was better when it wasn't. We internalized the message that we couldn't handle our own process, couldn't trust it. We muffled our inner voices.

"As adults, wanting to be in control of ourselves, we don't let ourselves see what is really going on within us," Anne continued. "We addict ourselves to drugs, alcohol, sex, food—anything that will keep us out of touch with ourselves. Our culture reinforces this denial because it is addicted to death and powerlessness. The best adjusted person in our culture is a zombie—not fully alive, and not yet dead—who listens to all the voices outside and none of those within."

**Jean Tait** used to be one of those people—until she almost died. In March 1982, doctors told her they couldn't cure her cancer. She had two months to live, and she went home to die. "I didn't know what to do," Jean said. "Madeline [a chiropractor] started working with me, and then I found several native American healers who agreed to help me. 'Why do you have cancer?' they asked me over and over. 'Disease is caused by attitude, and cancer is powerful medicine. Why do you have it?' I didn't know.

"Then they asked how I felt about my body. I hated my body. I wanted to be rid of it. 'Everything must be in total balance for total health,' they said. 'How do you stand in connection to other things?' As it turned out, I was out of balance with myself, with my family and friends, with my environment."

Jean's body continued to deteriorate, and one day that summer, in great pain, she thought she was dying. "I was in bed with a high fever," she continued. "I could feel myself slipping into another state of mind. I felt pulled backwards. The pain lessened, and I was euphoric. Then I looked around and saw people I knew who had died. 'I'm dead,' I thought, and I was so happy. I signaled them to help me, wanting to join them, but they shook their heads. I tried to run toward them, but my legs were stuck, like in mud, and I couldn't move.

"Slowly, I returned to the awareness that I was in my own bed, and I got terribly depressed. I had wanted so much to die. Instead, the message was, 'You want to go there, but they don't want you. So you're stuck here, sick or not. You'd better get well.' Within a week, my liver, spleen, and kidneys all began to improve. I decided that if I had to live, I wanted to be well." When Jean went to the oncologist in August, five months later, her cancer was gone.

Many women, refugees from media hype and fashion fads, are turning down the volume on radios and televisions and turning up the volume on inner wisdom. They are pasting "Question Authority" bumper stickers on their cars and minds, and they are taking sexual, spiritual, and psychic authority from inside. As they name their reality as women, they are teaching each other methods for paying attention and for healing from the inside out. "Our internal life process goes on unfolding," Anne Schaef concluded. "If we trust it, it will unfold more readily. If we stop and deal with what comes up in us, we can live more freely in the present."

## Listening From The Inside

**Jean Erlbaum,** yoga teacher in western Massachusetts, knows the truth of that. Like Jean Tait, she paid attention when she got sick. "I was very ill with colitis," she said, "and then I learned Hatha yoga. I practiced it regularly, and got well." When she saw other people suffering physically and spiritually, she decided to become a teacher. "It's painful when I don't share something that I have been given," she said. "If I don't, I get sick." What she shares are the techniques that work best for her—relaxation, yoga, self healing, breathing, Womancraft meditations.

And her insights. In the late 1970s, Jean lived in a spiritual community where members believed quiet meditation was the way to change. But she was also doing political work with feminists who believed the way to change was through direct action. Jean felt the pinch when both groups pressured her to be more fully on their "side." "I *knew*, from the inside of me, that politics and spirituality came from the same place," she said, "and soon I had to share it." She decided to write several articles about the dilemma, but no words came.

"I kept putting off writing because I wanted a vacation," Jean continued. "Then I got headaches, so I began. I wrote the first article with my foot on the brake and the gas at the same time, and I wasn't satisfied with it. But the second one, I just let come through. It was like taking a shit. It felt great. And it was a good article."

Jean talked about herself as though she were a channel. "I listen to God, Goddess, spirit moving me, life force," she said. "It feels big like a rushing river. It's not rationally based, and it comes from the inside out. When I was younger, I learned it worked for me, and for the last ten-fifteen years, I've felt propelled from the inside out. Of course, I kick and scream against it sometimes, but there is nothing more delicious than when I feel myself on the right path. It's like an ongoing process of *coming home*. And when I come home to myself, I open my heart and have compassion for everybody else."

What messages are coming from your inside now?"

"Slow down in my work."

"How do you know to slow down?"

"In December, I got a clear message to take six weeks off."

"Doing what?"

"I don't know."

"How will you support yourself?"

"I don't know."
"Is it scary?"
"Yes."
"Will you do it?"
"Yes, I have to."
Many women are feeling this compulsion to act from the inside out,
to shift, change, and adapt because of inner promptings. Some are
discovering it through body work. They embrace their bodies' cycles,
maladies, sexual impulses, hungers, and pain. They don't strive for
storybook measurements or Hollywood fantasies of beauty. They reject
the mixed sexual messages from Larry Flynt, on the one hand, and Jerry
Falwell, on the other. For them, the body is the ground of their being,
a source of deep knowing.

**Betty Dodson** is one of them. She became a sex teacher because she
was curious about her body. During sexual consciousness-raising groups
in the early 1970s, she was restless. "We were sitting around in circles,
talking and talking," she said. "Sex was hanging everybody up. We
couldn't talk about it; many of us weren't having orgasms. There were
a lot of sexual problems. So, I decided to open the can of worms."

Betty had no "teacher training." She followed her instincts, offered
classes in her New York City apartment, and discussed issues she wanted
to talk about. Since 1975, over five thousand women have explored
their sexuality in her Body/Sex Groups. "My workshops are conducted
in the nude," Betty said. "I begin with yoga or breathing exercises or
massages to get everybody relaxed. We look at and talk about our
genitals—how we feel about them and why. We discuss orgasms. Many
women don't have any sexual imagery; they don't know what an orgasm
looks like. 'What is an orgasm?' they ask. 'I'll show you,' I say, and
they sit and watch me. I teach women about orgasm by masturbating
to orgasm."

In *Selflove and Orgasm*, Betty wrote, "It is time to stop insisting
upon the romantic ideal of having all of our orgasms from Romeo's
cock inside of Juliet's cunt. If a woman can stimulate herself to orgasm,
she is orgasmic. 'Frigid' is a man's word for a woman who cannot have
an orgasm in the missionary position in a few minutes with only the
kind of stimulation that is good for him."[1]

Betty whole-heartedly insists that women be "cunt positive," use
masturbation as meditation, savor erotic drawings and paintings. And
most of all, she encourages us to have fun. "Sex is our core," she said,
"the life force. When sexual self-expression opens up, we relate
differently to ourselves and to others."

**Jacqueline Livingston**, Ithaca photographer, found out what Betty
meant. During a cervical exam, her doctor asked her if she'd ever looked
at her genitals. She hadn't. When he provided a hand-held mirror,
Jacqueline was enthralled. "The image I had been taught of my sex

Toby Z. Liederman. Untitled Sculpture. 1983. Clay.

being nasty and dirty was dispelled in one steadfast gaze,'' she wrote. ''I was pink, clean, and pretty inside!''[2]

She phoned women friends, arranged a ''genital show and tell'' session, and photographed female genitalia for the first time. ''Our colorations were unique,'' she continued, ''ranging from light pinks to delicate mauves, lavenders to deep purples. The sizes and shapes of vulva, its labia, clitoris, and vaginal opening all varied as much as our facial features. We were delighted in our differing forms of beauty.''[3]

**Parameswari Hhan** uses belly dance to keep in touch with her spiritual, sexual core. ''The belly is the center of life for all of us, particularly women,'' Swari said, ''and the universal symbols in belly dancing—snakes, veils, pots, baskets, fire, staffs/canes, swords, and the belly—all emphasize the power of feminine energy. We get in touch with this feminine power, the cycles of the universe, and the flowing energy of the life force through belly dancing. In belly dance, you have to let go, relax, and delight in being a sensual being.''

Swari has witnessed, often enough, the power released through belly dance. In one case, a woman in her dance troupe got pregnant even though doctors had told her she would never conceive. ''She began to lead a dance which I and the other dancers realized, after many performances, was a fertility dance,'' Swari said. ''As time went by, and we performed the dance on many occasions, at least two other women became pregnant in spite of sound birth control, and this one woman also got pregnant and delivered a healthy baby. Her doctor still doesn't understand her success.''

Our bodies are like the earth—rhythmic and cyclical. Vari-colored, textured, damaged, and whole, they suck in light, water, air, and give out, spit, shit, music, laughter, drawings on a wall, blood. As we understand and cherish our bodies, we stop giving Madison Avenue authority to tell us who we are. ''When women believe their bodies are sensual, sexual, and beautiful,'' Swari said, ''they are powerful. And when we know the power of our bodies, from within, we are less likely to let anyone take power over us.''

Betty, Jacqueline, and Swari listen to their bodies, take direction from them. **Ellyn Cowels** takes her cues from dreams. ''I learned to trust my dreams with great difficulty,'' she said, ''but the more attention I paid to them, the more important they grew. It was a matter of taking them seriously.''

She takes them quite seriously. In the early 1980s, she opened the Wholistic Resource Center because a series of dreams told her to. Today, she publishes a newsletter, *Wholeperson Communications*, and with other area teachers, leads workshops on dreams, therapeutic touch, herbs, iridology, humor and healing, and visualizations. The Center serves as a hub for alternative health care in conservative Lynchburg, Virginia.

---

Pat Christy. Goddess Woman Receiving. 1982. Clay.

This work has been a long time coming. "As a child, I was intuitive, but didn't dare talk about it," Ellyn continued. "Later, my husband brought a recurring dream to our marriage. I studied Jung because of his dream, but I never had any of my own. When we divorced, I began to have huge dreams, started taking dreamwork courses, and committed myself to dreams and their healing power. Now I teach people to incubate dreams—pray or meditate before they sleep, focus on what they want to know, and expect an answer. It's all about paying attention to what comes up.

"Dreams are gifts," she added. "They're free, and abundant, like solar energy. The more you love and use them, the more they bless you. Of course, you find some dark things in yourself that you'd rather not know about. But once you start naming those things, *owning them*, then they become a part of you, and you become more whole."

For oppressed and abused people, the process may be terrifying, but Ellyn believes it can heal. "I worked with a young woman who had been seduced by her psychiatrist and ended up in a straitjacket," she said. "As we worked with her dreams, she gradually regained her power. Now she doesn't give it away to anyone, doesn't look for anyone to fix her up. Later, I taught her family how to work together with their dreams, and it was very healing for all of them."

Ellyn wants to establish dream groups at the local Head Start program, with mental patients and residents in nursing homes, in public schools and churches. She talks about the politics of dream work. "Dream groups are empowering because you are sharing material about your life that you have generated out of yourself. Since the source is within and since dreams are in your own language, no one can tamper with them. In addition, it is empowering for individuals to share dreams. It builds trust, and ultimately, it has an impact on social issues. People living from the inside out help to make a better, safer world."

By turning down the external noise, by refusing labels plastered across billboards, by heeding dreams and orgasmic contractions, these women are learning to respect their inner wisdom. Jean Tait and Jean Erlbaum learned when they got sick. Betty Dodson learned because her sex life was unsatisfactory. Ellyn Cowels learned when dreams began to instruct her waking life. Whatever the path, once women tune in they rely more and more on what they know from the inside. As a result, they are less susceptible to external pressures. They find inside not only guidance about how to live, but also power to heal, teach, confront, create.

## The Implications of Listening

**Jean Mountaingrove**, editor with Ruth Mountaingrove of *Womanspirit* magazine, clearly understands the implications. "The basis for meaningful action comes from one's spirit, feelings, attitudes," she said. "*Womanspirit*, which has been a major part of my life, is a political magazine because it contains material to change our consciousness, to value ourselves and our intuition. It encourages us to rely, not on the crowd or on rituals or on airy-fairy spirituality, but on our own wisdom. The only way we can create a future that is different is by taking responsibility for who we are.''

With access to this power, women are taking control of their lives, beginning with their health. They are questioning the authority of medical professionals, and further, they are learning to prevent disease and heal themselves. **Sue Fisher** does all she can to encourage them. By sharing information in her university classroom and workshops, she helps demystify health care and the authority of doctors.

Her book, *In the Patient's Best Interest*, addresses how doctors use language to promote treatments that are often not needed, like hysterectomies; to withhold information about preventive precautions like pap smears; and to further their moral and social construction of the world. ''A world view based on science as a paradigm and sexism as a cultural reality determines the treatment doctors recommend to women,'' Sue said. ''I want women to know what they're up against.''

A friend of Sue's found out by experience. ''She had pelvic inflammatory disease,'' Sue said. ''The first round of antibiotics hadn't worked, and her doctor recommended a hysterectomy. My friend called me from the emergency room to ask me what to do. I told her to tell the doctor that she was engaged to marry a resident at the hospital, and he wanted children. Immediately, he changed his recommendation, and said, 'We'll try another round of antibiotics.' My friend was wheeled back to her room, the second round cured her infection, and she still has her uterus.''

When Sue's doctor advised a hysterectomy for her, she refused. ''The first thing he said was, 'At your age, you don't need your uterus or ovaries any more.' But when I asked him if I was at greater cancer risk than other women my age in the population, he said, 'No.' We eliminated the hysterectomy.

''Then he said he'd 'manage me on artificial estrogens,' '' Sue continued. ''He assured me that there was no statistical evidence of a relationship between cancer and estrogens except in the uterus, but I knew he was wrong. So I refused that treatment too.

''Women need skills to do battle with the medical system, so their health care is in their interest,'' Sue concluded. ''I had enough knowledge to ask my doctor the right questions, but many women just say, 'Yes, doctor,' because the threat of cancer is such a mighty one. But we can't be powerful patients if we collude with the providers who control the skills and knowledge.''

The women of **Morning Glory Collective** in Tallahassee, Florida, have devised one method for women to chart information about their bodies. Their Everywoman's Calendars give women a place to record menstrual periods and body/mood changes. As we traveled, we saw them hanging from bulletin boards, taped on refrigerator doors, and stapled to the insides of closets. ''Every time a woman goes in for a pelvic exam, doctors ask for the date of her last period,'' said Carol Calvert, one of the seven Collective members. "Nine out of ten women don't know. What would happen if she pulled out her charts for the last five years and said, 'Now, what information do you need?' Women can't be exploited when they have data that is *their own* about their bodies."

Pre-Menstrual Syndrome (PMS) has become a convenient ailment for doctors who want to continue their control of women's health care. Together with the chemical industry, they are raking in the bucks from women who suspect they are victims. Morning Glory members would like to see this exploitation end. "Progesterone therapy and PMS are the new catch-phrases in the gynecological game," Carol added, "and physicians and drug companies are going to exploit women's worries about it. But by charting, women can find out if they have PMS; then *they* can decide how to treat it."

Women protect themselves by listening to their bodies, and paying attention to information about them. They also seek alternative practitioners of medicine, especially those who further such listening. **Jean Tait**, who almost died, is an herbalist, and **Madeline Goulard**, the chiropractor who helped heal her, are two such women. They are redefining health care in their tiny desert town. When Jean told the oncologist she had changed her diet and worked with native American medicine men and women to cure herself of cancer, he walked out of his office and slammed the door. "He was angry with me for living because he had told me I would die," she said. "Most doctors don't listen to their patients, so they don't find out what's really going on.

"We listen carefully, and work slowly with people," she continued. "People come to us for alternatives—diet changes, herbs, nutrition advice—so we don't trust machines and charts; we trust ourselves and what we feel. And we're always learning from our patients. When a person has a problem that can be treated with five different herbs, we have to find the best one."

"We're like the turtle and the hedgehog in Kipling's *Just So Stories*," added Madeline. "They imitate each other so much they become like an armadillo. That's what we are—a chi-herbalist. We work well together, complementing each other's approach. Jean tends to think that the mind controls the body, and I tend to think the opposite. Between us, there is a balance."

"Women and men have been taught to ignore their bodies," Jean concluded, "though ignorance is harder for women, who bleed once a month and bear children. Most of us are out of balance, but when we listen we can learn what we need to know. Madeline and I encourage people to become sensitive to what they need and to use any techniques—taste, feeling energy, dreams, whatever—to listen to their impulses. We want to educate our patients so they can stand on their own two feet."

The ultimate in self-health care, of course, is knowing not only what we need, but how to provide it. **Billie Potts**, lesbian, feminist, mother,

Peggy Feerick. Hoopskirt, America 1880s.

artist, potter, gardener, goatkeeper, healer, author, and herbalist, is teaching women to heal themselves by using cheap and accessible herbs.

Mary Clare attended one of Billie's workshops. She and other participants, who wanted to become producers (gardeners), practitioners, and patients of herbs, gathered and identified herbs. They learned how to dry them, how to make tinctures and salves from them. Together they uncovered an ancient and powerful tool for self-healing. "My approach to health care ties in with the politics of questioning authority and our deep lifelong struggle to resist male authority," Billie wrote in *Witches Heal: Lesbian Herbal Self-Sufficiency*. "Many lesbians readily accept the slow, consistent, self-healing process of herbalism because the taking on of personal responsibility ties in with our feminist worldview. Healing ourselves is seen as a personal and political act of empowerment."[4]

Mary Clare adds a daily ritual of self-healing to her exercise routine. It is an interior, poetic monologue, in which she imagines organs, tissue, and bone washed in white light. "I swoop down through my body," she says, "starting with my brain—walnut in a hard shell—then through the small hammer and anvil of my ear, and the smooth, optic nerve in its sheath. I move into my chest to touch my pumping heart and gray lungs looking like plastic bubble wrapping material. I sweep clean my stiff standing ribs and lymph glands under my arms and breasts. My abdomen, full of stomach and tangled intestines, juicy organs— liver, spleen, gall bladder, and pancreas—I touch with light. Then I move over to my kidneys, hidden in the back, and my sleek bladder. I bathe my seed-bearing ovaries, flowering fallopian tubes, and muscular uterus in the light's heat before moving down my long leg bones to my sturdy feet. I have a healthy body. All the cells, tissue, and organs are doing what they are supposed to do. All harmful cells are being destroyed and carried out of my body. I am a well woman."

Attentive women not only care for their bodies, they also build healing and teaching centers. **Louise Grout** is a builder. Her parents taught her to do healing meditations as a child, and today she teaches others at her Sky Song retreat center in Issaquah, Washington. "Because I had such an open background, intellectually and psychically," Louise said, "I learned early to trust the wise woman inside, or the God part of me, and I have experienced it all my life. I can't always tell *how* things come to me, but there is something utterly natural and very compelling about my inner process. Dreams or meditations are what trigger the main things I do, and the small things of my life fit in around that— paying bills, splitting wood, cooking food. I've learned that as long as I keep clear of other people's shoulds and oughts—and my own—it works for me. I do what *feels* right to me."

Louise built Sky Song because she had a vision. She saw herself walking inside a beautiful, but unfamiliar, house. As she explored each

Blanche Derby. Herbalist Jacket. 1980. Silkscreen and Handpainting on Fabric.

room, she wondered whose house it was. When she went into a bedroom, her clothes were in the drawers and closets. She knew then that the house was hers and that she was being invited to live there.

She didn't act immediately. "I spent the next eighteen months putting everything in the way," she said, "my marriage, children still at home, no money. Until one night, I had a dream. I was shown the infinity of energy, a little like standing at the edge of a grain field in eastern Washington. Nothing was visible but the constant undulation of the grain—a living, pulsing, vibrating movement. A voice said, 'Energy is limitless. You can tap into all this if you will build a center of light.' "

Louise had neither the money to build such a place nor the expertise to oversee it. "But I knew the way would be cleared if I would be the outer member of an inner team," she said. "It was like being asked to sign a contract."

She began. And she never felt alone during the building of Sky Song. "Again and again, when we were stuck for something, down the driveway would come what or whom we needed. And sometimes, after the workers had left, I sat down on a pile of lumber and knew the space was filled with beings that were excited about what was happening. They were helping it to happen."

Today Louise offers retreats and workshops. "People I work with are always saying, 'What I really want to do is go to Africa, or study anatomy, or be with children,' " she concluded. "I ask them why they're not doing what they want, and they don't know. They have stopped themselves short of their dreams, but they know what the dreams are."

**Starhawk**, feminist therapist, witch, and author of *Dreaming the Dark* and *The Spiral Dance*, dreams of world peace, and she uses inner wisdom and power to work for it. "If we are to survive," she wrote, "the question becomes: how do we overthrow, not those presently in power, but the principle of power-over? How do we shape a society based on the principle of power-from-within?"[5]

Power-from-within, which has many names—spirit, God, immanence, Goddess—is "what we sense in a seed, in the growth of a child," Starhawk continued, "the power we feel writing, weaving, working, creating, making choices."[6] It is also darkness—fear, death, anger, hidden aspects of ourselves. Yet for Starhawk, power-from-within comes from a birth-giving dark, a place of transformation.

Magic, "the art of changing consciousness," is one way to get to this place. Magic can be prosaic—a leaflet, a lawsuit, a demonstration, or a strike. Or it can be esoteric—ancient techniques for deepening awareness, developing psychic skills, or heightening intuition. Whatever its form, Starhawk believes "magical techniques are effective for and based upon a calling forth of power-from-within, because magic is the psychology/technology of immanence, of the understanding that everything is connected."[7]

---

Sarna Marcus. Seed Atom VI—Study. 1980. Ink on Paper.

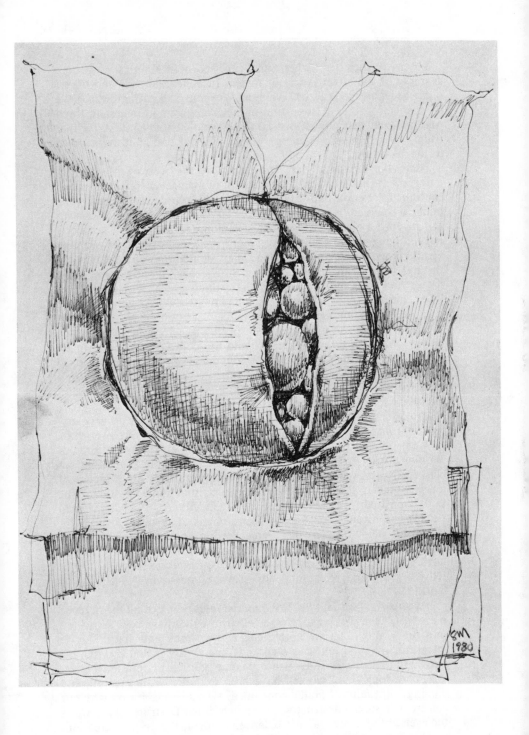

When we met her in her San Francisco apartment, she gave an example of the effectiveness of magic. In June 1982, she and others organized a blockade at the Livermore Weapons Lab in California. "We did a solstice ritual at three a.m. in the campground," she said, "and were amazed that almost one hundred people came to it. After that ritual, we grounded the energy, jumped in our cars, and went down to the blockade."

There they made a web, "symbolic of the web of life and its interconnections, into which we put a lot of magical energy," Starhawk continued. "People had woven ivy, flowers, colored cloth into it—the things we valued in opposition to the weapons lab. We got all set up and stopped a busload of workers by holding up our web. Then along came a flying web of policemen on motorcycles, who had been zooming up and down looking intimidating. They thought they could drive right through the web and smash it. But it caught them, and before we knew it, we had four motorcycles on the ground and a whole tangle of blockaders and police. The police pulled themselves up with string and yarn and ivy dripping from their boots."

Starhawk's power is based on her spirituality which, in turn, is based on her ability to listen. When she and her colleagues made a simple web, symbol of the deeper interconnectedness of all life, they stopped traffic. "In *ritual* (a patterned movement of energy to accomplish a purpose)," she wrote, "we become familiar with power-from-within, learn to recognize its *feel*, learn how to call it up and let it go."[8] Weapons designs still roll out of Livermore, but women are using power-from-within to confront them and other manifestations of power-over.

What does all this activity add up to? **Hallie Iglehart**, author of *Womanspirit: A Guide to Women's Wisdom*, would argue that sex classes, dream workshops, and self-healing practices are evidence of a new women's spirituality. "When the spiritual home is within," she said, "spirituality becomes a part of everyday life. A lot of what women do is very spiritual, but it has not been recognized as such. Giving birth, nurturing, being intuitive or psychic, feeling a connection with nature and all life forms—all of these are very important spiritual experiences. Giving ourselves cervical exams is a spiritual experience. So is rediscovering and reclaiming our heritage and ability to act in the world."

"Women's spirituality is based on the *integration* of all the parts of ourselves," she continued, "especially those that have been separated into inner and outer, receptive and active, body and spirit. As we integrate, we bring out our own and others' power and creativity— maybe in the form of inner peace, maybe political action, maybe art.

"For a long time, women have been excluded from creating and naming spirituality," Hallie concluded. "This is one reason why our culture is in such a destructive phase right now. Destruction *is* part of the cycle, but we are way off balance. Women, the original creation-makers, have been suppressed. Women's spirituality can help to restore that balance."

Because that spirituality is powerful and available and true. It is seed, source, spring, egg, well, fire, heart—so many metaphors describe it. It is like a spring rushing out of a rock. There is no spigot and no one ever turns it off. It comes naturally from the inside of a mountain, and life all around is watered by the flow. "You listen to yourself in little things," Louise said. "When you see that it works, you begin to trust your inner voice in bigger things. Then you just follow where that leads."

It is leading women to re-form religions, protest nuclear arms, heal bodies, celebrate sexuality, and challenge medical authorities. Women are questioning what is handed down, advertised, packaged, displayed, taught. They are taking down the signs, turning off the noise, listening, listening, all the time listening to themselves. And they are literally changing the world. "The new age is being brought about by ordinary people, not gurus or extraordinary people," said **Dorothy Maclean**, a founder of Scotland's Findhorn Community. "Ordinary people who are tuning into their divinity, ordinary people who in the course of ordinary living with ordinary things are enlarging their consciousness to include more and more of the world in their loving."

# 2

# MAKING LOVE

**H**uman beings are social animals. We mate; we befriend. We join country, bridge, and Elks clubs. We create support, therapy, and action groups. People of all sorts volunteer to campaign for one issue or another, one politician or another; to ride on buses to protest civil rights violations, or nuclear arms, or high farm prices. But mostly, we join groups because we like the company of our kind.

On a day-to-day basis, however, group life may not be intimate enough. We seek partners, companions, one or a few others with whom we can be closer. In Western culture, only one social form has been recognized to meet this need. It is marriage. In this institution where two individuals join in "holy matrimony" and promise to love and obey each other, the human animal has made a place to belong.

It is everywhere promoted. Turn on a radio, flip the dial from 88 to 108, and listen to rock and roll, country and western, jazz, punk, new wave, boogie, rap. The melodies, rhythms, and lyric lines may change, but the national mantra for loving and losing drones on.

Freshly sexual teenagers listen morning, noon, and night. They sing words extolling the virtues of romantic love and marriage. Movies, comic strips, romance novels, and television make the musical images real. When the youngsters grow up, they yearn for life partners to match the fantasies. Practically everybody is looking for Mr. or Mrs. Right and the life "lived happily ever after."

Preparation starts early. When Annie was a little girl, everybody in her family promised prizes when she got married. Her mother embroidered an Irish linen tablecloth, stitching a pattern of dark brown flowers on it. Her father said he'd refinish a cedar-lined "hope chest" for bridal bed linens. When Annie's brother built his family a coffee table topped with an old boat-hatch cover, Annie frequently admired it. He said he'd build her one when she got married.

Annie never did walk down the aisle. Her father went ahead and restored the hope chest and gave it to her for her first apartment. She found the finished tablecloth after her mother died and took it for her own. Her brother never did build the table.

Some people don't want to marry. Annie never did. The form doesn't fit everybody, but there are no socially acceptable alternatives. Singleness is suspect. Tired jokes about old maids and bachelors still pepper high school reunion chatter. A single woman is often described as one who "never married," and any woman in public without a man is suspected of looking for one.

On the other hand, multiple loving relationships imply promiscuity, wild abandon, and irresponsibility. Even though sex manuals urge couples to pursue other intimacies, being sexually involved in simultaneous relationships is still the stuff of romance novels and Hollywood B-movies. Coupled partners have secretive, deceptive, and guilt-ridden affairs, and most people don't think multiple relationships can work without sneaking around and lying.

Singleness looks lonely; multiplicity looks complicated. For fear of the new, we human beings stick with our his-and-her-towel mentality. The heterosexual marriage model prevails.

Many women are questioning this male-defined model, wondering if it's for them. They are noticing how they relate differently than men, how they don't love just one person at a time. Women are *inclusive* social beings. They give care and energy to all family members. Child-bearing women respond to children's demands for attention and love. They hold far-flung families together. And women's love goes beyond their families. Our friend Vera Pierce sends us birthday cards every year. We haven't seen her in four years, but our relationship goes on because she remembers us in this special way. Vera must keep a birthday calendar, tucked in a drawer of her desk, in which she has noted the birthdays of special people in her life. Her book, crammed with names and addresses, exemplifies women's capacity to love and relate to many people, all the time.

Women bring this heightened sense of inclusiveness to their intimate relationships. "My personal goal is to know as many women as possible in my lifetime, on a real, intimate, shared, friendship level," said writer **Nell Wagenaar** sitting on a sandy Lake Michigan beach. "To take whatever there is between two people—care and concern, not sleeping together—and spread that over the whole community. I'm looking for a family, a trusted circle of intimate friends."

More and more women, and many men, want the same thing. Instead of adopting the one existing, matrimonial model for loving, we're beginning to make our own. Make no mistake: this decision to confront the basic social unit in society, to question its application to everyone, is a *radical, political* act. We are creating new relationship forms because we believe we have the power to shift basic social arrangements to meet our needs.

We are breaking new ground. This ground is sometimes hard, and only pickaxes can crack it. Sometimes it is quicksand, and we run from its seductive look and feel. Sometimes, though, it is fertile river bottomland that we cultivate and plant. Whatever it is, by denying marriage as the *only* choice, and by looking for loving arrangements that reflect who we are—expansive, inclusive human beings—we are assuming power.

Some couples, heterosexual and homosexual, are scrutinizing and redefining the vows they once simply said. They are noticing that while pair bonding may be safe, it may not give them the freedom they want and need. They battle fusion and dependence and learn ways to be autonomous.

Some women, rejecting the almighty couple in favor of multiple relationships, are making sexual and non-sexual commitments to more than one person at a time. While working on this book, the two of us changed our relationship and formed intimacies with other women. Two of them in particular, **Ann Gibson** and **Sidney Oliver**, struggled with us as we wrestled with the issues presented in this chapter.

Multiple relationships are neither simple nor clearly understood. When we told one woman that we were opening our relationship, she quickly reacted, "Oh, really? It won't work, you know." Some women and men are convinced it *might* work, even though we have few models, and have to deal with jealousy and terrors of being left. We don't want to discard lovers like paper plates whenever someone new comes along. We do want open relationships that allow for change and diversity.

Still other women, celibate or not, choose no partners. They have plenty of friends and work to do. They may be lonely sometimes, but they like being without an intimate, daily partnership for a time or for their whole lives. For them, non-sexual relationships have equal value to sexual ones.

## The Tyranny of Language

Whatever form for loving they choose, whatever arrangement, all of these women and men face the tyranny of language. Words or phrases like "lover," "friend," and "falling in love" are not simple. They connote degrees of loving and sexual involvement. For example, "lover" is a sexual intimate; "friend" is intimate, but not sexual—our commitment to friends is often less than our commitment to lovers; "falling in love" implies passivity and powerlessness.

All words are limiting, but they're all we have to make sense of the world. Relational words often don't tell the whole truth. A woman asked Mary Clare if we were lovers. She said, "No." But later, Annie asked her why she said that—"We love each other, so doesn't that make us lovers?" And Mary Clare said, "Yes, but it was easier to use their language than to try and explain."

It may take years to explain, to make the switch. These old words are embedded not only in popular songs and CBS sitcoms, but also in myths, fairy tales, and history. To describe our relationship, Mary Clare would need a paragraph or a page, not a word. Who are our "lovers?" **Jere van Syoc**, an artist in Los Angeles, said, "My brother, my friends, my past and present sexual partners—everybody I love and who loves me—are my lovers."

Redefining old words is one task; inventing new ones is another. Nell wonders what to call the woman she meets every Monday night. They don't party, *or* sleep, *or* dance, *or* live together. They just talk and tell each other stories about the past week. They are intimate, close. Their relationship is like none other in their lives, but *what is its name*? Are they "girlfriends," "companions," "soulmates?" And for multiple relationships, **Anne Rhodes**, mime artist in Ithaca, New York, suggests "multigamy" because "non-monogamy" is such a negative expression.

**Sidney Oliver** looked for new definitions when she became involved with Mary Clare. "I don't want to behave with Annie, or without Annie, as though Mary Clare is a mansion," she wrote in her journal. "The issue isn't who gets the best room and which hallways we can walk down. She's not divisible into chunks. She's not a furniture store, or a supermarket, or a Holiday Inn. She can't say, 'This is the part of me that's for sale or lease.' Mary Clare isn't a structure; she's a process."

Old language keeps us trapped in old patterns. When **Ann Gibson** and Annie became involved, Ann saw herself as a "housebreaker" and "the other woman." While clinging to these descriptions, she remained powerless. She knew she wasn't "a bad girl," but she felt like one. And as long as Mary Clare bought the "affair scenario" complete with the "poor-woman-who-has-been-left," she felt victimized and in competition with Ann. In the presence of this kind of word/story tyranny, nothing new can develop.

Mary Daly, author of *Gyn/Ecology: The Metaethics of Radical Feminism*, and word-worker extraordinaire writes, "...deceptive perceptions [about ourselves as women] were/are implanted through language—the all pervasive language of myth, conveyed overtly and subliminally through religion, 'great art,' literature, the dogmas of professionalism, the media, grammar. Indeed deception is embedded in the very texture of the words we use, and here is where our exorcism can begin."[1]

## The Complexity of Sex

Words to describe relationships are almost all sex-oriented. "Monogamous" means having sex with one person. "Serial monogamy" means having sex with one person at a time. "Celibate" means having sex with no one. "Lesbian" is women having sex with women, and "gay" is men with men. Then there's "virgin" and "whore." In every case, the word denotes a degree of sexual involvement. If women and men are going to succeed at building intimate relationships based on freedom and trust, they will, sooner or later, have to deal with the complexity of sex.

Sex has power. Two bodies, naked together, touching each other, have an impact of their own. A perfectly sound relationship can be turned on its head if one of the partners has sex with someone else. Even the *idea* of extra-relationship sex, let alone the act, is enough to send most people into panic.

A friend, Cathy, married for over thirty years to Jim, felt this fear on one memorable occasion. Several years ago, she came home from a meeting late in the evening, and Jim wasn't there. He was having dinner with a mutual friend, a woman he liked. Cathy had told Jim when she'd be home, and she expected him to be waiting for her. The empty house fed her fears. On the one hand, she knew her relationship with Jim was solid and sure; on the other, she was terrified that he was being sexually intimate with another woman. By the time he came in, she was hysterical and furious. She and Jim talked about what had happened, and after a few days, she felt safe again. But she still remembers the ache in her belly on that long night and the terror that took over her mind.

Sex does that to people, to relationships. It has enormous power to disrupt, yet deepen; destroy, yet cement. And it must be dealt with. It can't be avoided. Anne Rhodes, who has two sexual partners, said, "When we acknowledge that we have sexual feelings for more than one person, everything goes berserk. But it's an issue we're going to have to solve before we can move on as women. Otherwise, we've got only two choices: serial monogamy—love'em and leave'em; or stick with the relationship we're in until it's dead, cutting off our feet to fit the golden slipper."

Sex salesmen around the world have convinced us that the idea of two naked bodies together is *the* ultimate. Is it really? And how do we find out for sure? Women and men are beginning to think about these questions and make conscious decisions about the place of sex in their lives—how much time it gets, and what it means.

**Elizabeth and David Dodson Gray**, married for several decades, described their sexual relationship as "erotic, playful, and changing. Early in our relationship," said Elizabeth, "we were more committed to intercourse and working out our orgasms. When we finally gave up orgasms as the ultimate goal, we were emancipated to try new forms.

For example, in the past ten years, we've become totally addicted to sleeping like spoons. If we had to choose between losing orgasms and that hour-after-hour intimacy, we'd lose orgasms.''

David thinks the urge to sexualize feelings that resemble tenderness, caring, and attraction is a male tendency. **Marjory and Peter Bankson** would agree. When they were first married, almost twenty years ago, Peter associated sexuality with genital excitement. "Everytime he needed touching, it turned into intercourse," said Marjory. "I resented it because it didn't feel right to me. Since we've taken a massage course and learned to talk about what feels good to both of us, Peter can separate a sensual need from a sexual one. He might really want a head rub or a foot massage.''

But deciding between intercourse or a foot massage takes some doing when the message blaring across the land is that bodies together equal sex, and sex equals ultimate pleasure. **Lenora Trussell**, Washington, D.C. masseuse, went on a weekend beach trip with six other women, and one night they all got in bed together. As they lay on the large-sized bed, talking and laughing, Lenora said, "What we're doing here, my friends, is making love. Making love is not just a sexual thing.''

Neither are "crushes" necessarily sexual. Anne Rhodes used to feel like "a sneak and a rat" when she had a "crush" on someone. She interpreted the attraction as a sexual need, until she realized that the feeling wasn't about falling in love. "Just because I felt attracted didn't mean I should have a sexual relationship," she said. "It just meant I probably had something to learn.

"I get so caught up in my schedule and emotional life—all the details of my life," she continued, "that I barely notice the things to be worked on in myself. The only way the goddess can get me to pay any attention is to give me a crush. A sexual relationship may or may not be part of it, but it's likely that both of us have something exciting to learn.''

Celibate women take Anne's idea one step further. They explore what can happen in relationships without sex. Lenora described her process. "I'm not in a relationship right now, and I'm finding it one of the most productive times of my life—in terms of my work, my friendships, and myself," she said. "When I'm in a hot, passionate relationship, that's all I think about. It's all encompassing, and I tend to get lost.

"Also, within the lesbian community, it's so easy to fall in bed with someone," Lenora continued. "You don't have to worry about getting pregnant or VD or about getting beat up afterwards. Things that contain heterosexuals, we don't have. I like containing myself. When I contain feelings, they intensify, and I know I'm really alive. Besides, I can talk about sexual feelings with others without having to have sex, without the heavy-duty stuff that comes down when you say you're sexually attracted to someone. So in some ways, I'm more intimate with people now than I am in a sexual relationship.''

One of our basic, human instincts is the desire to be related in intimate and loving ways with each other. When the only path to get this closeness is through sex, we want sex. Other relationships—friends,

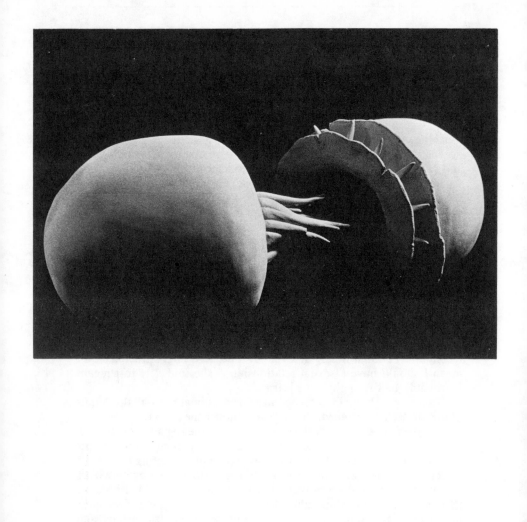

family, working partners—get less time, attention, value. And they know it. Yet when we can broaden our intimacies to include all of our loves, we dethrone sex. The idea of "just friends, lovers no more," can be turned around. "Glad we're friends," a greeting card proclaims, "not *just* lovers."

## Autonomy and Connectedness

Once we know what to call each other and our arrangements, and once we handle the intimacy that happens when naked bodies lie together, we face the tension between autonomy and connectedness. Walking the tightrope between the two is a balancing act—too much autonomy may lead to loneliness, and too much relatedness may lead to fusion. We risk our lives on this tightrope because we know that wholeness means being autonomous *and* connected.

The journey is never easy. We human beings may be social animals, eager for connection and love, but we are also solitary, single individuals entrapped in bodies with boundaries. We long to be a part of the whole; yet we strive within the whole to assert our individuality. **Rosie Thompson**, North Carolina artist, was the fourth of eleven children. "It was impossible for me to know who I was as a person until I left home," she said. "Until then, I was just part of a group."

When Rosie told her mother she had to leave home to find herself, her mother was shocked. She didn't understand what Rosie was talking about, perhaps because she had always subordinated herself to her family group.

Women learn early how to connect, conciliate, sooth, and negotiate. Our toughest task now may be learning how to be separate persons. "How can we live close to or with someone else," Nell wondered, "and not get into pleasing the other person? How do we keep our own friends and pasttimes? How do we still allow for our own individual development?"

"The family that prays together, stays together," old bumper stickers read. Togetherness is the American way. Carson McCullers' wonderful girl character in *A Member of the Wedding* wanted more than anything to be married to her brother and her brother's wife-to-be. "All people belong to a 'we' except me," she cried. "I love the two of them so much because they are the *we* of me."[2] Nobody likes being left out. Everybody wants to be a part. Being part of a group is often easy for women, but it can also be a stumbling block. Fusion, the opposite of autonomy, is our natural enemy.

Fusion comes in many forms, slips up on us when we least expect it. Our houses foster it. In single family homes, bedrooms are shared: children in one or two, a couple—usually—in another. There is only one kitchen and sometimes two bathrooms, but more likely one. "The

Lorene Senesac. Untitled. 1976. Clay.

little lawn," Nell said, "the double bed, and the social engagements—
the whole scene of togetherness—can become a wedge that drives you
apart."

Before we know it, we are calling ourselves "we" all the time. "We
have friends," "We're going on vacation," "We think the President
is a fool," "We spend our money on clothes." Whose friends? Whose
vacation? Whose ideas about politics? Whose money? Whatever
happened to the individuals who started out as separate "I's" in the
relationship?

Writing this book, the two of us are together day and night. Because
we have a habit of doing many things together, we have to make an
effort to be separate. We have separate rooms, we eat some meals alone,
we might go to movies alone, and occasionally one of us will take the
van and go camping alone. Whenever one of us starts saying "we" all
the time, the other says, "Hey, don't forget who you are." In this way,
we continue to teach ourselves how to manage separation.

**Jean Lawson**, financial advisor for small businesses and couples in
Seneca Falls, New York, battles fusion by teaching people to manage
money. She sits in her storefront office down the street from the building
where Elizabeth Cady Stanton and Susan B. Anthony declared equal
rights for women, and continues their tradition. For her couple clients,
Jean prepares a balance sheet, a weekly budget, and a list of estimated
expenses and income. Then she tells them that they must each have equal
allowances. It may not be much, but it will be equal. "It's like a cold
shower," she said. "But I insist. They've each got to have something
of their own."

She gets agreement, and they settle on an amount—five dollars, let's
say. "I write it down. 'That means five dollars for you (the man),' I
say, 'and five dollars for you (the woman)," Jean continued. "They
look at each other, then at me, and say, 'What do you mean?' because
this may be the first time in their marriage they have had equal amounts
of money to spend. Even if the wife has worked in the same business
with the husband, and thinks she is a partner in it, financially she isn't
anything except a pair of hands of unpaid labor. So I just say, 'You're
both working, and you deserve the same amount.' Most of the women
are working two jobs—one in the home and one outside, so really, they
should get two thirds and the men one third. Whenever I suggest that
arrangement, the men are happy just to have it equal."

Jean takes these lessons home. When she married her present
husband, he was tired from working to support his first wife and family,
so she thought they'd be able to skip over the old male, head-of-
household role playing. After the marriage, she took over the books,
figured out monthly expenses, and each of them deposited an equal
amount of money into a joint bank account. "It worked phenomenally
well," she said. "It left us free, without hassle."

When Jean got a notice from their insurance company offering a
reduced rate if all cars on the policy were registered to one owner, Jean
said to her husband, " 'Sounds good to me. You sign your car over

and I'll put it under my name.' That stopped him," she said. "Having his car under his name made a difference to him. It didn't make any sense financially, but it made a difference psychologically."

In Jean's opinion, "money causes more trouble in marriages than anything else, sex and religion notwithstanding. Too many women don't own any property, don't have their name on any documents. If the husband decides to leave the woman," Jean said, "she's left with nothing." Fusion can lead not only to loss of self but to loss of economic power as well.

For Marjory Bankson, the Vietnam War was the occasion for her developing autonomy. A few years after she married Peter, then an Army officer, he was sent to the war and she was alone. During that first, prolonged separation, Marjory discovered that she liked being on her own, responsible for bills and daily maintenance. She enrolled in pottery classes, recognized her talent, and quit teaching. By the time Peter got home, she had decided to give herself three years to become a production potter, and with his help, she succeeded. When Peter went to Vietnam the second time, Marjory's business life in the United States was active and stable. "Those early separations allowed us both to trust separation and growth, to stay married and allow for change," she said. "A lot of marriages don't get a chance to test that."

Over the years, Peter also kept a clear picture of his own path. Almost fifteen years after his first trip to Vietnam, and just before his military retirement, he was sent to Germany. Marjory could have accompanied him, but she didn't. During that separation, Peter discovered more about autonomy. He found his own apartment, decorated it, and stocked the kitchen. "I had to decide what kinds of spices I wanted in the cupboard," he said, "where to store the pots and pans. I did it differently from Marjory, but my way had a logic about it too. Men are really stuck until they learn to feed and wipe themselves, and I learned that I knew how to do both."

Taking care of mundane, day-to-day needs, *just for yourself*, is liberating for women and men who are just learning how. In Columbus, Ohio, poet **Margaret Honton** left home after thirty-one years of cooking and baking for her husband and six children. Alone at last, she swam, updated two years of dream notes, wrote poems, and went to $1.50 movies. "The first few months were euphoric," she said, "acclimating myself, constructing a garden, arranging rooms, rearranging my priorities, sleeping soundly every night." Even though she felt lonely at times, she was happy to be exploring her own life for a change.

**Elizabeth Wright Ingraham**, Colorado architect, knows just how Margaret feels. Married for over thirty years, and then divorced, Elizabeth keeps extremely busy with architecture and a summer school institute for graduate students. "I'm quite happy," she said. "Not having a husband anymore saves a lot of time and it gives me new freedom. I have good friends, four absolutely smashing children, and my work. I may need an intimate relationship again, but not now. I need a respite."

Widows, unlike Elizabeth and Margaret, don't choose singleness, but some learn to appreciate the benefits. Ruth Powell, Mary Clare's mother, became a widow in 1969 at age fifty-one. She has not remarried and lives alone. "What I like about the solitude," she said, in Mary Clare's book, *The Widow*, "is the chance for something new to pop into your head.... When you get a new idea, it's sort of like a little surprise, and you get the realization of *the abundance of good things*."[3] She, and all of us teetering on the autonomy tightrope, understand these lines from Asta's poem, "coming out celibate:"

> we must all be seen in
>           couples
>           families (even "broken families")
>           collectives
>           some sort of relationship
> all our lives
> whether we like it or not
> anything but as individuals   being glad in our one-
> ness
>           . . .
> imagine an epidemic of autonomous individuals
> and you're on your way to realizing
> a few feminist fantasies[4]

## Creating New Forms

Virginia Woolf said somewhere that before we can marry anybody else we have to marry ourselves. Once Mary Clare had a self-marriage dream. In the dream, she was eating breakfast with friends, and she suddenly realized she was late for her wedding. She sped out the door. In a rush, she forgot her green chiffon wedding dress and the organist's sheet music. A friend at the church had to drive back and get them. In spite of a jumbled beginning, the ceremony began. Mary Clare stood at the altar of the underground church in her tacky, green chiffon dress and said she would love and honor herself, stay with herself in sickness and in health. The music sounded, friends witnessed, and the union was made.

When we have strong relationships with ourselves, we are more able to form relationships with others. But learning self-love takes a lifetime, and while we're working on it, we join with others who are learning to love themselves. Together, we discern the forms that fit.

Some people like monogamous marriage. Much has been written about the inequalities for women in this institution—restriction of growth and opportunity, economic dependency, tyranny of roles, and often brutality. But Elizabeth and David Dodson Gray have consciously

Janet Braun-Reinitz. Olympia in the Four Poster. 1984. Acrylic on Paper. 39″ x 45″. (Photo: Andrew Gillis)

made their marriage an opposite of this description. Elizabeth writes and lectures on feminism and Christian theology and David, an Episcopal minister, does the same about history, futurism, and the history and philosophy of science. Both write and speak in the "futures" field, and David publishes and distributes Elizabeth's books. "When David left the parish ministry," Elizabeth said, "we decided not to accept many commitments where we had to be apart. We really like being together."

Some women suffocate in so much togetherness. They like living alone, not being responsible to or for anyone else on a daily basis. Nell, reflecting on her life in Grand Haven, Michigan, said, "I'd like to have a lover I didn't live with. Maybe we could be together, say, two or three nights a week, and live separately the other times. I like taking out my own garbage."

Still others like the freedom of forming more than one intimate, sexual relationship at a time. **Betty Dodson**, sex teacher and writer in New York City, "signed off on pair bonding in 1969. It was like breaking an addiction," she said. "I went one day at a time. 'I'm not going to fall in love today,' I'd say. Then it became a year, then another. There is no positive model in the culture for somebody who doesn't want to spend the second half of their life as part of a couple. But so far, I've been able to sustain it."

Relationships of all sorts work when the form fits the people involved. The people we interviewed have thought about relationships, and have shared with us what they've learned: each person must have equal power, each person must honor their commitment, and each person must let go of the other, loving the other with hands opened wide.


## Sharing Power

Elizabeth and David dealt with power issues that emerged from cultural expectations about men, women, and marriage. Elizabeth had been a professional before they married, but afterwards, she stayed home and took care of their two children. She shared David's ministry at many points because they had identical professional training, but she resented their own and society's expectations that she not only bear, but also raise children. She felt as if she were giving up her own life. Finally, she reclaimed her life and career when David left the parish ministry. "For years, Liz stood beside me in my work," he said. "When opportunities began to emerge for her, I felt a responsibility to help her re-launch her professional life, and to be as supportive of her as she was of me."

They began to work together, respecting each other's judgment and creativity as always. They each do tasks that they do best: David edits better, and Elizabeth outlines better. "We call this 'functional diversity,' " Elizabeth said. They also make sure that time, professional opportunities, and emotional space are available to both. They use words like "symmetry" and "justice" when talking about this.

But unlearning old lessons takes practice. The first time Elizabeth asked David to type a paper of hers, she felt guilty, even though he was the better typist. "Then I thought, 'This is ridiculous! I spent fifteen years of my life helping him do his work. I've got fifteen years coming!' "

**Sonya and Manning Dyer,** married for thirty-one years, have learned to negotiate for what they need, each from a position of power. Their working lives are full and separate, so they don't get much time together unless they choose it. "Manning asked me not to plan any outside activities during our regular dinner time if I could avoid it," Sonya explained. "He said, 'One of the most important times of the day for me is when I come home until we finish dinner. The rest of the evening doesn't matter to me. But that hour at dinner is important.' And that's something I could work with. It doesn't mean I never have supper with anyone else, but, generally, that's our protected time."

Ann Gibson described herself as "a woman who works with what is given," and though that receptive quality is life-giving and wonderful, she had to struggle to claim her right to be related to Annie. "For a long time, I felt powerless," she said, "like I had to wait for you two to decide when I could see Annie alone, or when I could see you both. You lived together, and had been partners for years. I really respected your relationship, and that kept me from saying what I wanted for a long time." When Ann settled in Massachusetts, she began to do her art work, and as soon as she chose her own life, she felt more powerful. As the road manager for our project, she had a role, and with it, power. "I had some standing then," she added. "I began to feel more equal."

Issues of power and access are especially complicated in multiple relationships. Somebody always feels left out. Because we were travelling, and then writing this book, Ann and Sidney always had to wait for us to say when we were available. We asked them to join in making decisions that would affect all four of us, and for a while, we sent letters back and forth, sorting out our feelings and chewing on joint decision-making processes.

But we failed for several reasons: geographical distances between us—we were on the road interviewing women for this book, Ann was in Massachusetts, and Sidney in Washington, D.C.; unequal knowledge and experience of each other—we had been partners for ten years, Ann had been a friend for four years, Sidney had known Mary Clare only a few months. Hard as we tried, we couldn't reach a feeling of equilibrium. But we made the effort because we believe successful multiple relationships require equality. Every person must feel they have a "right" to the relationship, and structures must exist that allow for resolution of differences.

## Honoring the Commitment

Marjory and Peter Bankson, because of their many separations, have
learned to honor their commitment over distance and time. Several years
ago, Marjory was invited to South America to teach pottery. While
there, she met a man she liked, but she didn't become sexually involved
with him. When she came back to the United States, another woman
was interested in Peter. Suddenly, Peter and Marjory had to examine,
on a deeper level, the basis of their commitment.

They decided to give each other *the first right to care*. "For example,"
Marjory said, "if I read a book or meet a new person or pursue a new
activity, I give Peter the first right to care about it and share it with
me. If he doesn't want to join me, I find other companions."

Being committed to another person is always a creative pursuit. Ann
Gibson, in a long-distance relationship with Annie for four years, had
to invent ways to stay connected. She used psychic skills like meditation
and "sitting with," as well as dreams and fantasies. And on a more
earthy level, the phone and letters were important links. "I learned that
an intimate relationship can exist," she said, "indeed can thrive, when
the people are far apart from each other. I learned that the definition
of being in relationship may not include physical presence at all."

**Susan** (last name withheld on request) now lives in New York City
and **Elizabeth** (last name withheld on request) lives in Atlanta, Georgia,
but they maintain a most special, intimate, long-distance friendship.
They write letters to each other. In 1977, they met briefly when they
read their poetry together in Atlanta. During the next few years, they
worked on projects together—in person and through letters—and got
to know each other slowly.

Several years ago, Susan's partner of twelve years suddenly decided
that she was leaving the relationship. Within a week, they had sold their
house, and within a month Susan had stored her belongings and moved
to New York. For five months, she had no job. For eight months, she
had no home. She slept on couches, paid strangers and friends to let
her stay in spare bedrooms. "All this time," she said, "I was grieving
for my lost relationship and learning how to go through things alone
for the first time in years."

But she wasn't alone. Her friends, mostly in other states, rallied and
helped Susan through the pain of that time. Elizabeth wrote letters.
"She brought such variety into my home with her letters," Susan
continued. "She wrote about her garden, her job, her political work,
her beautiful house, her cat, her past, her future, and thoughts about
things outside her personal life. I would picture her bright hair in the
Atlanta sun as she planted her huge and variegated garden. I would
picture her writing during a thunderstorm in her journal at the kitchen
table, holding the door while the cat decided whether to stay in or go
out. I can think of no topic we haven't touched on with extreme
honesty."

Susan thought obsessively about death. "I doubt if I would be alive today if Elizabeth hadn't gone through that time with me," she said. "She understood how important her steadiness was, knew how sometimes everything hung on it. She knew that it mattered that I would get my mail and there would be a letter—sometimes ten or more pages long—full of the liveliest accounts of life."

Susan and Elizabeth have seldom visited each other. They like the distance and perspective that letter writing brings. Their relationship stands as a model for all relationships. They rent instead of buy, and they are always letting go.

## Learning To Let Go

It is ironic that, after working through power imbalances and reaffirming commitments, women and men realize they have to let go of each other. **Elana Freedom** and **Elizabeth Freeman**, lesbians in their sixties living in Durham, North Carolina, have learned not to restrict each other. They've each been independent too long for that. Elizabeth, retired guidance counselor and administrator, has spent her life living alone, but with many friends and close family ties. Elana, peace activist and photographer/journalist, has had many friends and sexual partners, but no long-term commitments.

As a result of their histories, they pursue separate projects. Elizabeth has studied quiltmaking, Southern literature, and Italian in preparation for a trip to Italy. When she moved to North Carolina, she joined a white racism group to explore her own racism. She serves on foundation boards and works with money issues. Occasionally, she publishes a book of poetry with her small press, Crone's Own Press. Elana, a political activist, helped organize and walked in a Women's Peace Walk from Durham to the Women's Encampment at the Seneca Depot in New York. She regularly participates in civil disobedience activities, and attends lesbian/feminist gatherings.

Because they don't work well together, but have similar interests, they have learned ways to work alongside each other. In a demonstration, for example, Elana might be in an organizing group, and Elizabeth might be in an affinity group. Elizabeth takes over the photography tasks if Elana is arrested, and is part of her support group if she's jailed. "Our basic interests and values are the same," said Elana, "and we're very important to each other. But we're separate."

Sonya and Manning might describe their relationship the same way. They've been on parallel tracks ever since they were married. Sonya is co-pastor of an ecumenical church in Washington, D.C. and co-founder of a lay ministry project. Manning runs a family store. "Early in our marriage, I told Manning I didn't want to be involved in his business," Sonya said. "And because he's not excited about theology and the church, I don't get the same kind of stimulation from him as from other people. Sometimes, I'm sorry our areas of interest aren't

closer, but this is the way we are, and it works pretty well. Our model of a couple does not include bringing the other person along on your track.''

Elana, Elizabeth, Sonya, and Manning are letting go of each other in daily pursuits and career paths. David and Elizabeth are thinking about the ultimate letting go that comes with death. "We're both 54,'' Elizabeth said, while recovering from a mastectomy. "Learning to cope with being alone is part of caring for the other person, learning how to help one another function separately. I've encouraged David to think about coping without me, and I've done the same.

"For example,'' she continued, "we always thought we would retire to our summer place on the shore. But I realized that I don't want to be there alone. I want to be right here in Wellesley so I can go to stores or the library if I get depressed. David and I have chosen to be very close, and it's been terrific, but the separation—from life partner, sexual partner, working partner—will be inevitable and hard.''

These women and men are finding new forms for loving and for letting go. Why do they bother? Because they are social animals. They mate; they befriend. They like the company of their kind. They may babble in inadequate language, distort sex, and struggle against the monolithic marriage form, but they are choosing intimate bonds that fit them instead of going around in little boxes called couples. They are broadening their capacities to love.

Love, this thing the radio raves about, is more than we thought. It isn't something we fall into or out of as music makers would have us believe. It is not something that happens to us; it is something we choose. It is as limitless as the sky. No one form can contain it, no restriction stop it, no language name it. Sidney Oliver put it plainly when she wrote, "Mary Clare and I are intersecting rivers, each with lots more than one intersection. What would batter and wound me is if Mary Clare stopped up, built a dam right after the Annie junction. Or if I tried to bypass our intersection, I'd certainly end up choked in mud and silt and highly stylized. I'd have to gouge through somebody else's pastureland and maybe flood out their homestead. What I really, really want is to be a broad enough, fine enough, clean enough, and deep enough river that the few other big, fine, clean, and deep rivers out there would like to flow through me for awhile.''

Women are keeping their rivers wide.

Nancy Azara. Shadow Goddess. Wood, Paint. (Photo: Janna W. Josephson)

# 3

## NEW KIN

There's a rumor going round that the family is dead and that women killed it. "If women hadn't left home and gone to work," the tall tale goes, "there wouldn't be crime, child abuse, high interest rates, war. Children wouldn't be illiterate and into drugs, fathers wouldn't wander, and precooked frozen dinners wouldn't be shot full of microwaves."

Of course, the argument is ridiculous. In the first place, it reeks of elitism. It's only since white, middle-class women went to work outside the home that we've felt the flak. Working-class women have always worked, but no pious Right Wing or silent Left has been concerned because poor women have never had enough political clout to make a row. But now, with white sisters hacking away in the marketplace jungle, the societal costs and benefits of working women are hot topics for talk show hosts and publishing houses.

### The Myth Of The Family

In the second place, it's the *myth* about the family that is unraveling, not the family itself. Clarissa Atkinson, Harvard Divinity School professor, unfolds the fairy tale. "There once was a time when families had two parents and no latchkey children," she writes. "Kindly adults cared for children, who played in unpolluted meadows, learned the basics in neighborhood schools, and worked beside their parents in fields and shops and kitchens. Before the Fall [of the Family], children didn't celebrate Christmas Eve with Mom, and Christmas morning with Dad and his girlfriend. . . .

"Mothers helped their daughters to take care of the baby; children didn't watch violence on TV; people went to church together and obeyed God's laws for families. One's offspring were virgins when they married. Abortion, if it happened at all, happened to other people's daughters and in other people's neighborhoods. There were no homosexuals, and if there had been, they would not have been married in church and set up housekeeping together. Test-tube babies were for science fiction. God sent babies to people who deserved them, and they required neither nursery school nor orthodontia, nor car pools to hockey practice at 5 a.m.

"Some say the family Fell with the Industrial Revolution, when Father left home for the office or the mill," concludes Dr. Atkinson. "Some say it happened in the 1920s, when women began to cut their hair and drink gin. And some of us locate the Fall in our own memories, along about the time the Beatles landed, and kids took to the streets to tell their elders what to do. Whenever it began, it was cataclysmic. The American Family was driven out of Eden by an angel, an appropriately androgynous figure who looked like a rock star."[1]

Myths die hard, and pressure mounts for women to keep this one alive. Mothers press daughters to marry and reproduce. Unmarried women, over thirty and motherless, hurriedly scan male friends for fatherly qualities. Some of them mate and procreate, but soon find motherhood a two-edged sword. **Maggie McGuire** wrote her dissertation about them. "On the one hand, most mothers discover new parts of themselves as child rearing progresses," she said. "Some learn how to give themselves without giving themselves away. Others learn how to use their power and trust themselves when confronted by doctors, teachers, and other authorities. In essence, they learn what their limits are, and, at the same time, experience a new sense of spiritual, intuitive, emotional, and physical power. But on the other hand, especially at the beginning, many women with children feel frustrated, isolated, and impotent."

This latter bunch are burned out Supermoms trying to do it all. On "Saturday Night Live," a beautifully dressed comedienne acted out the dilemma. She sashayed into a huge, clean kitchen and put two grocery sacks down on the counter. While she unpacked them, she said to the camera, "Hi, I'm an astrophysicist and a mother of four. I'm also president of the local PTA, do volunteer work at the hospital, and drive the carpool several days a week. My favorite hobbies are deep-sea diving and sky diving." She continued putting away the groceries, then looked back at the camera. "You may wonder how I do all this," she said. "I'm on speed."

**Kathy Altman**, former Executive Assistant to Congressman Robert Edgar and mother of preschooler Max isn't on speed, but she understands the scenario. "There are some days when I don't feel like I'm pleasing anybody," she said. "I ask myself, 'How do I keep everybody happy? How do I keep my husband happy? How do I keep my in-laws, who think I should be a round-the-clock mother, happy? My parents? My boss? Max? Myself?' " She reads books about working parents, "latchkey kids," and tips on saving time. "The books tell me to order from catalogues and cook ahead on weekends," she said, "but most of the time, I'm doing my laundry on weekends and playing with Max. I don't have any time to save."

Guilt, frustration, and fatigue haunt these women day and night. The price exacted to sustain the fairy tale grows. And if women want to work *and* have children, as many now do, the nagging problem of child care rests on their already burdened shoulders. **Alice Cook**, former professor of Labor Relations at Cornell University, asked women around the world two questions: (1) "How do you manage to get everything done in the mornings and evenings?" The women answered, "We sleep four or five hours a night." (2) "If you had your wish, what kind of help would you most like?" And they answered, "Improved child care and part-time work opportunities." Alice found the problems the same everywhere, regardless of the political system. "Did you know," she asked, "that the United States is the only modern country that has no maternity leave provisions, and no national child care policy? The *only* one."

In reality, not in myth, more women are moving into the marketplace, but more men are not moving into child care. So every working day, women like Kathy drive their children to day care centers, or devise other arrangements. For four years, Kathy's son Max stayed with a woman who had relinquished a promising, career because she couldn't handle the struggle any longer. In the fall of 1984, Kathy caved in. She left her Congressional job and went home.

White, affluent women like Kathy are feeling the pressures that women with fewer choices have felt for decades. Six million black mothers raising their children alone often don't have the luxury of choosing between career and children. They have to work to pay landlords who may be reluctant to rent to them. Good, inexpensive child care centers are almost nonexistent, and those that do exist have rigid time schedules. Many poor women can't take higher paying jobs that involve overtime because their child care center hours aren't flexible.[2]

As for the "good old days," **Joan Hudyma Tucker**'s Polish grandmother, Vaga Nartowicz, lived to be 86 and raised six children alone in Hatfield, Massachusetts. "She never depended on a man," Joan said. "She never chose to speak English. She lived in a little gray house, maintained a garden, made beer, canned vegetables, and raised beautiful, fragrant violets." At first glance, the picture of this "self-sufficient'' woman in her quaint, rural garden looks different from Kathy's anguish or a black mother's dilemma, but it's the same.

"Drive to South Deerfield sometime," Joan continued, "and go up Mt. Sugerloaf. Look down at the Connecticut River and those fields and reflect on the women who tilled that land, raised huge families, never had any education, were indentured to wealthy families, married into labor and drudgery and pain, then died and were buried in the Polish, Ukranian, and Lithuanian graveyards dotting the landscape. My passion for change comes from these women. I wish for more options, more ways of being than they ever imagined.''

Don't we all? And the mythical family can never provide those options because it never existed. Behind the gloss of idyllic, Norman Rockwell scenes of family life were, and are, harried, guilt-ridden, exhausted, dying women maintaining the family with their own lives.

## Abandoning The Myth

Women are not abandoning the family. Far from it. Women are abandoning myths about the family and confronting the power relationships, sex roles, and competitiveness inherent in them. Where husband and wife have been unequal under the law, women are demanding egalitarian relationships. Where women have been primary caregivers for children, they are pushing for shared child care. Where a man has held power, women want consensus decision-making processes.

Women everywhere have stopped sacrificing their lives. Women of all classes, races, and political persuasions are rejecting the mythical family and creating new families. This is a powerful act, fraught with political and economic implications. Government services, tax breaks for dependents, welfare and social security policies, health care, and housing grants are determined by how "family" is presently defined. "To the U.S. Government, an 'intact family' consists of husband, wife, and children," said **Marsha Mabee**, staff member of the House Select Committee on Children, Youth, and Families. "The single-parent family is a 'non-intact family,' and other forms of family just don't exist according to U.S. domestic policy."

They just exist in real life. Women and men everywhere are creating them—stirring together a rich mixture of people to rely on, be companion to, build a history with. The families women make are not just the people they marry, live with, or give birth to. These new "kin" are people next door, across the assembly line, members of the same intentional community, neighbors down the street. "The false naming that creates the myth of the happy traditional family," **Karen Lindsey** wrote in *Friends as Family*, "has its corollary in the false naming that says life outside the family is miserable and empty, that people who choose childlessness have no real relationships with children or with the future, and that friends are never as fulfilling as family.

"Friends are who you pass pleasant time with," she continued, "who you like but don't love, to whom you make minimal if any commitment. Above all, friends are not family. Blood is thicker than water. Your friends are always 'other'; your family is who you are. But people are larger than the myths they try to live by. And the truth hidden by the myth is that people have always created larger families than the biological family—larger, and infinitely more diverse."[3]

Karen speaks from experience. In spite of pressure to conform to the myth, she never wanted to marry ("The law has no business in personal relationships."), or reproduce ("I had myself sterilized when I was twenty-seven."). She audaciously asked friends to give her a party after her tubes were tied, and they did. Several years later, she gave a party for a pregnant friend. "I wouldn't have felt so good about giving her a shower if I hadn't had one myself," Karen said.

Where did she get such ideas? From her parents, theater people who filled their Queens, New York home with other theater friends, a diverse group of adults who became part of Karen's family. And from books. Karen loved Louisa May Alcott's women characters. "Her spinster ladies had very strong women friends; they had roommates," Karen said. "My ideal was to grow up and have a roommate. We would live together, have our separate careers, and a wonderfully cozy domesticity. We would be life companions. I didn't call it family, but that was what it was, and it was as romantic a vision as walking off with Mr. Right."

To Karen, the choice not to have children is a respectable and honorable alternative. Creating family with friends instead of biological or legal ties is her way of life. "This vision of friends as family is profoundly feminist," she said, sitting in her apartment near Boston. "Women are told that our only major commitment is to our husbands and children, but it's not true, and really never was. When you name your friends as family, you give them a right; you legitimate them and give them the power of the traditional family."

## Elected Families

Compassion, consideration, and love are not restricted to the "intact family" fantasies of U.S. government officials and narrow-minded bureaucrats. Family feelings can't be contained in one, prescribed formula. "We need a new form today," Margaret Mead told Members of Congress before her death. "The extended family fell apart because nobody liked it. As soon as people realized they could get out, they left. Today, the nuclear family is too confining. We need 'elected

Charlotte Robinson (designer and cutter). Daphne Shuttleworth, Ruth Corning (assistants). Wenda F. Van Weise (silkscreen). Bonnie Persinger (piecing). Betty Guy, Gena Simpson, Lena Behme (assistants for piecing). Signature Quilt #1. from "The Artist and The Quilt" Exhibit. 1983.

families' made up of people we choose."[4] She would have liked the "families" we found.

• **Barbara Bailey** invited Eric, a thirteen-year-old son of a neighbor, to live with her and her son Rudy because Eric's mother couldn't give him the financial or emotional support he needed. He had gone with Barbara and Rudy on family excursions, and they were friends. "I decided I could help out," Barbara said, "so I asked Eric to come and live with us."

The first year was the hardest. Eric was new to the family. His mother moved out of the neighborhood. Rudy had to make room for another child in the family, and everybody had to get used to everybody else. But things settled down, and Eric found his place. He was successful at school, head of ROTC, and was the first person in his family to finish high school. Next stop—college. "I love him and I'm proud of him," said Barbara. "My investment of time, money, and support has been rewarded."

• **Sr. Diane Fassel** and **Anne Wilson Schaef** use the words "family" and "community" interchangeably to describe an assorted group of Colorado adults and children—a woman down the hill and her daughters, one woman in Greeley, a couple in Denver. "People come in and out," Anne said. "One person lived here last summer. A minister came for a week for help with his spirituality. At Christmas, we invited twenty people and thirty showed up."

"There are two requirements for belonging to this family," Diane added. "One is that each person lives his or her own process and respects others who are living theirs, and the second is that we will be honest with each other. These are the two basic commitments that bind us as a family."

• **Maggie McGuire**, in rural New Hampshire, has a group of women friends who help each other raise their children. "All are strong, compassionate women conscious of themselves as women," she said. She and her son live with another woman, Linda, and her daughter, Laura. Together they have made a family. "I'm Simon's parent, and Linda is Laura's parent," Maggie added, "but when I'm here, I'm in charge, and when Linda's here, she's in charge. Even when we are both here, it's nice to be able to say, 'I can't do it anymore. Could you please take over and be the mother for awhile?'

"Our family is based on a lot of love," she concluded. "By that, I mean not getting caught up in the little bitchy things like taking out the garbage and doing the dishes. We respect each other's privacy, and nurture each other, and ride through the hard times because we have a larger commitment."

• At the **Twin Oaks Community** in Louisa, Virginia, blood ties are deliberately blurred. Children born into this intentional community, one of the nation's oldest, are raised collectively by "metas," community members who want to be with children. Modeled after B.F. Skinner's *Walden Two*, Twin Oaks community members value cooperation, equality, nonviolence, antisexism, ecology, and noncompetitiveness.

**Peggy Fitzgerald** is a meta and a mother. She works a daily four-hour shift in the children's cottage, and spends several evenings a week with her two-year-old daughter. But her daughter has other primary adult relationships. During our interview, for instance, her daughter came walking along a path with a tall man in overalls. He was her caretaker for the evening. But when she saw our group, the baby left the man and came into our circle where she plopped down in Peggy's lap. They cuddled for a short time, the baby nursed, then she rejoined the man, waiting nearby. Peggy, free from child care for the evening, could eat dinner and talk with us about Twin Oaks.

Barbara, Anne and Diane, Maggie, and Peggy are living truths different from those *Family Circle* portrays or our nostalgic minds remember. They are not passively "making do" with what is given; they are actively choosing new families. In this creative furor, "the family" couldn't be stronger. Any rumor to the contrary is a lie. But new forms need new foundations, and families of choice need grounding. Traditional families have law and blood to bind; elected, intentional families have what they say to each other. That's all. Words of honor to live by.

There are no paths to follow, no models to copy. These women and men are creating families where members *commit to stay*, through thick and thin, for support in hardship and rejoicing in glad times. They are creating families where members *bend to difference*; where tolerance for, and celebration of, unique persons are the norms; where listening and decision-making skills reflect all points of view. They are creating families *committed to equality and cooperation*, where consensus, not conquest, is sought and where access to money, information, and power are shared. These three commitments are the bases on which new, elected families stand.


## A Commitment to Stay

No one functions very well without "home." But "home" is hard to describe. It is a feeling as much as a place—safety, love, some laughter, tears, a place of belonging. When we have this place, we build on it as though it were a cement foundation, or we grow up out of it as though it were a garden patch. Home doesn't fly apart in hard or easy times. It has weight, and in elected families, the weight is given by choice, not by law or blood. Karen Lindsey, members of Vancouver's Community Alternative Society, and Kathy McGuire are creating such home bases.

Karen had an emotional breakdown in 1977. "During that depression, I started phoning my friends," she said, "because I didn't want to commit suicide and I didn't want to be hospitalized. A community of people formed around me—mostly women, but a few men. For three months, every day, they came and took care of me. It was incredible; I felt so gratified."

They made vats of soup, cleaned Karen's house, held her while she sobbed, tucked her in bed at night. When Karen tried to cut herself with a knife, one friend took the knife away and put a pen in Karen's hand. "Don't cut," she said. "Write." These friends set limits for themselves, asked Karen to take some responsibility, and knew who to call when they had to leave her. But they agreed to take care of her until she could take care of herself. This experience led Karen to write *Friends as Family*.

**Val** (last name withheld by request), member of the **Community Alternative Society** in Vancouver, British Columbia, quit her job and exposed wrong-doing at her workplace with support from her community. "I was working for the local human rights commission, comparable to the EEOC (Equal Employment Opportunities Commission) in the States," she said, "and it was being put down the tubes by the government. I agitated inside the organization for about eight months, then I resigned and went to the media with my criticism. I could do that because I had both emotional and economic support here. My colleagues at work didn't have the freedom to quit or criticize because they had mortgages and families to care for."

When she resigned, Val's rent requirement dropped, and the thirty other adults in her rural/urban cooperative took up the slack. She had sympathetic friends to talk to during the transition period. "We stand by our commitments to each other," Val said. "Your idiosyncrasies and problems are part of the family and part of what we deal with. Once you're in, you're in."

**Kathy McGuire** is creating a similar, secure family for her later years. When she and six other women were in their early thirties, they formed "The Clovers," a women's retirement community. "We have made a commitment to be with each other when we are old," Kathy said. "We didn't want to lose each other over the years, and none of us wanted to end up being eighty years old and alone."

Each woman contributes $100 a year, and agrees to attend an annual reunion. "It's like a bedrock," Kathy said. "I have six women who are committed to me for my whole life. It has a big influence on my present life. I'm more able to make demands; I feel freer about changing jobs. It's possible for me to think about not having children as insurance for the future. And if I leave my husband or he dies before I do, those women will be there."

Karen's caretakers gave her permission to go crazy; Val's family stood

Olivia Bernard Wilson. Tree Figures. 1983. Plaster, Gauze, Wood, Wire. 10".

by while she opposed her government; Kathy is freer from worry about
the future. They have each cast their lot with people who used to be
strangers but who have become part of the ground they stand on. What
makes a friend family? "A family friend is someone who is accessible
in emergencies," Karen said, "and someone with whom you share some
history. In the traditional family, we put a lot of time into building
something, and we value it. We don't throw it away easily. In non-
blood families as well, people who are part of your life are to be
cherished and held onto as long as possible. If there must be a break,
there must, but it shouldn't be assumed or habitual."

"I want a blend of old and new," she concluded. "Sometimes when
people create alternatives, they feel bitter about the past and toss it out.
But we can keep what was useful from the past and use it to shape what
we want for the future."

## A Commitment to Diversity

Clearly, creating family with a bunch of strangers is not easy. Scores
of communes and cooperative houses fail because eager, idealistic
individuals don't understand that ideals have to be coupled with
sharpened communication skills. Elected, diverse families don't work
unless members listen carefully and lovingly to each other. Kathy
McGuire has been helping people form communities and intentional
families for over a decade.

"People are looking for intimacy," said Kathy, author of *Building
Supportive Community*, "and listening carefully to another person is
a very intimate activity. When you set yourself aside and understand
another's experience, a deep bonding happens. The person you're
listening to becomes transparent. You see how they see the world. And
they feel heard, deeply known, and understood. When people learn these
skills—both the sharing and the listening—they have the basis for
building a loving, empathic community."

Kathy encourages people to listen to their inner feelings. "A lot of
people act as if feelings don't exist," she concluded. "They talk about
what's on the surface all the time. But community can't be based on
surface material. Members have to listen deeply to themselves and each
other if any real bonding is to take place. Competition and hierarchies
are not part of it. Mutual respect and concern for the individual, one-
to-one, is the key to a successful community."

Family squabbles, feuds, and misunderstandings usually boil down
to matters of style and preference, not to differences in basic values.
In Vancouver, retired people and young activists, whose world views
are separated by several decades, share living pods. Some live in the
cooperative because they don't like living alone; others know that if
they pool their money, they'll have more to contribute to social causes.
"Some of us are saying we've got to be more political as a community,"
Val said, "while others are saying we've got to get the basement cleaned

up.'' In the end, family communities do both—clean basements *and* use group strength to change the world.

The **Sisters of Loretto**, have changed from a cloistered, habited, restricted group of women before Vatican II to a far-flung, brightly dressed collection of social and political activists. When the doors opened, these strong-willed women left convents in droves, learned to cook, drive cars, apply for jobs, write checks. But now, they wonder how six hundred, individual women no longer compelled to live together can remain a family in the wake of progress?

In the first place, they respect each other. Loretto anti-nuclear activists like Sr. Mary Luke Tobin and Sr. Pam Solo don't cut themselves off from Sr. Jane Marie Richardson and Sr. Helen DoBell who live as contemplatives in the woods of their Kentucky Motherhouse, because they'd miss the gifts of solitude and prayer that Jane Marie and Helen have found. Sr. Jeanne Deuber, Loretto artist, doesn't refuse to acknowledge the important work done by Sr. Anna Koop at the Catholic Worker House in Denver because she wants her art to be informed and relevant to the world into which it must eventually emerge.

In the second place, they initiate processes that give fast talkers *and* shy ones equal time in group discussions. Annual general assemblies now incorporate nonverbal sessions that employ dance, music, and visual art. President **Marian McAvoy** recently proposed ''Spinning and Weaving'' workshops to talk about issues of concern between annual meetings. Women could either participate in discussions in various cities or submit their thoughts in writing. ''As our ideas are shared with one another,'' wrote Marian in her letter introducing the process, ''the thread of each one's thinking will be woven together with others to reveal a fabric all the more interesting in texture and appearance because of the differences in individual threads.''

Like the Lorettos, members of the **Aradia** community in Grand Rapids don't live together, but they form one of the most varied, women-only communities in the United States. It is no simple task to keep their various threads woven together. Incorporated as a nonprofit organization in 1976, Aradia welcomes lesbian and heterosexual women. Community members publish two newsletters, sponsor softball teams, write plays, help produce the Michigan Women's Music Festival, lead racism workshops, and conduct healing rituals. Nine task forces include Charlotte Perkins Gilman Task Force for fund-raising projects, Patricia Neal Task Force for handicapped accessibility, Abigail Adams Task Force for internal group processes, and Wilma Rudolph Task Force for athletic events. Several members own ''The Ramblin' Inn,'' a cozy, good-food restaurant. Others own the ''Emporium,'' a clothing and gift shop. A music group, ''The Orgasms,'' meets regularly to make music. And Mary Ziederveen and Kit Dorsey turned their home into the ''Gallery for Wimmin's Art.''

Artist **Debbie Jones** initiated a corporate art project to help Aradian women deepen their knowledge and respect for each other. She asked women to trace their left hands onto pieces of paper, cut out the

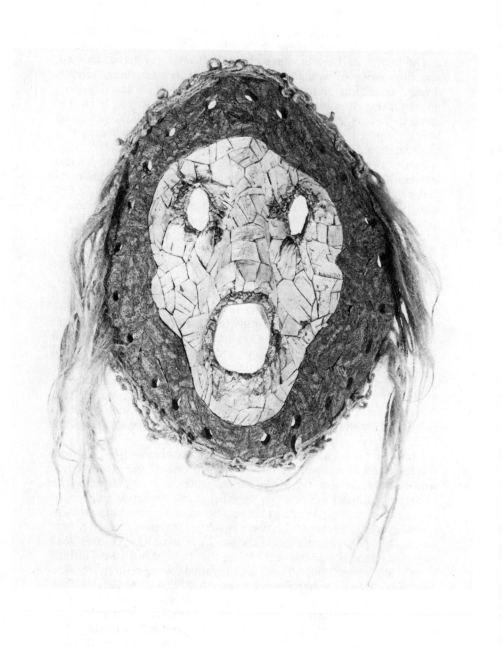

drawings, and decorate them. Debbie put the hands together to create a large mural.

Debbie learned who was timid and who was brash. She learned who was awkward with art materials; who reveled in paints and glue. And when she put all of the hands on the mural and listened to each woman describe her piece, Debbie knew that "art is a way we see and speak to each other. The diversity and unity of Aradia women was revealed in a strong visual way. The mandala of hands became a symbol of the collective energy generated in the community, and through the art, the women felt even more the special bonding between them."

Elected families use whatever they can to cement their connections with each other. They have to because diversity can blow a family apart as well as keep it lively. Members seek to honor their differences, temper the personal quirks and habits, and nurture individual gifts and talents. At Twin Oaks, **Trisha** explained how it works. "I'm grateful for Barry who keeps me up on native American issues," she said, "and for Mike who informs me about Central America. Because others pass around petitions and go to demonstrations, I don't have to. I can focus on my own interests and still support the larger 'causes' the community supports."

And **Taylor**, another resident, enjoys the options a large family offers. "Before I came here," she said, "I'd meet one interesting person once in awhile. Here, because we are a select group, the world of intriguing people is very large; there are always about thirty people I want to spend more time with." Living with many people is a break from living with only one person. "If somebody asks me to go to the movies, and I don't want to go, I feel free to say 'No,' because I know they can ask somebody else. I don't feel obligated to be anybody's companion."

When **Robin Moulds** lived at Twin Oaks, she found a group of people to meet her different needs. Women friends met her emotional needs ("We are more family than friends. We know each others' warts."), and other Twin Oaks members provided intellectual encouragement ("I seek out individuals who are stimulating.") Because there were many options for relationships, she could always be *with* someone. Knowing this allowed her to choose *being alone* when she really wanted that.

A mere tolerance for diversity gives way to an embrace. Kathy teaches others to listen; the Lorettos search for new ways to hear each other; scattered and diverse Aradians merge into a whole community; and women at Twin Oaks celebrate their options. Women are welcoming multiple and diverse relationships because they know the loneliness and isolation of the all-American family dream. By experimenting in living laboratories, day-to-day, these women are learning to cooperate and to share spaces, responsibility, and power.

---

Deborah Jones. Bark Mask #5. 1978. Wood, Bark, Ailanthus with flax fiber. 10" x 8" x 3". (Photo: Elizabeth Liaquer)

## A Commitment to Equality

We are one human family, all related, living communally on Planet Earth. Yet the affluent one-third of the world eats over half of the food produced.[5] This mania for consumption can't last if we are to survive as a species. One answer is to cooperate—internationally, interpersonally, interracially, intergenerationally. In elected families, women are caring for children and elders, pooling money, designing shared space, insuring equal access to opportunities, sharing daily tasks. "Communal life is a rational, efficient way to live for people who want to lower consumption and income," said **Sandra Boston**, member of the **Movement for a New Society** (MNS). "The fit will survive, and the fit are those who learn to share."

She learned just in time. She was mother of three children under six, married to a man who didn't believe her life should be as supported as his was, isolated in a Philadelphia suburb. She looked for an alternative, heard about MNS, and found there a model for the life she was seeking. Within three years, she had moved into a communal house in downtown Philadelphia. "It was the most soul-searching decision I had ever made," Sandra said. "It was agony to put what was good for me before what was good for my husband and children. I had seen myself as a good wife and mother, in a lasting marriage, struggling with my husband to break through the unfair social structures of marriage. So it was painful to realize that, in spite of our best efforts, patience, struggle, and determination, the glaring invalidation of my position as a woman remained."

MNS, a network of small collectives all over the United States, originated in Philadelphia and is peopled by individuals who are living the revolution now—simplifying and sharing their lives while they build a nonviolent, revolutionary movement. Sandra continued, "I wouldn't have moved out of my husband's house if I hadn't discovered actual people living like I wanted to live. With only my own experience and yearnings to go on, I would not have rent my family apart in an effort to validate my needs. But the MNS people gave me the support I needed to make the change in spite of the terrible costs."

MNS folks were alert to patterns of inequality. "The men had been getting proudly arrested at demonstrations," Sandra said. "Women got no glory or recognition and weren't making strategic, political decisions. Of course, while the men were in jail, the women were keeping it all together at home. But it was changing. Men began staying home with children while women led demonstrations."

Sandra started a collective house with people who wanted to share child care responsibilities. But child care wasn't her sole reason for living there. "It was living among people who were designing their whole lives consistent with a commitment to social and economic justice," she said. "This has to include shared child care if women are going to be liberated from exploitative, unpaid labor. I wanted a lifestyle that supported the liberation of all oppressed people, including mothers.

Because other adults helped with the children, Sandra could go out three nights a week, pursue her own career and education, keep up with local cultural events, have dinner with friends, do political work. "The whole experience revolutionized my life as a woman," Sandra said. "I felt like a normal person again, able to live my life fully. And living communally taught me how to cooperate, how to wait—for the telephone, the bathroom, the car—and how to contain my privacy in one room instead of in a whole house."

Just as women are creating new family structures to care for the young, they are also creating new spaces for the old. "Older women live by themselves in mansions on Long Island *and* in hovel apartments in the city," said **Jane Porcino**, professor of gerontology at the Stony Brook campus of the State University of New York and author of *Getting Older, Getting Better: A Handbook for Women in the Second Half of Life*. "They both wither away and age quickly because they are alone.

"Choice is the key issue for older women," Jane continued. "Older women, especially poor women of color, have few choices about who they will relate to, what work they will do, money, pasttimes, and housing. And the choices get slimmer as we get older, until finally we are totally cared for in institutions by others. By then, we have no choices at all."

Jane became an advocate for older women after a serious depression. "In my late forties, I suddenly felt totally alone," she said. "My children were leaving home, my husband and I were leaving the church. Some days, I thought I was going crazy in my own house. On top of that, I felt guilty about feeling bad. I had seven wonderful children, a husband I loved; I wasn't poor or sick. I couldn't imagine what was wrong with me. It took me a year to admit I was depressed."

Jane went to a doctor for help and didn't get any. "He just kept patting me on the head and prescribing estrogen," she said. "I couldn't find any information about depression, and at the time, there weren't any support networks for older women. The women's movement hadn't found us yet."

So she and a friend started a consciousness-raising group that included heterosexual, lesbian, divorced, widowed, and married women. "We shared very deeply," Jane continued, "and by the time I came out of that group, I had some good support for moving on. I went back to school, got my Ph.D., and decided to write a book about older women. I wanted to help them because if there had been another person to help me, I wouldn't have had to go through that depression."

Older women need loving, safe places to belong. Like the rest of us, they want companionship, work that allows them to give their considerable energies to society, and a sense of being valued by others. They need intimacy, someone who thinks they're special. "If we could put together groups of people in houses," Jane said, "some economic

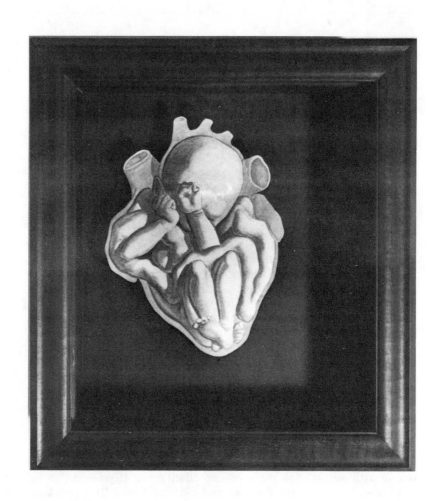

problems would be addressed, and some other problems as well. Everyone wouldn't need to have one of everything, and everyone wouldn't be so alone."

**Pagoda**, a lesbian community in St. Augustine, Florida, is determined to provide just that sort of space by developing plans for **Crones Nest**, a women's retirement center. Their brochure reads, "Our vision is to create a place that welcomes womyn, whether physically strong or not; of whatever color, creed or economic condition; lesbian or heterosexual—who choose to live their lives in common with other womyn." Natural health procedures will supersede drug treatments, and every resident will be encouraged to explore her fears, beliefs, and expectations about aging and death.

"Lesbian women are the models for us all," Jane said. "They are really addressing the question of how to take care of themselves when they are older. We straight women can look to them, and to women who have remained single, to teach us how to be alone because most of us have never had the experience. And we older women are going to have to strengthen our feminine companionships because we are going to be left with each other."

How hard the lessons come. How little trust we have in each other. In the Western world, competition, not cooperation, is the law of the land. Communism is for enemies; collectivity for science fiction utopias. Hierarchical social structures—churches, schools, governments, families—perpetuate dominant/submissive patterns: clergy over lay people, teachers over students, representatives over citizens, husbands over wives. It is radical to create structures where equality is the norm, where the foundation of our current social arrangements is undermined. Yet in elected families, equality, regardless of race, social class, age, physical condition or gender, is assumed even though individual members are products of the larger, hierarchical culture, who struggle daily to share power.

The sixteen **Pagoda** women, living together in ten beach cottages, deal with power issues all the time. "I come from money, from education, from law school, from yak, yak, yak," said **Lavender**, Pagoda resident. "I'm perceived as very powerful, and I'm not going to give away that power. I believe in strength. But I also understand more and more that many women who come here don't come from such privilege. They don't feel as secure as I do in certain settings. So, over the last six years, I've learned to keep my mouth shut more, to encourage other women to speak. I get involved, but don't assume that what I say has to be the law."

Sue Williams ("Rainbow"), Winter Park, Florida; Julia Jordan, trying to be queens. We just don't want to 'queen over' anybody else."

Aradian women, like their sisters at Pagoda, pay attention to queenly urges. They have developed an innovative, role-rotation system for their

Colleen Sterling. Inner Space. 1978. Watercolor on Paper, Cut-out and raised on foamcore, mounted in shadow box. 12″ x 15″.

meetings to address their needs. **Sherry Redding**, Aradia co-founder, explained. "One woman is the Maiden," she said. "She is the traditional facilitator. She plans the agenda and conducts the meeting. The Mother makes sure there's an opening and closing ritual, and her main function during the meeting is empathy—making sure everyone gets heard. The Nymph takes care of fun, food and breaks. By establishing these roles and rotating them, we insure that individual needs and community concerns will be taken care of. Otherwise, we can get bogged down in one or the other."

At Twin Oaks, all jobs—tuning up a car, cow milking, child care, and gardening—are equal. The task of overseeing the half-million-dollar a year hammock business has the same value as kitchen clean-up. Yet power struggles continue. When we asked what issue continue to need attention, Peggy answered, "Power. I've always felt strong, but how do I empower others? We still struggle to know how we can be a leader-full society rather than a leader-less one."

"This can only come about when each member is responsible for him- or herself," Taylor said. "Before coming here, I could say, 'If I had another job or if I lived in a different place, I'd feel better.' But here, I can't say that because nobody's stopping me from making things better. It's up to me."

Learning to cooperate takes courage. Older and younger women work on ageism while they plan for retirement on the Florida coast; Pagoda and Aradia members explore privilege based on education and class; and traditional "women's work" is equally valued with other Twin Oaks tasks. Women, men, and children are forming places of belonging that look like families—that provide loving contexts; continuity; history; emotional, financial, spiritual support.

Community building is future building. We live on one planet—old, young, animals, trees, Russians, sand, and stone. Women and men pioneering new family structures are preparing themselves for a future in which communality will be the norm, not the exception. They realize they are joined by 4.5 billion other people on the planet, and that by the year 2000, another 1.5 billion will join them.[6] There isn't time to argue about blood kin or restrict relationships by law. It is time to write a new story about corporateness and collectivity. It doesn't mean we turn into communists, or lose our individuality. There are times for arias and times for choruses. All operas have both.

The family isn't dead. But the old building that was "marriage and family life" is undergoing renovation. Some women are sweeping out the place, repainting, taking down a wall or two. Some are abandoning the old structure altogether and building their own-style houses down the street. In every case, the arrangements we are making are exciting and positive, though not without struggle or pain. "We women are beginning to test ideals, our utopias," said Maggie McGuire. "We are saying, 'We can do this so much better than it has been done.' We aren't throwing out the ideals. We are just tempering them without being cynical. And we are finding our way, little by little, step by step."

# 4

# THE GRASS IS GREENER HERE

Our psyches, shaped by stories of continents explored, the American West "settled," and space colonized, long for "elsewhere." "If only I lived there," "If only I could go with you," we utter. Striving after something "other" is commonly called progress—onward to the next mountain, upward to a bigger house, outward to the planets. Itching to shift from A to B, to get more, to be better, we overlook what is. Dissatisfaction and restlessness set in. We devalue our own lives. In contrast to color spreads in slick magazines and televised reports about the rich and famous, our daily lives seem pale and insignificant. We lose sight of the power and glory within ourselves. We think, "The grass is greener *there*."

Some Denver artists, settled between coasts, read *Art News* reports about art movements in Los Angeles, Sante Fe, Chicago, and New York, and wonder why the national art spotlight never focuses on their Colorado art base. "I'm not on the cutting edge," one woman said. "I read magazines about what's going on in New York and France, and I wonder if it's all passed me by. Is the *true* avant garde on the West and East Coasts? Do artists in New York and Los Angeles live in the *real* art world? I never feel like I know what's happening."

If the art centers appear to be in New York and Los Angeles, the political center seems to be in Washington, D.C. Congressional offices represent every section of the nation. On one floor of the Rayburn

House Office Building, name plates announcing Arizona, California, Florida, Hawaii, Illinois, Louisiana, Michigan, New York, North Carolina, Oklahoma, Oregon, South Dakota, and Wisconsin adorn doorways.

Inside each door is a microcosm of a state. Pictures of governors, state flags, samples of tobacco leaves or corn stalks, and posters of sandy beaches, steel mills, crawfish dinners, or skiers swirling through snowbanks establish tone. Receptionists greet visitors with back-home accents, while legislative assistants scurry back and forth teletyping press releases to district offices. In every way, the Congress looks like the hub, and ordinary citizens are awed by its scope. When Annie worked there, people continually asked, "What's it like to work at the center of power?"

Inhabitants of these mythical centers perpetuate the awe. Politicians in Washington like lofty, high-ceilinged committee chambers in which to do the nation's business. Art critics and gallery owners in New York and Los Angeles profit when Denver artists feel on the fringes. Government officials and art dealers keep power because their constituencies are off balance. Seduced by the lights of New York, the sprawl and speed of Los Angeles, and the wheeling and dealing of Washington, we stand like Dorothy before Oz, unable to see that the Wizard's magic is a smoky, audio-visual extravaganza.

But it is. By the time Dorothy and her friends reached their promised land, they possessed what they sought. The Lion had shown courage, the Tin Man love, the Scarecrow intelligence. And Dorothy, who wanted to go home, already wore the magic shoes that would take her there. If the women in Denver knew Oz was not New York, their art would change. They might write articles about themselves and get newspapers and magazines to publish them. Their unique exhibits might travel around the world. They would be excited. They would feel powerful. They would flaunt Colorado's effect on their imagery. Many of them do these things already, of course, and one woman we met explained her understanding. "There is a geographical imperative here," she said. "I can see for miles. As an artist, this expansive landscape makes me feel adventurous, like a pioneer woman. And like one, I have to find my own resources—inner and outer—to work with the scale, the light."

For decades, **Maryat Lee** has helped people appreciate where they live. First in Harlem with the Soul and Latin Theater and now in West Virginia with EcoTheater, she has written plays based on the lives of ordinary people and turned local citizens into performers.

Everywhere she goes, she uses the same process. She tapes interviews with local residents. Then she listens to speech rhythms, phrasing, and content. She distills the stories into five- and ten-minute scenes and looks for players, "untrained actors indigenous to the community to act as experts in their own play."[1] In Hinton, West Virginia, home of

---

Arlene Hartman. Soul Compressions. 1984. Graphite on Basinwerk.
5″ x 38″.

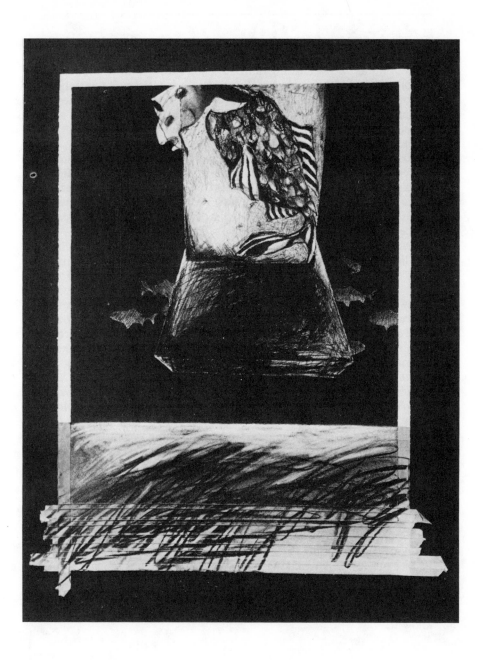

EcoTheater, Maryat cajoled, persuaded, and begged local people to join her. Enough of them did, and in 1975, EcoTheater was born.

Hinton was once a bustling railroad center through which thousands of tons of coal rolled each day. But today, it is a sleepy Appalachian hilltown, reduced to fading memories by the development of the diesel. When Maryat arrived, the economy of the region was depressed and the citizens were despondent. Maryat set about to help restore pride in their home place.

Today, the stories of Hinton, of its people and history, are told to audiences every week during the summer at Pipestem State Park, fifteen miles south of Hinton. Universal themes of love and loss, life and death, come alive as local non-actors tell how the railroad yard buzzed with seven hundred men before the coming of the diesel, how two opera houses competed for the boom town's entertainment business.

One night we sat underneath a cool, late summer sky, we watched and listened to Hinton citizens tell us about local legends and ordinary people. Kathy Jackson, a young mother, became the legendary John Henry who died after beating the spike-driving machine. Lucinda Ayers, for twenty years a single parent with four children, made us weep when she remembered the loveless life of a waiting wife. And Joe Bigony, part owner of Hinton Builder's Supply and vice president of the Chamber of Commerce, sat on a stool and thought out loud about how the man who finally comes home had "sold out his family for things."

Hinton citizens are no longer victims of change or depression. By transforming local stories into theater, they gain self-respect. "EcoTheater is an occasion for the people of a community to explore its own stories and history with fresh perception," Maryat wrote in *CoEvolution Quarterly*, "and to find comfortable ways to express it with integrity in public presentation. Attention, pride, and a certain excitement come to the whole community that sees that its own stories, perceptions, and its own plain people without theater-training are worthy of interest."[2]

The center is where we are, doing what we do daily. Good artists live and work in New York, but they also reside in St. Louis and Denver. Entertainers flock to Los Angeles, but dance, music, and comedy are not confined to the hills around Hollywood. Washington, D.C. may be a center for policy making, but every New England town meeting and Southwest community block party are examples of political power. Major urban centers are receptacles for activities generated somewhere else. Fact is, the grass is greener *here*, and increasing numbers of women know it.

## Putting Down Roots

**Judy Smith** is one of them. Though the scale of the West welcomes and dares, Montana has won her heart. She's dug in her heels, sunk roots down, called it home. Her friends think she's crazy to live in a state with a brutal climate, vast distances, conservative politics, and only 700,000 people. Yet there she stays. What does this doctor of biology, community organizing whiz, and feminist theorist find in Montana? "A viable state community," Judy said. "The population of the whole state is small enough, and we have enough traditions in common to make us one people. People here still believe they have the power to make change."

She hates going to national conferences because of the political polarization—radicals vs. liberals, straights vs. gays, environmentalists vs. labor unions. "In Montana, you can't just work with a little core of people who are 'right,' " she said. "There aren't enough of them. I work with very diverse groups, even members of the religious right. In Montana, you have to have very flexible working relationships and learn to complement each other."

She listens for trends, and then she acts. When lawyers around the state told Judy they were getting inquiries about incest, she asked a student in her feminist theory class at the University of Montana how to approach the issue. "She'd written a paper on incest," Judy said, "and she said we should focus on public education."

Judy put together a broad coalition—educators, church people, social service agents, state government representatives, psychologists—and asked some of them to serve on the Board of Directors. Together they named themselves the Montana Incest Prevention Coalition, wrote a grant proposal for a conference, and invited people from all over the state. "Over five hundred people came," Judy said, "and two other projects spun off—a set of workshops to go into smaller communities and a video program from the conference."

Judy believes in Montana—its people and its issues. She resists the temptation to move on. A friend of hers said, "Judy is so capable, so smart, so powerful. She's an expert on appropriate technology, incest and teenage pregnancy, and energy, among other things. She could be a national leader in any one of these areas if she chose." But she stays where she is. "I work on a local/state level because I can make a difference here," Judy said. "For me, it is the only way to go. It keeps me sane."

**Malissa Burnette**, a South Carolina lawyer, stays in a state where Southern attitudes deny women and minorities equal rights. Yet she uses her power to make a difference there. In the early 1970s, fresh from college with sociology degree in hand, she became a guard at the women's prison. Within a few years, she was principal of the prison school. "I saw how women prisoners were treated differently from men," she said. "In job training and schooling opportunities, they are not getting a fair share. I saw that blacks were one-third of our state's population, but two-thirds of the prison population. I saw that if you had money or were white, you probably wouldn't be there. The whole experience opened my eyes."

When she left the prison, she directed a senior citizens' center, then got involved in the battered women's shelter when her husband began to batter her. "At one point he tried to kill me," she said. "I locked myself in a room and left the next morning. If prison work opened my eyes about racism, having my life threatened by my husband opened my eyes about sexism. It changed my life. I quit my job and enrolled in law school. I was mad as hell and determined to do something about injustice."

She worked on the campaign to pass the Equal Rights Amendment in South Carolina, became active in the state's National Organization for Women chapter, and graduated from law school. When Nancy Stevenson was elected lieutenant governor, the first woman elected to statewide office, she hired Malissa to be her deputy. From that position, Malissa wrote legislation for displaced homemakers and authored a marriage license tax bill to provide permanent funding for domestic violence programs in the state. "I loved working with Nancy because we had power to do things that benefited women in the state," Malissa said. "A lot of women have to do their political work on their own time. I was free to do mine on work time."

Today, Malissa is a lawyer in her own firm, arguing cases on sex and race discrimination. She's active in state politics and is building a political base. She helps other women wherever she can. When the Business and Professional Women's Club sponsors a program for young career women, she encourages women to apply. "Women need to get into the system," Malissa concluded. "One way to do that is to meet people, be involved in legislative activities, then accept invitations to serve on committees and boards. I see more women in business, more women on state commissions. What a pleasure it's been to notice how I am less frequently the only woman at meetings."

**Eleanor McCallie** left her home in Chattanooga, Tennessee, at seventeen and stayed away for seventeen years. She wanted to shed the heavy overlay of social class and racial tradition common to her Southern heritage. "I was glad to leave the South and the restrictions of family and class," she said. "People in the South ask, 'Who is your family?', and they really want to know your credentials. Our family's been here for generations, so I know my place."

She landed in California, moved into a women's communal house, taught self-health classes, and started Earthwork, an organization that distributed nutrition education, organized food coops, and established direct markets for farmers. But at age thirty-four, Eleanor returned to Chattanooga. "I had actually come to value a community with roots," she said, "networks of relations and people you've known a long time, especially ones you don't agree with. I also began to realize

that change happens more slowly, and more deeply than I once thought.
I saw change happening here in the South, and I was ready to return
to it."

Chattanooga was different. Whole neighborhoods had been torn
down, and suburban malls occupied once green pastures. The Tennessee
Valley Authority's solar-powered office building dominated the center
of town where old stores, bars, and movie houses once stood. New roads
and bridges tricked her sense of direction. Though class and race issues
were still evident, the traditional industrial base was eroding and with
it, the old alliances. Schools and businesses were integrated, and new
people had moved to the area. Chattanooga was in transition.

Eleanor settled in, attended the women's network lunch meetings,
started a black/white dialogue group, and conducted an oral history
project for the library. She joined Vision 2000, a project calling for
broad public participation in setting future community goals. "From
those years away," Eleanor said, "I gained an awareness of the
possibilities for the future. As a result, I've returned to Tennessee to
build it slowly, very slowly, because it must be done at home."

Judy and Malissa, trained in science and law, keep their focus at
home. Eleanor, broadened by being away, chooses to return. They each
understand national and international trends; they follow political,
scientific, and economic events outside of their state lines. But they
are committed to their neighbors. They stay put. **Hattie Williams** does
too. Her commitment to the poor in Chicago's South Side is passionate
and total. Like Judy, Malissa, and Eleanor, she works on behalf of
the folks next door.

She was born on Lake Park Avenue in Chicago's South Side sixty-
odd years ago. She still lives there. Over the years, she has watched
her neighborhood become one of the nation's poorest ghettos, sitting
on some of the most valuable, lakeside real estate in Illinois. She figures
that by 1992, when the World's Fair is scheduled to come to the South
Side, her neighborhood will be destroyed and replaced by expensive,
high-rise condominiums for the rich. This suspicion about the future
does not stop her in the present. Years ago, Hattie survived two brain
tumor operations, blindness and paralysis, and made a vow to God
that she would commit her life to helping her people.

Some of her people need all the help they can get. In the sixteen-
story projects across the street, eleven-year-old girls have babies, and
incest and child abuse are common. Nervous young mothers, stupified
by prescribed Valium, lose control of their children. "They don't see
that their kids get to school," Hattie said. "They don't know the
teenager's having sex in the back bedroom. They don't know nothing,
they're so dulled out. Pretty soon, the youngsters are selling their
mother's pills to other kids."

When Hattie recovered from her surgery, she proclaimed her block
and all its inhabitants as "family." and opened her house as a Christian
center, a place of hope and help. "I was just a black woman in a
neighborhood, a widow living on a widow's pension," she continued.

"My kids were grown and this house was empty. So I decided to do my work right here." She hung a fish, a Christian symbol, from her living room window, went across the street to the projects, and invited the neighbors into her Shalom House. She's been busy ever since. "The way I look at it is this: if Jesus was born in a manger, this house don't have to be so hot."

Eudora Welty said once that she never left Jackson, Mississippi, because she knew she'd never run out of stories there. Women centered in their neighborhoods and states dig around where they are to uncover stories, pain, possibilities, and history. They make a difference. They are effective and powerful. They participate in change. Maryat, Judy, Malissa, Eleanor, and Hattie are proof. By staying where they are, they are stimulating creativity, building pride, healing divisions, teaching skills, and staying sane by working on a scale that has meaning.

## Solving Local Problems

And there is plenty of work to do. Their home bases are fraught with problems. Substandard housing, poverty, injustice, crime, and an inequitable distribution of wealth challenge them and all their neighbors. In most cities, too many young people waste their lives on drugs, alcohol, and gang warfare. Women rooted in their neighborhoods, state politics, and community affairs are tackling these problems with a vengeance.

In Chicago, Hattie Williams opened Shalom House, but her people need more than prayer to get them through each day. Many of them don't have enough to eat. They need confidence and training, jobs and child care, transportation and housing, self-respect. When a local Catholic divinity school professor approached Hattie and suggested they start a program called "mission in reverse," Hattie accepted the challenge. Seminary students would live with Hattie and work with people living in housing projects. Shalom House would be the base. "I didn't want seminarians coming in with preconceived notions about what would be good for the poor," Hattie said. "The people in the neighborhood are the *teachers*, and when they are listened to, you find out how to implement a program that will be self-sustaining after you're gone. I wanted seminarians to learn *from* the people they had come to serve."

Hattie and the seminarians have started clothing and food banks. Seminarians have taught project residents how to sew, renovate old buildings, get their GEDs. "One sister taught the people in a six-family building about receivership," Hattie said. "When they didn't have heat, they took their rent money, put it in a fund, and bought a furnace. Now they are turning the building around, and the people living there are doing their own renovation."

Janet Braun-Reinitz. Empty Bed of Roses IV—Geometry Quilt. 1981.
Colored Pencil on Paper. 27″ x 39″.

Trust and skills are building. Poor blacks learn that whites aren't always out to exploit them. White seminarians learn the reasons for angry behavior. When one young man cursed a seminarian, Hattie discovered that his home situation was deteriorating. "The night before, his father had beaten his mother," Hattie said. "This young kid had to jump in and beat up his father to protect his mother. I told the young man he didn't have a right to take out his anger on the seminarian, but I also told the seminarian what the situation was. They've got to see what it's really about here."

Because of her commitment to the local community, and her ability to match white, middle-class students with poor, black ghetto residents, Hattie can see practical results for the future. "The skills that my people are learning can go *anywhere* with them, and that's what gives me hope. Also, the seminarians who've been here leave with new respect for those they came to serve. When they move away to live all over the world, the Shalom House key is everywhere."

Half a continent away in Los Angeles, Chicana muralist **Judy Baca** hits the streets every summer looking for teenage gang members who will help her paint the history of California on the Tujunga Wash Flood Control Channel in North Hollywood. Since 1976, young dropouts with police records have learned to read Judy's blueprints, calculate complicated math problems about scale, and prepare an outdoor, sometimes underwater, surface for paint. They have also learned to trust and work with kids different from themselves.

In 1974, the U.S. Army Corps of Engineers asked Judy to design a mural along the flood-control channel. A founder of the Social and Public Arts Resource Center (SPARC) in Venice, California, Judy works on issues that affect the varied peoples of Los Angeles. The Great Wall of Los Angeles, as the Tujunga Wash Project is called, turned into her biggest project.

But not her first. Since 1970, Judy has painted murals in East Los Angeles barrios. There she found young people drinking wine, sniffing glue, playing idle games. Unemployment, drug use, and violence prevailed. "There was nothing for them to do in the parks—no programs, no jobs—not then and not now," Judy told editors of *La Comunidad.* "No one was taking an interest in them, and I got the idea of trying to relate to them through art."[3]

Many of the young Chicanos and Mexicanos were artists. Formed into fiercely territorial gangs, they established boundaries with graffiti-covered walls. Judy capitalized on this inherent artistic talent and asked gang members to help her paint a mural. At first, the atmosphere was charged—members of one gang didn't trust members of another. But they trusted Judy, and gradually, by using improvisational games to defuse tension, she helped them trust each other.

When the Tujunga Wash project came along, Judy was prepared. She knew that racism was created by isolation and misunderstanding.

Judith Baca. The Great Wall of Los Angeles—Detail Olympic Section. 1983. (Photo: Gia Roland)

"The black, Asian, and Chicano communities are miles apart," she said. "There's terrific geographical and cultural isolation; the people just can't read each other at all. One sentence can mean three different things, depending on who's talking and who's listening."[4] By inviting minority group members to paint a mural about the history of minorities in California, she knew she could heal wounds.

As an urban artist, Judy cares about the whole fabric of Los Angeles—the physical, the social, and the cultural. "Art is not just for the rich, the educated, or five of my friends," she said. "Art is vital to the spirit of human beings, rich or poor." And she knows that public, blank walls do nothing to address the depersonalization already felt by urban residents. Art on those walls changes everything. It expresses a people's experience of place and reduces cultural isolation. "Space is power. Take over a big public space and you've got power."[5]

To prepare for the Tujunga Wash Project, Judy called community meetings and asked for money and support. She explained that mural-makers would be low-income youths between fourteen and twenty-one, many of whom had had trouble with the law. She outlined her strategy: form racially mixed crews, set aside one day a week for study, and use improvisational drama to handle personal problems.

Some of the kids had never met a person of another race, let alone worked with one. Creating mixed crews of Chicanos, blacks, and Asians encouraged familiarity. Interracial friendships developed, along with interdependence—it took teamwork to erect scaffolding and paint eight-foot walls. Lives were changed. One young Chicana with a troubled past, including incest, self-torture, and armed robbery, announced at the beginning of the summer, "I ain't *never* gonna work with them niggers." By summer's end, she was teamed up with an all-black video crew.[6]

Fridays were "study days." Judy recruited dynamic teachers to talk about the economics, politics, and social history suggested by the mural. When the crew was working on a panel about fascism, the first speaker was a historian specializing in the Holocaust, the second was a Holocaust survivor, and the third was a relative of a displaced European Jew.

One of Judy's major goals is to root out racism. Using dramatic improvisation, she teaches problem-solving and conflict-resolution skills. During group role-plays, teenagers write down their ideas about other groups, then act them out. " 'Chicanos are lazy and dirty' becomes hilarious," Judy said, "when it's being acted out by kids so energetic you sometimes want to hogtie them."[7]

The energy and power of the mural are impressive. When we visited on a muggy Los Angeles afternoon, we couldn't believe its detail *and* scope. Bright, aggressive colors swayed and surged, coattails became railroad tracks, outstretched hands became flames of fire. Decades unrolled down the channel, and successive panels depicted dinosaurs, goldmining, industrialization, depression, war, and prosperity. When it is finished in 1987, the mural will be one mile long.

Over the years, kids return to tell Judy Baca how their work on the Great Wall changed them. By confronting racism, they have explored and exploded stereotypes about others. By learning reading, math, and communication skills, they have a chance to move out of the ghettos and into mainstream Los Angeles life. By painting a history of their people, they have applauded their heritage. "The racism directed at these youngsters leads to self-hate, which amounts to a death-wish," Judy said. "There's no way they can participate in the American dream of 'work hard and get ahead.' Painting the channel widened their scope. Before they would say, 'We can't move all that dirt.' They now say, 'We'll get it moved today.' "[8]

Poverty and low self-esteem can be overcome, but for undocumented Mexican women who cross the border into El Paso, Texas, it is an uphill battle. In constant fear of deportation and exploitation, without language skills, passports, or money, these women are their community's most vulnerable citizens. Workers at the ecumenical **Liceo Sylvan** offer refuge and help. "Word got out that the center was a place where the undocumented were not persecuted or taken advantage of," said Sister of Loretto **Mary Peter Bruce**, "and women began coming in with their problems."

They have plenty. Hired in El Paso as domestic servants, the women are practically enslaved by employers who deny them time off and pay them fifty cents a day. Many quit in anger and frustration, but stay in Texas. Some get married, then pregnant, and are eventually abandoned by their husbands. When they find Liceo Sylvan, "they have children and no support," Peter said, "no language, no skills, no money. We begin at the beginning—delayed birth certificates, health care, schooling."

Freed from fear, treated with respect and love, the women blossom. At the center today, Mexican women are teaching Spanish to United States women. The sewing teacher is a woman who landed on the doorstep several years ago, beaten and alone, with three hungry children in tow. "The women are taking things into their own hands," Peter added. "They are becoming what they should have been all along— happy, contributing people."

## Empowering Local Citizens

Enabling women to take community leadership is the goal of the **National Congress of Neighborhood Women**. They are dedicated to the nurturance and empowerment of neighborhood residents and to confronting political issues that affect local citizens. They've combined a senior citizens and day care center, reopened a neighborhood library and fire station, and liberalized loan policies at local banks. Their battered women's shelter welcomes children. Grants from city, state, and federal agencies fund job-training and educational projects.

Headquartered in the Williamsburg section of Brooklyn, the Congress is staffed by dynamic working-class women who focus on education and skills training. Because many neighborhood women dropped out of school to support their families, they are paid a minimum wage when they reenter the workforce. Many of them want to return to school. Ever ready, the Congress started a community-based college program with LaGuardia College, part of the City University of New York. Students and Congress staff interviewed LaGuardia professors and selected the curriculum. The local senior center contributed a room, and fifty women began college.

By 1984, over two hundred and fifty women had graduated from the Associate of Arts Degree program, and four hundred more were enrolled. A Bachelor of Arts Degree program had been added, and **Sally Martino Fisher**, Congress administrator and resident of Williamsburg, was enrolled as a community development major. She began college when her fourth child was three weeks old. She worked all day, stayed involved in the community, and took care of her family. If her classes hadn't been in the neighborhood and related to her daily life, she wouldn't have been able to continue.

Once when neighborhood women were picketing for day care services, Sally told her professor she wouldn't be in class that day. He asked her why. "I told the class what I was protesting and what the issues were," she said. "The lessons we learned that day were much more informative than any traditional class, and the community is so much richer when that kind of learning takes place." Her health teacher encouraged Sally to research a mysterious disease that had suddenly killed her six-year-old girl. "Because the classes are interrelated," she said, "you can work on things right here in the community that already interest you."

Since college is part of the neighborhood, physically and psychologically, students apply their skills to Brooklyn. For Brooklyn, the rewards are obvious. "We aren't sending fifty people to school to get degrees to go off and work for Exxon," Sally concluded. "We're getting an education that we can put back into our community."

And what comes back into the community are powerful women. The National Congress staff likes nothing better than strong women. "Women are the natural leaders in neighborhoods," said Sally. "We set the agenda, say what's important. Many organizations have started when women got together under a streetlight because a child was hit by a car or something. They demonstrate, start a little group, apply for money. The group gets bigger. But when money comes in, women's roles diminish, and most of the time a man will step in as president. Eventually, the women disappear."

If local communities are to be the base of women's power, women must run the organizations they begin. "Our goal is to train women as leaders in neighborhoods," **Jan Peterson**, one founder of the Congress, continued. "And because most of us have been so hurt by the abuse of power, we have to develop new leadership forms."

The problem is, women often aren't their own best allies. Sometimes when they lead, they are criticized. Occasionally neighbors harangue Sally for working at the Congress. "Some people say, 'Those women you work with are all lesbians,' or 'What kind of Communist organization are you?' " she said. "We even get criticized from the other side. The radical feminists think we kowtow too much to working-class values and don't spend enough time marching for the ERA and abortion. Anytime you're not on the line where people think you should be, you're gonna get it."

"Women are used to dealing with their families in a personal way, and sometimes they deal the same ways in the community," Jan said. "If our friends don't agree with everything we do, for example, we may assume they don't like us. But families and communities are different. You have to learn to handle it when you have a fight with a friend on one issue and work with her on five others. It's easier to work on an issue with somebody you're not living with. It's harder when you've lived down the street for fifty years."

In spite of the nit-picking, women are building powerful coalitions with neighbors. And in areas like Brooklyn's Williamsburg section that means working with diversity—blacks, Hispanics, Poles, Italians, Jews, gays, rich, and poor. Handling difference is a major challenge for neighborhood groups.

Sally sat with Jan at an outdoor cafe on a sunny spring day, and told about her Italian-American support group. "We were bad about supporting each other," she said. "Many of us would rather help a man. So the first thing we had to do was build trust. Our meetings depended on confidentiality, which is difficult in a small neighborhood, but we needed to know we had a safe place to go.

"This trust took a long time to develop," she continued, "but it did happen. Once, when I was chairing a meeting with a group of blacks, whites, Spanish, Poles, Italians, and Irish, I knew I was going to be attacked. I was very uncomfortable until I looked around the room and saw five women from my Italian-American support group. Suddenly, I felt very strong. The dispute turned out to be a small thing that I could have handled by myself, but having my friends there felt great."

Congress members encourage ethnic support groups like Sally's, because they are convinced that women must feel grounded in their culture before they can be effective allies to other women. They sponsor weekend retreats to build trust within and between ethnic groups. During one such two-and-a-half day event, women from six different groups met separately and told each other stories about how life had been as part of that culture. Inevitably they acknowledged pain and feelings of discrimination. But instead of unloading their hurts onto the other groups, they each gave a presentation to teach the others about themselves. "It was one of the most powerful ethnic-sharing events I've ever seen," said Jan. "Each group had an hour-and-a-half to do their presentation. Nobody accused anybody. Nobody blamed or shouted or hated. Instead, the women told each other who they were. By the end, people were crying."

What began as a local effort has grown, and today Congress affiliates flourish in Ohio, West Virginia, Oklahoma, Missouri, and other states. Jan and Sally and women associated with the National Congress are providing education and job training, teaching political skills, restoring feelings of power, and saying in unison:

We are sisters raising
A banner of love
Before all nations
Colors of the rainbow
Keepers of the earth
Invisible no longer
Grassroots women leaders
*Getting it all together.*

Because Jan and Sally, Judy Baca, and Hattie Williams believe that they live in the center, women of Brooklyn and children of Los Angeles are creating works of art and political coalitions where none existed before. White seminarians are learning from Chicago's poorest. Because these community-based women affirm their locales as centers of power, they don't see insignificant neighbors when they walk down the street, people waiting to be served with newer and more innovative programs. Instead, they see neighborhoods filled with people rich in resources and creativity, ready to give.

This regard for the lives of local people is a most respectful and loving stance. And a contagious one. If women in Brooklyn understand leadership skills, they won't give leadership away to men. If inhabitants of South Side Chicago projects teach somebody something, they have contributed to another's education. If an undocumented Mexican woman can learn a new language and find support for herself and her baby, she is on her way to feeling like a full human being. Unleashing the power of individuals is heady stuff.

**Deloris Brown** ought to know. Ropes of oppression that bound her were untied some years ago. Ever since, she's been blooming. There are thousands of women like Deloris in the United States and Canada— overlooked by government authorities, disconnected from their communities, used as statistics during political campaigns. She lived for years in a Washington, D.C., two-room apartment with five children. She wanted a place of her own, but welfare checks wouldn't cover mortgage payments, so her dream remained a fantasy.

When the owner of her apartment building decided to renovate, Deloris had to move downstairs to a one bedroom unit. Everyday she went upstairs to see how the contractor was doing. Then one day she told him she wanted a house. "I would like to have a house of my own," Deloris said, out loud. "That sure would be nice."

The man she said it to was director of **Hope and a Home,** a black/white coalition working to help families stay together. The group is part of a larger group, FLOC (For Love of Children), committed to advocacy and care for abused and neglected children in Washington. Hope and a Home sponsors parenting groups and family camping trips, helps families get access to city and federal services, and buys and rehabilitates houses for low-income residents. When Deloris told Jim Dickerson, Hope and a Home director, that she wanted a home, he said, "We'll have one available within the year."

Deloris could not believe her ears. "I waited," she said, "and when the house opened up for me, my dream came true. Good thing, too, because just as soon as I moved in, another woman with eight kids got evicted. I was able to take four of her kids to live with me."

No government bureaucrats at the Department of Health and Human Services noticed her, though they sent her money every week. No politicians were representing her interests, though she voted for them every two years. No futurists were plotting graphs of her life in the 21st century, though she looked at her children and saw the future. A group of ordinary people, committed to the people in their community, looked at Deloris Brown, face to face, eye to eye, and said "Hello." And Deloris Brown looked back and said, "I want a home for myself and my children." She got it, and she also got a community, training, and self-confidence. Today she works for Hope and a Home, giving back what she once received.

Her dream was not small. Neither is Judy Baca's nor Sally Fisher's. But they come true because these women believe that change begins in kitchens, not in cabinet meetings. Instead of fleeing to greener pastures, they implant themselves right where they are. They affirm their power and notice others. They teach skills. They share personal and cultural gifts, hold them out for others to see. They believe in the local. They believe that change in one life matters. They know it comes from within, begins at home, and transforms the planet.

# 5

# MEETING AT THE
# INTERNATIONAL WELL

Some years ago, R. Buckminster Fuller gave a speech at a small Midwestern college, describing geodesic domes, tetrahedrons, enclosed cities with climate control, and his vision for global interconnectedness and peace. He was a patient man, with a charming, childlike manner, and at the end of the session, several students came forward to talk further with him. As the crowd scattered, the last questioner, a woman, stepped forward.

"Dr. Fuller," she said, "where do you come from?"

And without any hesitation, Bucky leaned over to her and answered, "I come from a little spaceship called Earth. Where do you come from?"

Where, indeed.

It is easy to forget. Too often, home means neighborhood or town— Seattle or Toronto or Dallas or the Coast. Buckminster Fuller usually didn't think like that. He probably answered "Philadelphia" every now and then, but for the most part, he saw himself as a citizen of a planet— a self-contained greenhouse in which all things grow.

Whenever astronauts photograph Earth floating in space, they see neither neighborhoods nor nations. No drawn, artificial lines delineate nations. Boundaries are mountain ranges, rivers, oceans. If these

Helen Redman. Hand Mandala. 1980. Collage. 20" x 20".

photographs hung from every bulletin board, refrigerator door, and alongside portraits of presidents and prime ministers, more earth-bound citizens might catch Bucky's perspective.

Held by gravity, protected by layers of clouds and ozone, we frail human beings are surrounded by a vast, cold, and forbidding universe. There is no escape. The space shuttle may rocket free of gravity and fly into outer space, but it must ultimately land again on California's desert floor. We have no other place to go. We are in this together. The big, blue marble is home.

Whole world awareness is necessary for survival. Without it, we pollute the earth's atmosphere, oceans, and land. Without it, people of one country hate people of another and don't even know why. Without it, *Time* magazine stories of starving thousands in Africa go unread. Without it, we don't see the connection between goods stamped "Made in Taiwan" and the women and child labor that made them. Without it, governments armed with nuclear warheads threaten to end all life.

## Cultivating Whole World Awareness

To develop this awareness, women are getting to know each other, woman to woman, culture to culture. They are exchanging visits, information, business cards. Opportunities to meet internationally have increased dramatically in the last decade. Mexico City in 1975. The Brussels Tribunal on Crimes Against Women in 1976. Copenhagen in 1980. Peace camps in England, West Germany, Seneca Falls, Puget Sound. Nairobi in1985. Women are joining together for political rallies, to boycott harmful products, to bring about international peace. The isolation is ending.

**Catherine Menninger** is a relentless connector. She has spent the last thirty years introducing Russian and United States citizens to each other. She began in the 1950s by asking the Soviet ambassador's wife to visit her in Kansas. "She had just come to this country," Catherine said, "and I thought it would be a good way to expose her to the reality of the Midwest and America."

The people of Kansas welcomed her to their Grange meetings and Methodist sewing circle. They cooked for her, entertained her, invited her into their homes, introduced her to their children. "Some of these people were members of the John Birch Society who endorsed the local billboard saying 'Get U.S. Out of the United Nations,' " Catherine said. "But once they were face to face with her, a fellow human being, a woman, they found her acceptable. They still didn't like Communism or Russian politics, but they liked *her*."

The experiment was so successful that a series of delegation exchanges between Kansas and Soviet women began. "The whole experience convinced me that people, on the surface, are afraid of differences,"

Catherine added, "but in a context that is non-threatening, they can learn to trust."

In the summer of 1982, Catherine organized a meeting in New Hampshire between Russian and United States newspaper editors. At first, the editors were reluctant to participate, but by the meeting's conclusion, they were suggesting story ideas—the birth of a first child, fishing tales, recipes, pictures of families—for an exchange of newspaper columns portraying life in the United States and the Soviet Union. "Do you think this sounds simple-minded?" Catherine asked. "It is, but when you have as little trust as we and the Russians do, you start very simply."

In 1984, Catherine coordinated another exchange between media representatives—ten United States and eleven Soviet broadcast journalists. They met in California to view each other's television news and documentary reports, read each other's news stories, and talk about differences and similarities in their approaches to their profession. They discussed varying concepts of news presentation and different ways of handling a major news story, such as the Soviet shooting down of the Korean airliner in September 1983. Sometimes they were polite and guarded; other times they were frank about what they liked and didn't like about each other's methods, philosophies, and techniques.

The most significant business of the thirteen-day meeting, however, was the human exchange. "Through all of their talks and time together," wrote Catherine in the meeting's report, "there ran a thread of amazement, that they were talking—and listening—to each other at all. Side by side with that amazement was a growing sense of discovery of one another as individual human beings....It was quite simply people-to-people, though it involved high-level media folk from two far-off and sadly far-apart lands."[1]

Catherine fosters global understanding in her particular way. She doesn't participate in demonstrations and mass rallies. She can see that others are mobilized by them, but she finds them abstract ("like Pentagon war games and defense strategies"). She wonders what people do when they get home from a march ("How do they make peace then?"). "I choose to put my energy into projects that link people, that build personal trust," she said. "I'm attracted to the small scale, the human level, the earthiness of my projects."

She calls her work "the feminine component of peacemaking—foundation building—which is slow and respectful of the human being. We, as women and as people, have a role to play in improving climate," she said. "We know the most about life—daily life. And until the climate between the U.S. and the Soviet Union is improved, the larger political solutions can't happen."

**Martha Stuart** (who died on February 15, 1985) was an independent video producer committed to building the same foundation as Catherine. Rather than person-to-person gatherings, Martha used video technology to broaden global communication. "Because video is easy to learn and use, inexpensive to repair, and durable," Martha said, "users don't have to be technological wizards to grasp the fundamentals. Since videotapes don't have to be processed at a laboratory, users replay footage immediately, learning as they proceed."

Martha trained villagers in China, India, and Mali to record projects, stories, and cultural activities. She was so excited by the outcomes that she wanted the villagers to share their tapes with people of other countries. "The Chinese tended to be non-visual but technically proficient," she said, "and the Malians were non-technical but visually creative. I thought they could learn something from each other. Besides, if they knew each other, the tapes could go back and forth directly, without me as the middle person." Martha, ever the entrepreneur and innovator, assembled representatives from each country, and convinced the United Nations University in Tokyo to co-sponsor the Village Video Network. Today, it trains Third World people in video techniques so they can directly communicate visual information about their development solutions to villagers in other countries.

Twelve nations, including China, Egypt, Mali, India, Jamaica, Antiqua, and Zimbabwe, participate. Tapes about a Chinese energy-efficient village, workers at an Egyptian family planning agency, and teachers in a Malian literacy project are examples of video projects. Network members exchange tapes and also distribute them to broadcasters, universities, corporations, and development agencies.

"People are telling their own stories in a form I call 'self-documentary,' " Martha explained. "Most documentaries are based on observation, and I'm opposed to that method because it's not quite real. Self-documentary is a truly democratic information exchange, where people are doing, rather than being done to or done for. No one is printing something about them they can't edit. The people making the tapes are the subjects, but they are also the producers."

At the time of her death, Martha was completing arrangements for a television series about Soviet women, retired generals, survivors of World War II, and farmers. "By people encouraging other people, we can tap a pool of human energy and healing power of untold dimension," Martha wrote in an article for *Intermedia*. "I find it hard to imagine a more powerful method for establishing world peace and supporting human health and growth everywhere."[2]

North Carolina artist **Rosie Thompson** employs art making, the only technology she knows, to develop international relationships. For one project, she sent blank books to artist friends in Brazil, Canada, England, France, Germany, Ireland, Holland, Italy, Yugoslavia, and the United States. She made the first entry in each book and asked other artists either to complete the book themselves or pass it around. She called the project, "Time-Space Works," and named herself "The Processor/The Witness." When the books returned, she organized a

Mariagnese K. Catteneo. Installation I (Lesley Collage). 1985. Cheesecloth and Acrylic. 120″ x 120″ x 120″. (Photo: Nora Charleston)

traveling exhibit, added two more blank books, and invited viewer participation. "The books from various countries seemed to have a coherence," Rosie said, "almost a national identity. When I looked at any one of them, it was like taking a time-space-idea (mind) flicker trip."

Rosie undertook this international project because she wanted a tangible international support system. She also wanted to encourage others to make connections across cultures. "Each book had lots of names and addresses," Rosie said, "so anyone could get in touch with other artists, share concepts and research, or find a fellow artist to visit. I've always felt *love* is overcoming the otherness of the other. Only then will international peace and humanistic ideals be secure."

## Developing Cross-Cultural Understanding

Peace and understanding are goals that Catherine, Martha, and Rosie share. They count on direct communication without intermediaries, insist that person-to-person meetings are vital environments in which to cultivate whole world awareness. But this work can also be done at home, within the United States and Canada, to convey a unity of purpose, to work in solidarity with those who need support, or to educate a wider audience. We found two projects that were examples of this cross-cultural sharing.

In 1975, a group of women dancers formed the **Wallflower Order Dance and Theater Collective** to address issues of women's oppression. **Moli Steinert,** managing director at the time of our interview, described the group's breadth. "Wallflower is not just a dance group, and not just a women's dance group, and not just a political women's dance group," she said. "What we do breaks all the rules of form. We combine comedy and theater and martial arts and sign language and whatever else we need in a presentation."

In 1981, they also combined their dances with Latin American music and formed an alliance with Grupo Raiz, a group of exiled musicians. Grupo Raiz introduced them to new sounds and rhythms and heightened their awareness of other cultures. They toured the United States, Europe, and Nicaragua, performing benefit concerts for the people of El Salvador and Chile. Feminist and Latin American communities had to collaborate to produce the concerts, and audiences were invariably rich in color, gender, and cultural tradition.

"Making this alliance affected our understanding of politics in Latin America," Moli said. "In the 1970s, we women developed our own music and art and spaces, and we needed to do this. But if we stay in our old contexts, we tread water. Women at Wallflower thought feminism, as we had come to know it, was too ethnocentric, too American. So now we take what we know into the world and translate it into larger terms. We see that women's oppression is undeniably linked to class oppression, racism, imperialism. Working with Grupo

Raiz was a way for us to broaden our commitment to liberation.''

**Vincente Tang** and **Genny Lim**'s project, "Chinese Women of America, 1848-1942," broke through a barrier of ignorance within the United States. They conducted over two hundred interviews, and collected stories, documents, and photographs of Chinese women immigrants. By collecting such materials, they unearthed a part of their history unknown even to themselves. They traced the effects of immigration and exclusionary laws during the so-called Exclusion Period from 1882 to 1942 and recorded the improved status of Chinese-American women since 1942.

They arranged a traveling exhibit, sent it to ten American cities, and wrote a book which was published by the Chinese Culture Foundation of San Francisco. Vincente and Genny want Chinese-American women to feel good about their contribution to American life—to see it, to know it, to be proud of it. And they want non-Chinese Americans to understand these strong, tenacious, "iron butterflies."

Women are building bridges between cultures—sharing art, teaching communication skills, raising consciousness about global issues. They are helping us understand that we don't live on Spaceship Earth alone. When Catherine Menninger wrote about the media exchanges between Russian and American citizens, she spoke for all these efforts. "We are talking about locating in ourselves, and in each other's societies, that better part," she wrote, "the part which is warm and generous, curious, open to learning, which can grow and change, and can adapt to new circumstances.

"But, as in coming to know deeply and well another person, there can often be pain along the way as we discover things about one another which we find hard to take or bewildering: attitudes of mind, habits, pieces of past history which affect present behavior, absence of feeling in places where we feel a lot, presence of strong feeling where we don't understand, and surprises, always and inevitably surprises.

"Yet," she continued, "as with any relationship worth having, worth building, worth preserving, the idea seems to be to persevere....Our goal, our hope, is three-fold: for us, the American people, to reach the Soviet people that we may know them more fully; for them, not to abandon the good will and friendship we know they have held for us for a long time; and that we may begin to learn from one another many truths, the first of which most surely will have to be that we are all fellow sufferers on this planet—and that we need one another."[3]


## Women Helping Women

Women especially need each other because we are an underclass everywhere. In many countries, we have no legal rights, own no property, are refused health care and education. Reports of murdered girl babies in China, of genital mutilation in Africa, of the absence of economic aid in Nepal are frequent and verifiable. And in the United

States, women are not protected by the Constitution, are not even mentioned. "Because feminists are always in a minority," said **Nellice Gillespie-Woltemade**, "they need support from a larger community in order to survive."

She has studied how women's issues move from country to country. "I wondered how word got around about battered women's shelters, or about forced sterilization, or about female sexual slavery, or about contraception," Nellice said. "Where did the idea of Take Back the Night Marches start, and how did it travel? What I found was that reading is tremendously important to women, and from reading, women contact each other."

Women's issues are similar in all cultures—child care, poverty, health care, reproductive rights, peace. Feminist activists develop strategies for these problems, and Nellice found evidence of much cross-fertilization. "Women's groups in one country are appealing directly to feminists in other countries," she said. "We are asking each other to help with letter-writing campaigns, fund raising, and demonstrations."

This support is happening all over the world—in Portugal, with the Three Marias in prison; in North Carolina with Joanne Little; in South Africa, with the struggle of Winnie Mandela. In 1985, international feminists called a "girlcott," urging United States women to buy New Zealand products if the United States government imposed a trade embargo because New Zealand refused to accept nuclear-armed ships. Women want to support New Zealand's stance.

Nellice's latest project is a Comparative Women's Studies Program sponsored by Antioch College. United States feminists spend four months in Europe doing research, attending conferences, festivals, and classes. They see exhibits by European feminist artists and compare social change strategies and perspectives on motherhood, sexuality, aging, racism, and education. As women find each other and identify common issues, they are sharing resources. Those with information, money, and political know-how are making them available to women who don't have access.

When **Michaela Walsh** listened to women at the 1975 conference in Mexico City, she decided to do something about women's lack of economic control. Her background on Wall Street, at a major foundation, and at the U.S. Congress's Office of Technology Assessment gave her the experience and confidence she needed to start an international banking system for women.

But it was her five years in Lebanon working for an international investment firm, that introduced Michaela to the realities of small-scale village economies. There she began to understand the layers of a multi-tiered economy—the centralized, credit-based, macro economy; the small-scale, micro-entrepreneurial cash economy; and the nonregistered or underground sectors. This knowledge led her to practical, reasonable

Elizabeth Vail. Orange Kimono. Full Kimono is 7'x 8½'.

goals. "I can't create an equalized economy in the world," she said, "but I can provide one alternative for women who have little access to the formal economy and are a major productive force." By 1981, she had formed Women's World Banking (WWB). Today WWB, with twenty-eight programs and a capital fund of several million dollars, is broadening production and consumption bases for women by making loan guarantees to banks in countries around the world.

In her New York office, Michaela described two projects funded by Women's World Banking. "In Columbia, a woman owned a bicycle shop, and she wanted to expand," Michaela said. "She knew she could sell and repair more bicycles if she could hire more people and buy more equipment. But she needed more money to do that. Her bank told her about loan guarantees from WWB; our local monitoring group checked out her situation and recommended that she receive one. Now she has hired two more workers, doubled employment, and her sales have risen one hundred percent. Any banker will tell you that's good business."

In India, **Ela Bhatt** created India's Self-Employed Women's Association to organize 16,000 market women who make pennies a day selling food from carts. Before the Association was formed, the women gave their earnings to their husbands each night, then borrowed bank money at ten percent the next day to replenish their carts. Now they take their pennies, put them into a bank, and borrow against their earnings each day. They earn interest on their savings, and with this extra money, they buy shoes for a child or put a new roof on the house. "This method of self-help support is so much more positive than the more common experience of a foreign corporation coming into an area and hiring laborers to work on assembly lines," Michaela said. "We are strengthening local economies by creating new businesses in a community."

Economics is closely related to environmental concerns, and in many countries, ecological imbalances are chronic. Women and children suffer the most from resulting famines, floods, declining soil fertility, and erosion. Most people in poor countries depend on firewood for fuel, and eighty percent of that wood burns underneath cooking pots. Because the need for wood fuel is outpacing nature's ability to provide it, people at **Aprovecho Institute** in Eugene, Oregon, decided to address women's need for fuel-efficient cookstoves. They called their stove the Lorena. "The idea began after the Guatemalan earthquakes in 1976," said **Laurie Childers**, Aprovecho consultant at the time of our interview. "We began by helping with reconstruction and ended up working with local people to design a fuel efficient stove."

Aprovecho means "I make best use of" in Spanish, and Institute designers apply appropriate technologies that *make the best use of* users' skills and resources. The Lorena stove is cheap and simple to build. It is made of local materials—eighty percent sand, twenty percent clay, and because it is never fired, it can be broken down naturally, recycled, or rebuilt. Since it is energy efficient, it isn't a burden on the environment. In addition, the stoves are designed to suit different cultures. A Senegalese woman cooks differently from a woman in the highlands of Guatemala. Therefore the design for one culture is slightly different from another.

Laurie is interested in the Lorena for practical reasons—she helps people design and build them. But she is also an artist/potter, so her enthusiasm for it is broader. She studied the stove for a graduate degree in fine arts and explored the connections between pottery making, the nature of clay, the uniqueness of cultures, women's work of cooking, the economics of firewood, the physics of combustion, and the relation of families cooking dinners in woodburning stoves to the biosphere. "The ultimate art is the world we create," Laurie said. "The Lorena is an aesthetic integration of human needs into the cyclical flow of materials of the earth."

Wholistic approaches to women's issues, such as the Lorena stove, are becoming more common. When storyteller **Cathy Spagnoli** lived in India, she wrote *Listen to Our Voices*, a booklet about women's position there, past and present. Concerns for Indian women haven't changed much over the years, but new solutions are always being discovered. Sometimes these solutions address women's universal needs. Cathy saw how women construction workers solved the problem of child care.

Many women are active in India's construction trades. They scale bamboo scaffolding, haul bricks on their backs, mix cement. And they also have children to tend. Cathy described the Mobile Creche, India's on-the-job day care system. "In the year of the Gandhi Bicentennial," she said, "an Indian woman was trying to think of what to do in Gandhi's name. One day, as she was going out to a Bicentennial committee meeting, she passed a construction site and saw a baby crying on top of a pile of bricks. She watched as the child's mother stopped working and walked over to nurse her baby. When she had finished, the mother put the baby down in the rubble and went back to work. But the baby kept crying.

"The mother was frustrated," Cathy continued. "She had to keep working, but she also had to tend to her baby. The committee woman, watching from across the street, got an idea. She walked over to the pile of bricks and picked up the crying child. Then, taking a sari, the traditional cradle, she hung it from a tree branch. She shaded the sari with another piece of cloth and laid the baby down. The baby slept. On that day, the Mobile Creche was born.

"Today, Mobile Creches are visible at most construction sites throughout Bombay and Delhi," Cathy concluded. "Women build the first floor of a building, then turn it into a Creche. Infants lie in one corner. In another, toddlers play in a day care center. In a third area, older siblings, mostly girls who care for the younger children, do their lessons on slates. In every case, women and their children are together— working and growing up."

# Developing A Consciousness of the Connections

Just as women's issues are the same culture to culture, so is the exploitation of women. For example, when American women started dying from Toxic Shock Syndrome because they were buying and using Proctor and Gamble's Rely tampons, the company yanked them off grocery shelves. But instead of destroying their stock, they shipped boxes of Relys to women overseas who are not protected by government health agencies. **Charlotte Bunch,** New York City feminist writer and theorist, is acutely aware of problems like this one as she builds an international feminist network. "It's not that our lives aren't connected to women elsewhere," she said. "They always are. It's that our consciousness has been kept separate and therefore our ability to fight back has been kept separate. Global feminism is not just knowing what's happening in far away places. It is not about a few privileged women getting a piece of the pie while the rest remain destitute. It is the connection between what's happening there and what's happening here. We have to develop a consciousness of the connections if we are going to break down the barriers. Networks are crucial to get us beyond the limitations that patriarchal nationalism puts on our ideas and actions."

Charlotte, a spokeswoman for the feminist movement since the late 1960s, was a founder of *Furies*, a lesbian feminist publication in Washington, D.C. and of *Quest: A Feminist Quarterly*. She began meeting women from other countries in the 1970s when she traveled to Thailand, Australia, and New Zealand. In 1980, she helped organize international feminist workshops for the women's conference in Copenhagen and afterwards worked with the International Women's Tribune Center in New York, a center for international networking.

Charlotte created Interfem as a way to consult with women internationally. She's been able to use her experience and contacts to become a clearinghouse for women around the world. In this capacity, she refers women of other countries to feminists and publications in the United States and Canada and vice versa. "I'm interested in going into places where feminism is being discovered anew," Charlotte said, "where there are women with an overwhelming desire for change in the world, not just bettering their own personal situation. Interfem engages all the interests I have and involves seeing what feminism means in a global context.

"Feminism is a transformational force, an individual and social force," Charlotte concluded. "It is a way of looking at the world—a questioning of power/domination issues, an affirmation of women's energy. In this country, it has its roots in the civil rights and antiwar movements—roots that connect it to an *international* struggle for

Anita Segalman. Rodomishl. (detail) 1983. Silk, barbed wire, wood.
(Photo: Douglas Parker)

change. Don't let anybody tell you that feminism doesn't mean anything in the Third World. Don't let anybody tell you that the feminist movement has died. Don't let anybody tell you that a global feminist movement hasn't begun, because it has. And we are creating global feminist visions.''

Once a friend of ours was visiting a group of women in a developing country. One morning, the women asked her to come with them to the village well where they filled their pots and jugs with water. As they sat talking, the native women asked their guest how she got her water.

''I have a wonderful room in my house,'' she said, ''where there is a metal bowl with two metal handles. In between the handles is a spout. Anytime, day or night, I turn the handles and fresh water flows out. When I'm finished, I turn the handles off. That's how I get my water.'' She waited for the women to exclaim, thinking, ''surely, they will be impressed.'' But there was only silence. Finally, one of the women looked at the Westerner, proudly dressed in her fine clothes, and said in a quiet voice, ''How lonely for you.''

In spite of angry posturing between governments, thousands of women are reaching across oceans and land masses, artificial boundaries drawn on the globe by governments. Cathy Spagnoli brings words, Michaela Walsh money, Aprovecho a better cookstove. By touching our whole family, as Martha Stuart's videotapes and Charlotte's feminist networks do, we remember where we live and why. Big, blue marble consciousness begins here.

''Where do you come from?'' the woman asked Bucky.

A spaceship called Earth.

We women are stretching our hands, minds, hearts around this spaceship, enclosing it in a band of woman-knowing. We are working hard at it too. This is no simple daisy chain. ''Brotherly love'' pales in comparison.

We are building a future from the ground up—piece by piece, woman by woman—laying the foundation for peace. We are meeting our sisters at the well. No longer lonely. No longer alone. And we know it. And neither are they alone. And they know it too.

Shereen LaPlantz. Untitled. Basket—plaited, sewn, and knotted flat paper fiber split, half round and round reed, sewn with waxed linen. 9″ x 17″ x 17″.

# PART II:
## WOMEN CREATE

*We dedicate this chapter in loving memory and gratitude to Martha Stuart who died on February 15, 1985.*

# 6

# HOW DO YOU PHONE THE WOMEN'S MOVEMENT?

This century's explosion in communications technologies has shattered distance and altered time. By 1900, men tinkering with copper and current, sound waves and magnets had made mincemeat of the pony express and smoke signals. Suddenly, poles and wire strung the landscape. The jangle of telephones interrupted quiet afternoons, and newspapers reflected daily events teletyped across mountains and plains as they happened. Radios crackled with recorded music, and still and moving photographic images mirrored the world as it was, without the blur of paint. Today televisions, computers, and telephones join together to transmit visual and word information at the speed of light.

As scientists continue to fiddle with wires and glass and sand, science fiction fantasies will become present-day tools. Wrist-sized watches will serve as two-way telephones and data centers. The old, familiar morning paper, rolled up in the grass, will appear electronically on computer terminals at 6 a.m. Robots, programmed to simulate humans, will clean floors, deliver mail, and weld car parts. New technologies will not only change personal lives, they will also change government. When voting day arrives, registered citizens will sit at computer terminals and speak directly for themselves. Political leaders will become teachers, educating the voting public about issues, and democracy will become participatory rather than simply representative.

Dick Tracy watches, artificially intelligent robots, and personal computer voting booths are light years away from the timepieces, brooms, and ballots they replace. And though they are still uncommon, they continue the revolution in communications technology that is affecting every person on the globe. When Annie lived in Taiwan, she explored remote villages where aboriginal farmers gathered taro and hemp from mountain slopes. Women wove colorful fabrics using dyes from bark and roots, and fashioned jackets for markets far away. No one owned a car and one bus traveled the dusty road. But every village had a television set, and at night the villagers would gather and watch "Gunsmoke" or "I Love Lucy" or "Bonanza." As the blue light flickered against the faces of Chinese peasants isolated from the world, Annie understood Marshall McLuhan's notion of a "global village."

The new communications tools are powerful; they enable their owners to send messages to millions. And unfortunately, only a few white men decide which messages to project. In North America, they own television and cable networks, computer companies, telephone services, entertainment facilities, newspapers and magazines, and publishing houses.

They aren't shy about communicating their points of view, or claiming that they have a corner on the truth. Walter Cronkite's closing line used to be, "That's the way it is." National Public Radio's major news show is "All Things Considered." And editors of the venerable *New York Times* proudly announce on page one that they cover "All the news that's fit to print." If a few men, speaking in One Voice, convince the rest of us that their perspective is "the way it is," we will buy their products, support their candidates, agree to their distribution of wealth, worship their gods. They will control our behavior. We will feel free, as if we are deciding for ourselves, but we will only regurgitate what has been fed to us. When there is only One Voice, there is only one reality.

Evidence that we are moving towards One Mind is everywhere. Newspaper interviews with people on the street invariably sound like rehashes of the previous evening's news. Junior high school kids running for student council mimic hackneyed political slogans they've heard on TV. Ethnic groups are reduced to the lowest common denominator. Italians with black, wavy hair are plump if they're women, gesture wildly with their hands if they're men, and eat spaghetti with Mama's homemade sauce. Blacks are either poverty-stricken (news stories) or middle-class ("The Jeffersons") or absent. Native Americans are alcoholics or gurus. Women, though visible, are either young, smooth-skinned, and sexy, or old and arthritic. Professional women are often ruthless megalomaniacs who've abandoned hubby and kids for the high life. Many stories fit to print end up on the editing room floor, and too many voices aren't considered at all.

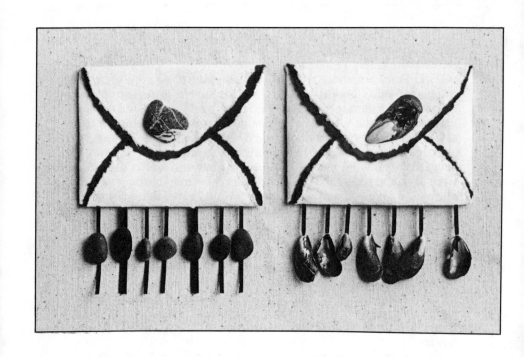

# A Range of Voices

Freedom is based on choices and citizens need to hear a range of voices if they are to make good decisions. The perpetuation of One Voice by the mass media does not further a free society. "To make a viable democracy, we need information from the most number of people," said **Donna Allen**, founder of the **Women's Institute for Freedom of the Press**. "To get it, people have to speak for themselves. When people speak for other people, stereotypes are maintained. People know their own information best, and neither the person with the information nor the public who wants it needs an intermediary reporter to interpret. All that person needs is some help getting her account on paper, on the airwaves, or on film."

Everywhere we went, we found women's accounts on paper. Newsletters and newspapers for every conceivable purpose and audience provide forums where women are telling their stories and getting in touch with each other. Z Budapest and the Susan B. Anthony Coven #1 in San Francisco circulate news of the Goddess movement in *Thesmophoria*, a "voice of the new women's religion." Margaret Sprague publishes *Amie*, a magazine for Madison, Connecticut's middle-aged, middle-class, suburban, working women. *Between Our Selves: Women of Color Newspaper* comes from a cooperative of Hispanic, black, Asian, native American, and Arab-American women in Washington, D.C.

*Broomstick* is a magazine for women over forty, edited by a San Francisco collective. In Lynchburg, Virginia, Ellyn Cowels publishes *Wholeperson Communications* to encourage wellness and the prevention of disease. Jane Porcino's *Hot Flash* is a newsletter mailed to over 6,000 older women in every state and ten foreign countries. Jane includes articles about mental and physical health, legislation, sexuality, and other issues important to older women.

**Anne D'Arcy** edits California's *Telewoman*, and her goals are similar to all of the above. *"Telewoman* is a personal connection for lesbians, particularly isolated, elderly, disabled, and closeted lesbians. A woman is warmly received from the time she sends for a sample issue. We aren't a commercial establishment looking for dollars. Instead, we welcome her with her needs and offerings from the start."

The Women's Institute for Freedom of the Press also has a newsletter, *Media Report to Women* (MRW). Each bimonthly issue reports "What women are thinking and doing to change the communications media." A sample copy carried advertisements for media jobs, reports on international efforts to end sex-stereotyping in the media, statistics about media ownership, and articles about pornography. Publication was

Ann Taylor Gibson. Earth/Sea Ritual Pouches. 1984. Mixed Media—
hand made paper, ribbon, thread stone, shells. 12″ x 16″

sporadic for the first two years. "I sent out the *Report* whenever I got nine pages together, because nine pages took two stamps," Donna said. But by 1974, women and men in journalism schools, television networks, major newspapers, women's studies programs, and members of the alternative press were subscribers.

Donna and Associate Editor Martha Allen use three "principles for feminist journalism" for the selection and presentation of news items. (1) No attacks on people. The MRW neither judges nor criticizes articles. Donna and Martha report what is said or done and let their readers judge the merit for themselves. (2) More factual information. The MRW includes full texts whenever possible, avoids repetitious information and editorials. Martha and Donna don't draw conclusions about stories, but present the facts about the issue. (3) People should speak for themselves. "We don't write about groups because *we* think they are important," Donna said. "We wait for women to contact us. We want them to write about themselves, speak to other women directly, not have us speak for them."

In women's newspapers, longer versions of the newsletter, issues and events are treated comprehensively and with respect. They usually reflect the Institute's three principles.

• The *Valley Women's Voice*, begun as a newsletter by women at the University of Massachusetts in Amherst, has become a full, eight-page tabloid. The university subsidizes the *Voice*, and additional support comes from advertisements and subscriptions. Its 6,500 copies are distributed free to the public each month. "Most women who work on the paper have felt, at one time or another, that we didn't care about their particular issue," said **Kathleen Moran**, editor at the time of our inteview. "For example, I didn't think the *Voice* printed enough about single parents. But when I started producing the paper instead of just reading it, I found out that each issue is a compilation of articles women write and send in. When someone submits an article and it's published, we broaden the paper and the information available to women in the Pioneer Valley. It's really up to each of us to talk about whatever is on our minds."

• *Sojourner*, born at the Massachusetts Institute for Technology in Cambridge in 1975, became self-supporting after three issues. The board of directors opted for a for-profit business structure instead of nonprofit status and sold shares of stock. This approach has been successful. Boston-area women have supported the paper throughout its decade of publishing.

*Sojourner*'s editorial policy is inclusive. "We don't accept or reject articles based on their political content," said **Martha Thurber**, former Managing Editor. "As long as it's not racist or sexist or homophobic, we'll take it. We want to give women a

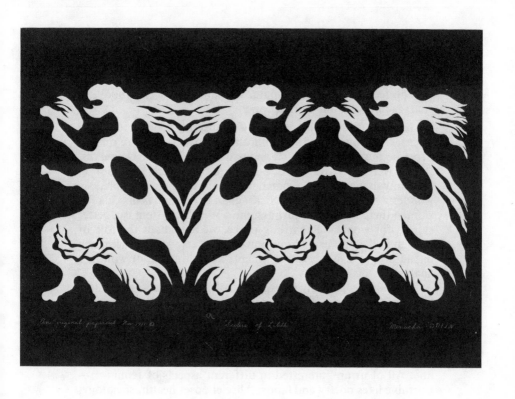

An original papercut Nr. 1951 D          "Sisters of Lilith"          Menucha מנוחה

place to air their views in a rational manner. Most of our writers
have a certain political viewpoint—left of center and feminist, but
we are committed to talk to and with more than just the feminist
community. We don't want to close anyone out, or have any
woman feel she can't participate. We can't please everybody, of
course, but we want to keep open."

• Members of a Washington, D.C. collective produce *Off Our
Backs*, a national monthly feminist newspaper. "We're on this
paper because we're feminists and writers," said **Tacie Dejanikus**.
"We cover many issues, but our unique approach is to look at
how any issue affects women particularly. For example, we
wonder what difference the Nicaraguan revolution is making for
women there. We don't just assume a socialist system is a better
system for women. Regarding peace, we ask about the role of
women in the military, about how women are working with men
in the progressive peace movement, as well as about women's
analysis of peace."

To produce a monthly newspaper, collective members volunteer
hours of free time and meet every week to produce, analyze, and
plan issues. They develop story ideas by consensus, but individual
writers write them. "A newspaper is uniquely suited for collective
decision making and individual achievement," Tacie said. "I
decide what to cover, write the story, see it printed with my by-
line. All of us are interested in different aspects of feminism—
Lorraine likes poetry and labor; Alice chooses health, sociology,
and math subjects; Vicki is interested in anarchism and Carol Ann
covers international stories. We have highly developed individual
styles, and we respect and admire each others' minds. But we are
also experts at compromise, and we trust each other. Out of
consensus, a newspaper created by all of us emerges every
month."

Even though these newsletters and newspapers aren't sold in most
big city newsstands, even though many teeter on the brink of collapse,
and even though some have small, specialized audiences, publications
by, for, and about women are bringing new values to the print media.
In them, all things female are considered, and articles deemed by readers
as fit to print see the light. "We should be celebrating every new
women's press and journal," declared Donna Allen, "and every one
that survives another year or five years or decade. Too few people realize
the crucial importance of having our independent means of
communication, how massive that power is, and what it does for us."

## Speaking For Ourselves

**Martha Stuart** understood. Before her death, she worked relentlessly as an independent video entrepreneur to put television technology into the hands of ordinary people. She was best known for her forty-nine "Are You Listening" tapes which reveal the common experiences of individuals. She gathered people in a television studio, arranged them on raised platforms in a semi-circle, and asked them to discuss candidly one aspect of their lives. Series titles include: *Black High School Girls, Children of Working Mothers, Freaks, Household Technicians, Jamaican Women, Judges, Mujeres Colombianas, Older People, Widows, Prisoners, Shop Stewards, Prison Guards, People Who Have Epilepsy, Women in Middle Management, Women Who Didn't Have An Abortion, Women Who Did Have An Abortion, World Feminists.* "When I began," Martha said, "people told me, 'Martha, a series of talking heads will never work.' So I called my format, 'feeling faces.'

" 'Are You Listening' started as a woman's series to show real women who were changing and doing something concrete," Martha continued. "Television is a great tool to get people turned on, but mainstream television turns people off because it shows women who are too perfect or problems that are too big to solve. Instead of saying to people, 'The solutions are all the different things you do in your own life,' television teaches that solutions come from those in positions of power. That's not the way change happens. The way things get solved is by everybody learning from what other people have found. I did 'Widows' because I had friends who were widows. They were used to functioning with men, and suddenly they had to function without men. I wanted to hear them talk about the experience. The program on epilepsy shows how a small, diverse, articulate group of people feel about having epilepsy, what it means to their lives. It's a much better way to learn about epilepsy than to see a documentary on it."

The mass media "feeds" its audience. Reporters analyze, recap, and comment on the news. Martha didn't play an analytical role. She sat with participants in the "Are You Listening" series, asked questions, helped clarify if someone was stuck, shared her own material. But when she edited the final tape, she often left herself out. "I let the people on the camera do the talking because talking is the most appropriate way, short of making love, to exchange feelings," she said. "We need to exchange feelings, not facts. Facts lead to understanding; feelings lead to action. When your consciousness overlaps with somebody else's, you start to move. The reason you think you can do something is because someone like you is doing something."

Martha generated ideas for production, then raised money from corporations, foundations, national, and international government sources. She distributed the award-winning tapes to commercial networks and to Public Broadcasting System stations. "Commercial stations have very small budgets for public affairs programming," she said, "and no funding for human affairs. Their news departments focus all our attention on government, figuring out who is in power, or who should be. That is not my focus. I want people to talk about their own lives."

Martha's philosophy about sharing, which she developed in an article for *Intermedia*, guided her work. "The desire to share ourselves with others is at the root of all communication," Martha wrote.[1] But she felt that *personal* sharing and *social* sharing processes are different. Personal sharing operates informally, person-to-person, extending in many directions at once. It concerns matters of small—i.e., specific, individual, and local import—and may be transmitted in a conversation or a phone call. Social sharing is a more formal information dispersal system, devoted to grander matters of public policy, and proceeding in a one-way flow. This is the form of conventional media.

The differences center around equality. In personal sharing, the parties are more or less equal, but in social sharing, equality dissolves. Life stories shrink to seeming insignificance next to earth-shaking events, and experts seem to know everything. People lose sight of the connection between their own lives and the problems and possibilities of the larger society. "All my work as a videotape producer," Martha concluded, "has been devoted to bringing the personal and social forms of sharing and communication into greater contact and harmony with each other. The underlying objective is to make social change through human exchange."[2]

Martha Stuart did not interpret. Neither do Donna and editors of women's newsletters. They trust the voices of individuals and want them to speak directly. They are committed to the individuals Martha Stuart videotaped—"people who are talked about, not listened to."

And sometimes those individuals speak for themselves. They are women self-publishing records and books, establishing their own mail order companies. When Mary Clare was producing *The Widow*, a book about her mother, she learned, step-by-step, how to publish a book. A graphics artist helped with paste-up and typesetting, her printer explained his technology and what he needed her photographs to look like. She sent a fund-raising letter to friends, and applied for a small grant from her church. And as we traveled around North America working on this book, she distributed it to women's bookstores. "By publishing and distributing my book, I learned how to get my word out directly," she said. "Nobody could edit or squelch me. Now I know that whenever I have anything to say I have the power and the knowledge to get it to other people."

## Connecting With Each Other

When women speak directly through print and videotape, we begin to see who else is "out there." We appreciate each other's struggles, grasp the commonality of issues, and eventually, learn to be allies. Donna Allen and other founding board members started the Women's Institute for Freedom of the Press to further and deepen the bonds between women. "The purpose of the media is to divide us," Donna said, "not just women, but all of us." By keeping us outside and off the pages and screens, men who control the media keep us from power. We have no way to connect with each other because we don't know who's doing what. It's a vicious circle, and women are the losers.

"Our criticism of men isn't that they portray us wrong," Donna added. "Of course, they portray us wrong. The problem is that we don't have enough information about women. If women are to get political power, we have to get access to the media. We have to be able to tell each other what we are doing and why. That's the only way we're going to change policies."

To insure that their information about women would be readily available, Donna and Martha decided to index *Media Report to Women* when it was two years old. "If women are to be included in history, as we have not been in the past," Donna said, "we have to index our material. People who write history always go to the index of the *New York Times* because if it doesn't appear in the *New York Times*, it didn't happen. So we created an index, and while we were at it, the *Directory of Women's Media*, which has helped enormous numbers of women find each other."

It definitely helped us. We pored over the *Directory*'s thirty-five pages of women's periodicals, library collections, film projects, writers groups, distributors, media organizations, and individual women in media when we began our Future is Female Project. We sent press releases to many listed there and received enthusiastic responses. Donna published our release in the *Media Report* as well. "I see your whole project as a communications phenomenon," Donna said. "You're not just going around and collecting information. By writing a book, you are passing the word along so others can know what's happening. In that way, you are making possible all sorts of connections."

Women with information pass it on. They don't want to give it to passive masses, but to people who want it; they want the sender and receiver to "meet" in a two-way exchange. **Jill Lippitt** and **Deborah Brecher** created the **National Women's Mailing List** (NWML) to help women's groups and advertisers reach 50,000 women who are ready to receive.

Their premise is unique. Women who fill out the NWML registration form answer, "Who can mail to you?" and then they check areas of interest—politics, women's culture, sports, health, education, violence against women, and work. If the registrant wants information about lesbians, women of color, or women's organizations, she can mark appropriate boxes. "A woman should choose what information she wants to come to her," Jill said. "In this case, the woman receiving the information should always be in control."

When groups use the NWML to contact these individuals, Jill and Deborah keep control. Groups must submit copies of their mailing package plus a written promise that they'll use the list only once. Because women on the list expressly want information from women's groups, returns from mailings are high. "If you're a small organization, like *Broomstick* magazine," Jill explained, "you can't afford to do a big mailing and only get back the average one-and-one-half percent. When the *Broomstick* collective used our list, they got a five percent return rate, and it's still growing. Women are reaching women who want to hear from them, not selling products to strangers. Our list service isn't just a mailing list exchange. It represents women *exchanging* information."

Distribution companies run for and by women share Jill and Deborah's values. In 1974, several women in Vancouver started a video production group, but learned, after a few productions, that if they didn't develop an audience, their tapes would sit on the shelf. Today, **Women in Focus** distributes women's film and video around the world. "The videotapes and films I have produced, and those we distribute for many other women producers, explore women's visions, lives, and experiences," said **Marion Barling**, founder and director from 1974 to 1984. "They challenge the dominant view of women which is crystallized in stereotypes presented by films, TV programming, magazines, and all other symbolic representations of society's values. As women we must develop imagery that reflects our lives. Then we must circulate it."

Thousands of miles across the continent, North Carolina's **Ladyslipper** has grown from a loose collection of women supplying bookstores with women's albums to the nation's largest distributor of women's music. Established in 1976, and incorporated as a nonprofit organization in 1979, Ladyslipper has a conscience. "Our goal is more than selling a record to make a buck," said **Liz Snow**. "We're feminists and we're interested in the herstory of women in music. Since 1975, 'women's music' has become a recognized and established genre of music, primarily fueled by lesbian energy. Our basic purpose is to heighten public awareness of the achievements of women artists and musicians and to expand the scope and availability of musical and literary recordings by women."

Their *Resource Guide and Catalog of Records and Tapes by Women* is evidence of their success. Page after page of listings for classical, new age, punk, new wave, rock, gospel, jazz, blues, folk, and country music invite women to listen to their own music. Children's records, music from other countries in languages other than English, and spoken records are also included. This catalog, mailed to thousands each year, gives women access to women musicians and composers, poets and writers, in ways unheard of a decade ago.

## The Power of Networking

The world of women's information came late to **Elizabeth Wright Ingraham**, granddaughter of Frank Lloyd Wright. When she decided to go to architecture school, she was one of only two women in her class. Her world was full of men, and her prejudices against women were deep and real. "I didn't like being with women," she said. "I thought they were boring, and their voices were too high. Because of my career, I was with men all the time, anyway—designers, architects, builders and financial backers. I didn't become conscious of women until I had my first daughter. She and my other daughters have taught me a great deal."

So did Elizabeth's good friend Elise Boulding, who challenged Elizabeth to create and chair the Colorado Women's Forum, a network modeled after the Women's Forum in New York City. Seven months after announcing the formation of the forum, Elizabeth, Elise, and several other founders were joined by eighty women. "They came from everywhere," Elizabeth said. "All of a sudden, we women had an important club."

And power. "This new sense of community among women is *the* most important thing that has happened to women," Elizabeth continued. "It allows us to have power, and I'm interested in power. Absolutely. I'm fed up with the abstraction of power. I'd like to see women in places of power. Until then, we won't know what effect women will have on war and peace, freedom, equality, beauty, goodness, and truth."

To get women into those positions, Elizabeth uses the Forum's directory all the time. "I think about what woman I could put on this or that committee," she said. "I never had this before; I didn't know where to find women. So to me, this networking is unbelievably strengthening. It makes you a whole person and gives you confidence in what you're doing, no matter what it is."

**Ann Weiser**, San Francisco therapist and networker, said almost the same thing. She's developed a "many-to-many" process to help people talk about ideas through the mail. In 1980, at the World Future Society Conference, Ann made friends with a group of people who wanted to stay in touch with each other. Since they all lived in different places, they needed a structure. Ann knew about a process used by science fiction fans to exchange amateur magazines, and she suggested they try it. She agreed to be the first organizing editor.

Every month, each person sent a page of writing to Ann, who xeroxed and collated the pages, and sent the package out to everyone. Each month, members of the group wrote again, commenting on the previous month's material and adding new ideas. "A group conversation developed, even a group consciousness," Ann said. "When some of the people saw each other at the next World Future Society Conference, they felt as if they'd been in a group process that hadn't been broken.

We even used the many-to-many process to organize two panels and a networking room at the Conference. The whole experience was much more than just seeing each other again; it was continuing a conversation.''

Ann uses the many-to-many process with the Action Linkage Network, whose purpose is to help community groups discuss their future. *At the Crossroads*, a document produced by one community group in the Pacific Northwest, has been distributed. ''We need to know we're not alone,'' Ann said, ''to connect with each other, to discover that other people are thinking about what we're thinking about. We need allies. The many-to-many approach is a way for people to talk to each other as equals and not have one person or several expounding to the rest.''

**Kathryn Girard** wondered how women might use telephone technology to influence federal legislators, and she invited women in and around Amherst, Massachusetts, to form telephone trees of six to ten women. In all, her **Equity Network** included fifteen circles.

The Network's first order of business was to help rescue the Women's Educational Equity Act (WEEA) from proposed budget cuts in 1981. Kathryn called her Washington contact to get the latest status of the Act, then she called the telephone circle heads and told them what to do. ''I'd say, 'The strategy today is: Call the White House in the next two hours, and make this point . . .' The circle heads called their groups, and those women called the White House. Women who were afraid to call the White House, did it,'' Kathryn said, ''and they were so excited when they did.

''Political networks can't be too time consuming,'' she explained, ''and they have to be small enough so the message can get around quickly. Everyone doesn't have to know everything about the issue; they just have to know enough to make an intelligent phone call. I got an overwhelming response to my telephone circles because women wanted to do something, but didn't want to work independently. We helped save WEEA, for the time being, because we avoided paralysis and depression, and made our voices heard by our representatives. Each time the Network was activated, I got back to all of the circle heads and told them how their influence had been felt in Washington. They passed that message on to their contacts, and everybody felt they had helped. An added bonus was that the D.C. lobbyists were delighted with all the local action.''

Over the next several years, the Network changed. Occasionally somebody passed along the wrong information, and Network members made incorrect requests. Kathryn assumed that passing information verbally was the problem, but she didn't want to return to print media. Today she is thinking about developing a private computer conference for legislative alerts. Always she searches for the best technology to influence public policy.

Heather Howarth. Saturn Cycle. Oilstick craypas on paper.

Whether women use mailing lists, directories, catalogs, or Xerox machines, they are getting their messages out and listening to messages that come back in. They are saying what they want from each other and they are building relationships based on common interests. Along the way, they are using new and traditional communication tools in creative ways. "How do you phone the women's movement?" asked Jill Lippitt. "How do we find each other for mutual support, for empowerment, for ideas and resources? How do we stay in touch once we have made the connection? The answer is simple. We learn to use computers."

Jill and Deborah Brecher believe women's organizations must control their information. If they each can't afford to buy a computer, Jill and Deborah urge them to pool resources and share one. "As long as women don't have access to computers, they can't control their data bases," Jill said. "They have to hire somebody to develop their mailing lists. This means that large companies using expensive computers handle women's data bases. It's a mistake for women's groups to rely on these outsiders. When our information is in men's control, it can be erased. That's cultural imperialism. Controlling our own information, our own data banks, is crucial for women's groups."

To educate women about computers and launch their **Women's Computer Literacy Project**, Deborah and Jill took to the road, crossing the country offering computer demonstrations. We bumped into them in Milwaukee and Washington, D.C. before our interview at their San Francisco office. "A lot of women's groups want to use a computer," Deborah said, "and need training, but they need help to take the first step. And that might be just to see a computer demonstration."

When they got home, they opened a computer school for women in the Bay Area. Students, particularly women over twenty-seven, sat down in front of ten computers and began to learn a new language. None had taken any of the many free computer classes offered in the area. Many were anxious. "It's like math anxiety," Jill said. "Women need a safe space to learn to use computers."

"I have dreamed about community computer centers for years," Deborah added, "and the Women's Computer Literacy Project is a model. We want women to participate in the computer revolution from the beginning. Computers are benign, wonderful tools, but they're used mostly by men with male values. When a technology is new, it's important to create viable models that are people-oriented, not profit-oriented. If we can get women's values institutionalized early on, we won't be knocking at the doors of computer companies twenty years from now saying, 'Things ought to be different.' We can make them different now."

**Sr. Elizabeth Thoman** doesn't confine herself to computers. She is willing to take on communications technologies of all kinds. "Computers, satellites, even newsletters—I'm interested in the values

Laura Catanzaro. Amazon. Mixed Media on Plywood. 1980.

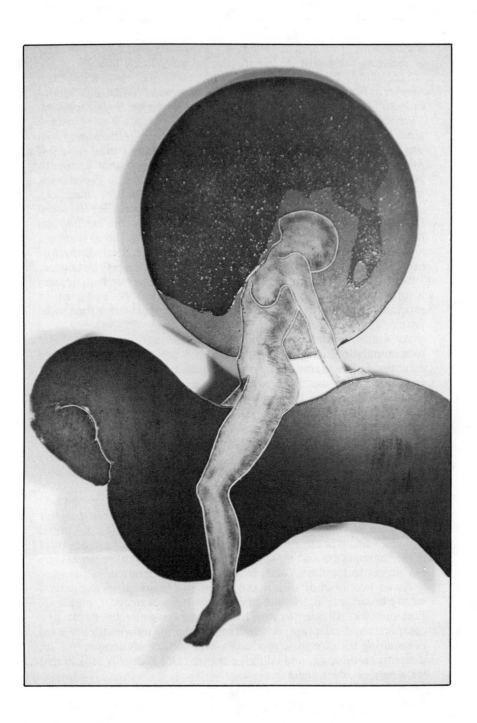

implications of *all* media," she said, "especially how new technology is changing the world we live in even as we're living in it."

Since 1977, Elizabeth has edited and published *Media&Values*, a quarterly magazine. At first, her audience was women in religious orders. "They deal with the casualities of the media age," she explained. "Families torn apart by consumerism, elderly persons who've learned from television that the world is mean, kids who can recite commercial jingles but can't read." But the audience grew, and in 1984, *Media&Values* merged with the Media Action Research Center to become a magazine for all major faith groups—Catholics, Protestants, and Jews. Today, its circulation includes readers in fifty countries.

Issues are stimulating and provocative, covering topics like the social impact of the telephone, media in the nuclear age, media exploitation of women, violence in rock video. The format is lively, full of graphics, and well written. "We raise questions about the long-term impact of new technology and media images of human life," Elizabeth concluded. "We are all fighting an entrenched patriarchy, and our best weapon is information. We have to know how the media works and use it to proclaim women's view of the world. We simply cannot afford to be passive consumers any longer."

As women actively communicate their views, they are less subject to manipulation, *and* they get power. And power is the name of the communications game. "If women could reach sixty-three million families a night," said Donna Allen, "day after day (as the TV networks do), we could change the world. Power is the ability to move something in the direction you want—a physical object or an idea. The more people you can reach to help you move something, the more power you have. Outreach is political power. In a democracy, where political power is supposed to be equal, no one individual or group should be the only one able to reach sixty-three million families every night. Anybody with something to say should be able to say it to just as many."

Women are talking. We are forming film and record companies, publishing houses, magazines, and newspapers. We are reviewing our books and buying them in our bookstores. We are singing our music and recording it in our studios. We are reading reports of our activities in our newspapers and making films about our lives. We are adding our voices to the One Voice, telling our stories straight.

As we take hold of silicon and copper, telephone lines and lasers, we are broadcasting, live and in color, from coast to coast, on paper, film and disk. All over the world, we are speaking directly, harnessing computers and videotape, controlling and sharing information. We are not waiting for directors, producers, and editors any longer. We are directing, producing, and editing our own. Our silence is broken and we won't be silent again.

# 7

# BE DISARMING—CREATE

Artists, we think, are different. They work odd hours, don't hold "normal" jobs. They are always trying to get some body in New York City to recognize them. They like cities where they go out at night with artist friends to gossip about each other. Sometimes they dress funny. They have "studios" with big windows and mess all over the floor. Out of the mess, beautiful things come to decorate walls, rooms, sides of buildings, traffic circles in cities.

Artists shop at special stores for colored pencils, huge pieces of mountboard, strange-looking carving knives, glue. They cart their finished work to quiet places with white walls, tracklighting, and wooden floors. They hang their art on the walls, and people shuffle around rooms looking at it.

Art also happens at fine arts centers. You need a ticket to get in. When you get one, you sit down in a big room with a lot of other people and watch somebody else do art. Sometimes the art is fine and sometimes it isn't. Afterwards, you go home and watch TV. Nothing on television is art.

Art is a luxury. Poor people don't make art. Art isn't work. It is a frill, a decoration. It can be cut out of school curricula without any loss to students, and young people should not be encouraged into it. If they go the way of art, they will crave colored pencils and studios for Christmas.

So it goes. Myths and prejudices about art and artists abound. Art is something other, "set totally outside daily life," wrote **Lucy Lippard**, author, art critic, feminist, and political activist, "either above it all, as the product of some mysterious superior activity, or below it all, as 'useless.'[1] " Artists are affected by this cultural schizophrenia. Watch any portfolio-bearing artist scurry down a city street, and know that she, too, wonders what her art has to do with life.

In Washington, D.C., Mary Clare squeezed two days a week from her harried editing and teaching schedule to photograph at her studio. At one end of the city sat the White House, and at the other, past prostitutes and drug dealers, her darkroom slumbered in a former Oldsmobile warehouse. Drunks slouched against a multi-colored mural on the corner building.

Three door locks away from the drug dealers outside, Mary Clare developed rolls and rolls of film, prepared slides to send to New York City galleries, and wondered what difference art made to the pimps, prostitutes, and homeless drunks below or to the Pentagon madmen across town. When Sotheby's auctioned a Turner painting for $3 million, while the women's center needed $5,000, she wondered if she were in the right profession. Was art a frill after all?

Lucy is obsessed with this question. She can't stand the separation between art and society. She wrote *Overlay* "on the premise that art has social significance and a social function. I resist the notion that in modern times the task of image and symbol making should be relegated to one more frill on the 'quality of life.' "[2]

Because "art is still overdefined in Western society," she continued, "to the point where its function is limited to decoration or status sysmbol," modern artists have had to shake loose art school educations and society's trivialization of the creative process, and reintegrate art with life. Those artists who succeeded became "disgusted with the star system and the narrowness of formal 'movements.' They began to ask themselves larger questions. When they looked up from their canvas and steel, they saw politics, nature, history, and myth out there."[3]

We are beginning to get the idea. Our lives and art are one. Witness: **Leslie Labowitz**, a performance artist, grows sprouts for a living, but it is more than a business. **Faith Wilding**, California artist and writer, explained. "Leslie is combining her art with her interest in nutrition, food shortages, and feeding the world," Faith said. "She became a member of a farmer's market where she sells sprouts, but she also does performance pieces with them—feeding sprouts to people and making images with them. It's a whole amalgam of art and life."

Witness: **Kathy Schilling** embroiders fiber foods which she shows and sells in New York galleries. "If I'd gone to art school, I would never have had the courage to call these art," she said, referring to her exquisite red and green peppers, a half lemon, and sea shells. "I've

---

Kathy Schilling. Peppers. Embroidery sculpture.

sewed and knitted and macramed for years, and my art just came naturally out of that.'' Her original fiber food was a pizza. While she
was helping a student do stitchery, (Kathy is a learning disabilities
teacher), she paged through a magazine, looking for a subject. '' 'Why
don't you do a pizza?' '' I asked, and the student laughed. I did the
pizza myself, and began to think of myself as an artist.''

Witness: **Bonnie Sherk**, New York environmental performance artist,
was a waitress and short order cook in an all-night coffee shop. She
turned the jobs into a series of performance events. She dressed for
each part, wearing ''cultural costumes,'' documented her night shift
with photographs, and included them in her portfolio. ''I'm a
performance artist,'' she said, ''and over the years I have explored the
nature of performance, from the creation of tight vignettes to the life
work of ''being.'' For me, the ultimate performance is being a total
human being, interacting with others. The performance is ongoing—
it's working to make your life and what you produce a gorgeous,
effective, and transformational art form.''

Witness: **Jere van Syoc**, Los Angeles sculptor and innovator in many
fields, works as a medical technician forty hours a week. For this job,
she wears solid white. But on weekends, she paints ''death toys'' solid
black. ''These toys are 'boundary pieces,' '' she said, ''about the transformation from life to death—about *eros* and *thanatos*—the forces that
keep life moving and changing. I'm glad the things I make are being
looked at and understood, but I'm still stronger and more interesting
than they are. What I really want is for *me* to be looked at and understood, and for my contribution to a new paradigm to be picked up on,
modeled after.''

Clearly, there is spillover for Leslie, Kathy, Bonnie and Jere. Their
art work and their lives aren't two delineated sentences separated by
a period. They hyphenate what they do for a living and what they do
for art. Years before Carol Gilligan described women's ethical reality
or Charlene Spretnak collected articles about women's spirituality, women artists painted and danced and wrote from the inside out, expres-
sing their reality obliquely and indirectly through art. They began with
what they knew.

Many of them have known pain. But, by transforming this pain into
art, they turn negatives into positives. As they tell the truth about their
painful past, they touch the rest of us who suffer too. And we are all
healed, restored, able to claim our history, and move on. To work outward from a personal base is a loving gift from the artist to all of us.
Here are some giftgivers:

• A man broke into her home and raped **Nancy Dahlstrom**, art
professor at Hollins College in Roanoke, Virginia. Afraid of being
alone in the house at night after that, angered by the trial process,
her hair cut short, and outfitted with new clothes, Nancy began

Nancy Dahlstrom. When Is the Time to Take Off the Bindings? Rape
Journal Drawing. 1982.

when is the time
to take off the
bindings? only when the
wounds are
healed.

"The Rape Journal," a series of thirty-four drawings. On the final piece, she scribbled, "When is the time to take off the bindings? Only when the wounds are healed." One way of healing was to create art out of hell and let her feelings emerge in the work.

• **Susan** (last name withheld by request), a poet, is working on an autobiographical prose piece describing her years in a mental institution. Susan wanted to tell the story from the ward women's point of view, but realized she only knew the story told by men doctors. To find the perspective she was after, Susan wrote daily pieces to her friend Harriet, prefacing each with how she felt that day. "Here I am in this dark, rat-infested basement in New York writing the hardest part of the story," she would write. "Why am I doing this?" Then she would proceed with the narrative. Harriet gave feedback, "but mostly she gave the opinion that what I was doing was important," Susan said. "I learned that I could define my own values, figure out what *my story* was and tell it my own way."

• **Endesha Ida Mae Holland** writes plays about her hellish past in Greenwood, Mississippi, where she turned tricks for $5 as a teenage prostitute, went to jail for shoplifting, and was radicalized and empowered by the Civil Rights Movement. At the University of Minnesota in Minneapolis, she has written about her own life— vivid and violent. "The Reconstruction of Dossie Ree Hemphill" explores the consequences of father-daughter incest; "Requiem for a Snake" is about drug addiction; "Second Doctor Lady" tells the story of her mother, a midwife who delivers a breech baby using magic, herbs, charms, and skillful hands. Endesha ("driver" in Swahili) scoops back into her life and culture for art material.

While women like Susan, Nancy, and Endesha go down and dig around their deepest roots, using life experience as subject matter, **Nancy Azara** pushes women until they *see* what is in their minds. She is a New York City artist, teacher, and co-founder of the New York Feminist Art Institute. Her own art describes women's strength and wisdom in such images as the Sun Goddess, using shapes and forms from her unconscious. In classes, she shares her process with other women. Nancy joins her students in a circle, introduces techniques of consciousness-raising, and helps them talk about their experiences as women. As they talk, they draw in visual diaries. "Their drawings reflect what is in their minds, and they see things they haven't dared look at before," Nancy said. "The drawing is there and can't be denied. In this way, the students see their visual language in relation to themselves.

"As women, we're not going to effect change unless we look at our unconscious and re-program some of the deep feelings and ideas instilled in us," Nancy concluded. "We can keep working on the rhetoric of change, but it won't happen unless we change our minds. By reaching into the unconscious through art, we can rethink our position in the world, both personally and politically."

## Supporting Each Other

The traditional art world, of course, laughs at such talk. Women's images and processes have been ignored and/or misinterpreted, and women artists have been consigned to the fringe. Blatant, personal material won't wash on 57th Street or at the Kennedy Center.

Realizing that it was crucial to have colleagues, these societal "extras" turned to each other, and asked for encouragement to make the images inside themselves instead of images that sell. They created support groups by the dozen. **Elizabeth Vail**, Washington, D.C. artist, has three that nourish her. "One group meets to critique art work," she said. "We're all women about the same age and level of development. These women are aware not only of the creative aspect of art-making, but also the aspect of promotion. We are fellow travelers in the struggle to be self-directed and self-validating."

The second one started as a feminist artists' group at the Washington Women's Arts Center. "This group is more diverse in age and life experience," Elizabeth continued, "and we share the connection between our lives and our art. We encourage each other to create and to risk changing our work. We're interested in what each other has to say, rather than in our levels of expertise."

The artists' group in Elizabeth's church "has more to do with relationships than with art products," she concluded. "It's an investment of time and energy and prayers in each person. We are three painters, a potter, a writer, and a person who hasn't found her medium. We assume the power of the Holy Spirit to mold our lives. Spirituality is present in the other groups, being very much present in creativity, but it is the power of explicit spirituality that forms consensus in my church group."

**Women Exhibiting in Boston** (WEB) is a network of visual artists who show together and separately. They also help each other bridge the span between the single-minded artist on the one hand, and the weekend artist on the other. **Antoinette Winter** explained. "Over the years, I've learned, with the help of other WEB members, to do my art *and* maintain my relationships *and* teach," she said. "I try to keep the art in perspective, as part of the rest of my life."

She was pregnant when we met, anticipating her child's demands on her life. "I am an artist, and I will continue to be an artist," she said. "But I will also be a mother. WEB members are integrating friendships, children, partners, and art. We don't want to be single-minded artists, but none of us would have developed that awareness without the support of one another."

Art making is a lonesome business. All the more reason for help along the way. **Rosie Thompson**, a North Carolina visual artist, plugs into every situation where she can engage with people and creating. Besides writing and exhibiting, Rosie is artist-in-residence at colleges and universities around the country. Infected with the love of making things,

Rosie packs her classes with young art students and community citizens looking for a fresh perspective. There she cajoles, teases, prods, and urges on everybody in her path. "Everyone—women, men and all children—are artists," she declared. "When I can help release that creative energy—in myself and in others, I feel like a new person."

Rosie took us to see "roadside art" in the back country of Orange and Pitt Counties. At our last stop, artist Clyde Jones was at home, recuperating from a workplace injury. His art work—painted, prehistoric animals hewn with chain saws from logs hauled out of the Pee Dee River—wrapped around his yard and presented a surrealistic mosaic of pastel colored beasts. Everywhere, whimsical creatures winked, perched, prepared to pounce. We were enchanted.

Clyde was shy at first, apologized for not being a "real" artist, but Rosie would hear none of it. She insisted that his work, playful and humorous, was art of the highest form, and that he should make it with a vengeance. She offered to deliver paint, suggested he come to Chapel Hill for a show, invited him to teach one of her classes. By the end of our visit, he was chattering away about this and that, rummaging through old boxes of photographs, telling Rosie about a a piece he wanted to do. It is likely that after she left, he went out back and began it. Her excitement about the creative process has that effect on people. It's contagious.

And it's healing. Clyde was depressed when we arrived, animated when we left. Rosie's enthusiasm and excitement about his work changed him, healed him somehow, so that he could proceed. "There is no private artist club," Rosie said, "no exclusive membership. We must help each other tap our creative energies if we are to change the world."

**Debbie Fier** is a singer, pianist, and percussionist in western Massachusetts, known across the country through her album, *In Your Hands*. Through sound healing classes, she leads participants back to their voices. "When we were three feet high," she said, "many of us were told that we sang off key or couldn't sing at all, so we just stopped. I'm reminding people that making sounds can be a release and channeling of energy. I start by doing toning exercises—feeling sounds come from different parts of the body, focusing on one part, feeling it, and letting the sound out."

When she plays in a club, Debbie hands percussion instruments to the audience, and asks people to sing and chant with her. "Get everyone involved—that's my philosophy," she said. "Try to bridge the gap between performer and audience. I want people to become non-mental, unintellectual, unselfconscious for a while, letting the energy come from their hearts as well as from their heads. When this happens, music is a powerful, magical experience."

To the women artists we met, the art world isn't a pyramid where only a few reach the top. It isn't a matter of getting the right people to notice, or write reviews, or offer gallery showings. It isn't being a solitary artist struggling in the lonely garret to make a masterpiece. To them, art making is a way of being connected to all things, of living their lives more fully. Women artists are leaving garrets in droves, and are joining with each other to create new masterpieces based on cooperation and collaboration.

## Collaborating

The impulse to collaborate flies in the face of societal jokes about artistic cooperation. (Remember the one where two people are looking at a piece of art or a building or a book, and one says to the other, "This whatever-it-is looks like it was done by a committee." Obviously, in tone and assumption, this comment is the ultimate criticism.) Individualism, almost a Western motto, is hard to resist. But tenacious women artists are succeeding. They stand in the rain, on concrete, paint their bodies and bombs, shout songs from mountain peaks, dance under moons ringed with clouds. "We are not separated from life, streets, cities, nature, each other," they are saying. "And we will prove it by joining our disciplines, media, hearts, and minds." Women artists, more interested in relationship than fame, are blending and merging instead of disconnecting.

When Massachusetts papermaker **Ann Gibson** wanted to do a thirty-day mask-making project, she had to collaborate because she couldn't make masks of her own face. She asked Mary Clare, a photographer; Annie, a basketmaker; Melissa Tefft, a potter and masseuse; and Vicki Hovde, a performance artist to come to her house on a full moon in April, and she explained the process: one of us would come each Sunday in the month and make seven masks of her face and one of our own. She would decorate one of the seven each day, and we would decorate our own sometime during that week. At the end of the month, on the next full moon, we would meet as a group and do a corporate mask of Ann. "It was the first time I'd ever asked for help with my art work," Ann said. "It was scary and exhilarating at the same time."

When we gathered at Ann's the following month, we saw that the masks had become more abstract and less complete as the project went on. By the last week when Mary Clare was making masks, the whole idea of mask as covering had broken down. She made a cast of Ann's hand touching her mouth, and a half mask that left the right side of Ann's face exposed. During the month, we had unconsciously, but corporately, moved from a traditional rendering of Ann's face to our own designs.

We each controlled only part of the process. We maskmakers could make any design we wanted, but we had to use Ann's body. She, in turn, could decorate the masks any way she wanted, but she was limited by our designs. "I began to see your masks less as *structures* for my artmaking," Ann concluded, "and more as *art* for me to respond to. Our work was thus bound together as one work."

The play, "Stell and Miss Reen," was a joint project between Washington, D.C. poet and filmmaker, **Michelle Parkerson** and **Joanne Jimason**, publisher and writer. Stell, the owner of a beauty shop, and Miss Reen, a school teacher, have been lovers and have lived together for twenty years. Michelle wrote Stell's part and Joanne wrote Miss Reen's. Over a period of months, they passed the script back and forth, carrying on a written conversation. The final result, produced in the spring of 1984, moved forward "using exchanges of letters, dialogues, material from their past," said Michelle. "The play is really a composite of voices—mine and Joanne's and, in the end, Stell's and Miss Reen's. Because before it was all over, *everybody* had something to say."

Women's theater groups sometimes collaborate to develop their plays. The women at **Rhode Island Feminist Theater** (RIFT) are good examples. "Creation of a play takes about four months," **Sherry Brown** said. "We begin with an idea. For example, 'One Is Silver,' our play about women's friendships, started at a party when a woman described a yearly ritual with a friend. We all chimed in with stories about rituals we each have, and how central friendship is to our lives. Before the evening was over, we had begun the play."

"After we get the idea, we research it," **Barbara Conley** said. "We read and talk with people about the subject. When we began 'Paper Weight,' a play about clerical workers, one RIFT member had a lot of information because she was writing a thesis about that subject. She taught the rest of us about the issues. This is a period of consciousness-raising."

Eventually, the actors get to their feet, bringing to life all that has been digested. "Our best plays and characters come from the hidden places in our own lives," said Sherry. "We don't put ourselves on stage, but rather take parts of ourselves and hold them up. I discovered a character in me, Mary O'Malley, who dresses in polyester pantsuits, wears a blond wig, and has been working for an insurance company for twelve years with no raise. She is opinionated, stubborn, impossible to be around, and I love her."

To prepare a script, the writer and director review the character work done by the actors and begin suggesting improvisations. "We go back and forth between improvisation and writing," Barbara explained. "It's a very intuitive process. When we need other people to see it, we invite them to give us feedback. At that point, we are wondering, 'Is this really a play? Is it going to work? Do we have anything here?' Finally we rewrite the script, make it as tight as we can, and copyright it. The last piece of our process involves conversations with our audiences after our performances. There, we just listen."

Throughout the development of a play, RIFT members engage with people outside their own circle. They ask other artists to give feedback before they complete the play; they welcome audience reaction. Many

Nelleke Langhout-Nix. Phases of the Moon. (detail) Mixed media wall hanging. 80″ x 62″. 1978. (Photo: Roger Schreiber)

woman artists enjoy the give and take that such collaboration brings. Ten years ago, **Nancy Dohlstrom** decided to use the U.S. Postal Service to help her reach artists far removed from her graduate school art class. She and a friend generated a mail art idea that continues to this day. They chose an image for other people to play with—the gingerbread man—and mailed kits containing ceramic gingerbread men to thirty artists around the country. They asked for responses, and proclaimed November 17th, National Gingerbread Day.

All year, the original thirty and their friends played with the gingerbread man image and mailed their renderings to Nancy. The next year, she sent out real gingerbread cookies to forty artists, broadening the base, and continued to document the responses. The third year, Nancy was a visiting artist at Alfred University, and with the help of students, she sent gingerbread art to two hundred and fifty artists.

Each year on National Gingerbread Day, Nancy shows slides to her art students at Hollins College, and sends more gingerbread art invitations. "The gingerbread figure is a light, positive, apolitical symbol," she said. "National Gingerbread Day and this on-going project are about communication and fun. I like making things with other artists. I stay fresh and in touch with others, not always isolated with my own work."

Some women collaborate with people not considered artists by the mainstream art world. **Charlotte Robinson** invited eighteen well-known artists to design quilts, and she found sixteen needle artists, most of them unknown outside their field, to sew them. The former understood the art world; the latter were not even considered artists. Together, they hauled up from history a functional craft and catapulted the lowly quilt, a folk art, into high art.

The visual and needle artists conferred. When artist Lynda Benglis sent bold Indian silks and satins to Amy Chamberlin, her quiltmaker, Amy had a hard time with the flashy material. She was used to working with soft, soothing cottons. But once Amy started putting the blocks together, she felt the energy of the material, added glittery thread on her own, and sewed stitched patterns that gave the quilt even more movement. In the end, Lynda, a "fine" artist, got to play with an unfamiliar medium, and the "craft" artist, Amy, had an opportunity to move beyond traditional patterns and techniques of quiltmaking.[4] Together, they and the other ninety-four women working on the project, made history. Alfred A. Knopf published a book about the quilts, and they are booked in museums until the end of 1986.

Another fiber artist, **Anna Dunwell**, designed a limited edition coverlet and found factory workers to produce it. First, she used a computer to find all the possible permutations of the design. Then she developed a durable three-thread construction weave. Next stop, the factory. "I wanted to work with other people," Anna said, "so that my art process wasn't a solitary thing. I also wanted to create fusion where there had been a schism—between artist/designer and craftsperson/technology."

But it wasn't easy. She had a complicated pattern, natural fibers, and a product that wasn't cost effective. But she was determined to work with craftspeople, not just give them the design, and leave them with the production. It took two years to find a factory willing to collaborate. "They were curious," she added. "The owner was an old style mill owner; I was a black women with a preposterous idea. He did it because he was curious."

When they began to run the coverlets, the machinery wasn't equipped to handle weaver's wool, so it ran slowly. Anna left her Boston home at five each morning to get to Connecticut in time for the seven o'clock shift. It took three years to produce two hundred pieces, but the factory workers exclaimed over "real cloth" and took pride in this part of the process. For Anna's part, "It was fantastic!" She said, "I loved it. I enjoyed bringing all of the people into the process."

Collaboration, of course, does not always produce a high, clear feeling. Often it is difficult. Women who engage with the process agree to hang in and sort through different media, egos, and styles of working until the true, collective voice is heard. This is not a simple thing to do. It doesn't come naturally to us, schooled as we are in competition. But women are managing.

In Seattle, **Faedra Kosh**'s friend Eleanor gave her a poem, and Faedra created a painting from it. Eleanor was horrified at the result; it seemed the opposite of her meaning. But as they talked about the painting and read her poem, they realized that while Eleanor used movement images in her poetry to free herself from formality and tightness, Faedra used controlled, precise images to stabilize her center. "It first appeared that we were disjointed," Faedra said, "but in fact, we were evenly balanced at the opposite ends of the pole. Complementary."

The collaborative, complementary bond between **Anne Rhodes** and **Barbara Anger** is so strong that when another woman arrived in Ithaca, New York, to apprentice, neither Barbara nor Anne could tell her what they did. Their **Mischief Mime** theater pieces are "started, not with written scripts," Barbara said, "but with our bodies, dreams, sensations. We work so intuitively, without explaining things to each other, that it was hard for our apprentice to engage with us."

Sometimes, Anne and Barbara follow an idea to a dead end and start over. Other times, the original kernel of the idea drops out, but leads them somewhere else. "We each have to let go," Anne said, "and not get stuck on what we individually brought in. We improvise back and forth, changing the original, individual material until we have something that belongs to both of us."

Women members of the **Heresies** collective watch their feminist publication change with each issue because they invite a new editorial staff to write it. And consistently, the two collectives produce the only existing publication to probe the connections between art making and feminist politics. Committed to broadening the definition and function of art, the group believes that art has a political impact, and that in the making of art, our identities as women play a distinct role. The

collective seeks to stimulate dialogue, document the art of women, and generate new creative energies among women. Every issue, filled with exciting ideas and images, becomes a definitive resource on the topic covered. This vitality is a direct result of the collaborative publication process.

"The core collective, which originally began *Heresies*, decides on topics," explained **Patricia Jones.** "Then they call together an issue collective—women interested in the topic. Because members of the issue collective have a lot of emotional commitment to the issue, we get a lot of creativity. And this process allows us to bring in different voices, not the same old people all the time. The process of working together, in a temporary collective, is a valuable one for most everybody."

But it isn't always easy. **Eleanor Batchelder,** a New York feminist, helped with the "Women Working Together" issue. "I've worked in several collectives," she said, "and have found that political understanding is not enough. You can know how you want things to go, but they still don't always happen that way. Working together can bring out personal insecurities, bitterness, and terrible intolerances. We flounder, look for explanations and solutions, and lash out at each other and at ourselves. We need good work structures, good models of women working together, to help us through that."

Patricia acknowledged that perfect communication between the two collectives has never been the norm. "It's not an easy situation to work in," she said, "but the creativity that happens offsets the personal problems. *Heresies* is still publishing after eight years because we believe in getting other people involved."

By the nature of their medium, musicians have to get others involved. Without people, black dots on a page of sheet music don't mean much. When **Beth York,** Atlanta composer and musician, was asked to open Kay Gardner's Atlanta concert with a new "classical, jazzy chamber music" piece she'd written, Beth had to become an administrator, conductor, and peacemaker in creating one, big, collaborative sound played by thirteen individuals.

It took four months to find the musicians, and that was only the beginning. "We had to work out our politics," Beth said, "work out our money issues, work out how we felt about the piece." But as they talked, politics began to fade, and the piece and what it said to people became all important. After the performance, everybody in the auditorium stood and cheered. "Five hundred people had heard and liked the music," Beth said. "It freaked me out, and I cried all the next day. I had never named myself composer before."

New responsibilities come with the title. To coordinate a collaboration is no easy feat. Women who know what they want and how to get it also are learning to let go of their original, individual ideas. They give all members of the team both direction *and* a feeling that their styles,

Mischief Mime (Top: Barbara Anger, Bottom: Anne Rhodes) (Photo: Connie Saltenstall)

voices, ideas are heard. Whenever this balance is found, and women
are finding it, collaborative pieces have power and cohesion.

## Getting the Work Out

Art is a gift, the fruit of a person, and it is intended to be given away.
Watch a group of children put together a backyard play. First, they
dig around in a trunk for costumes, then they push together cardboard
boxes and chairs for a stage. They may yell at each other during practice,
but by curtain time, they are a team. Somebody sells tickets, and suddenly, everything comes together—the too-long costumes transform
Mary into a Queen, Cynthia into Robin Hood. The stage, draped with
tattered sheets, bounces with bodies running forward to deliver lines.
It is inconceivable that those children will dismantle their stage and
return their costumes to the trunk without first performing for somebody else. The very act of creating calls for sharing.

Women artists are no different. Whether they make art collaboratively or independently, they want it to reach an audience. Artists may
delve into life-changing events like rape and mental illness, or together
make a piece that is more profound than any of its parts, but all of
them need and want their work to be seen, heard, read by someone else.

No longer content to store finished art underneath their beds, no
longer satisfied with yearly recitals at local garden clubs, no longer
willing to write gossip columns for town weeklies, no longer satisfied
with a show once a year, resourceful and creative women artists are
thinking about the "art game" and how they want to play it. "It's like
shooting craps," said **Janet Braun-Reinitz**, Ithaca painter. "You're on
a roll; you think you're going to win $5,000, so you take more risks.
Because you place more bets, you win more money. Because I go to
more places and say to more people, 'Look at my work. I'm wonderful,'
more people look at me and say, 'If she says so, with that confidence,
then it must be so.' The more powerful the *person* is, not the work,
the more the work gets looked at. I don't like it, but that's the way it is."

**Myrna Shiras**, Los Angeles artist, doesn't like it either, but she still
spends eighty percent of her time getting her work out. She sends dozens
of slides. "We reduce our powerful images to little celluloid strips,"
she said. "We don't protest. Then we send them to this person who
doesn't give a damn about us, hoping some magic transformation will
take place. We imagine him holding them up to a lightbulb and saying,
'Oh, God, this is what I've been waiting for.' "

"I don't like the hustling," Janet said, "but I'm willing to do it
because I want to make a living as an artist. And I want as many kinds
of people in as many different settings to see it as possible. The world
is not going to change by my sitting here doing nothing."

Pat Vecchione. Ice Environment From a Future Time. (detail) Polyester
resin.

But what to do? Go toward the traditional "art world" audience found in big city museums, galleries, fine arts centers, *or* toward an alternative audience through self-publishing, women's galleries, or art in the streets? Women artists are walking both paths, controlling as much of the art delivery system as possible and creating their own alternatives.

## Into the Mainstream

**Mary Beth Edelson** has been on both paths. Eighteen years an artist, she began as a traditional painter, art school-educated and gallery-oriented. Then, in the 1970s, she broke out of the pack, hit the streets, and organized full-moon rituals, earth goddess dances and performances, and workshops at colleges and women's centers. Today, she is back in her New York City loft studio painting huge paintings and looking for a gallery to show her work. "I started to paint again because while we women were out experimenting with collective ways of creating, men in the art world were stealing our initiative, making big paintings built on our ideas. They have been getting incredible press, power, money, recognition, and exposure for this work, and we women have been left speechless. What do you say when someone has stolen the words right out of your mouth?"

"I'm looking for a gallery to represent me, but I haven't sold out; I really want to change the world," she said. "But I don't have enough power to do it. Alternative gallery spaces are like ghettos. I want more access, more power. And the way I get that, as an artist in New York City, is to find a well-heeled, commercial gallery to show my work."

But suppose your work is too big to photograph and too complicated to be understood in parts? How to convey it to the powers that be? Large-scale sculptor **Pat Vecchione** couldn't ask Chicago gallery owners to drive to Madison, Wisconsin, to see her installation/environment, so she took it down to see them. "I bought an old moving van," she said, "and installed my work. Then I made an appointment and drove the van to Chicago."

She got there, and asked the gallery owner to step outside. "When I opened the van door, smoke from dry ice and my clear, fiberglass work created a fantastical environment," Pat continued. "It was so dramatic and unusual, I suppose, that they offered to show my work in a future exhibition." The gallery owner across the street saw the excitement, and went over to peek inside the van. "She and I ended up talking for two hours," Pat said, "and she took some of my work right then. My methods may have been a little flakey, but my work is serious, and I'm determined that it will be seen."

**Laura Shechter** is just as determined to be successful in the traditional art world. First, she and her husband studied *Art News*, and made a

Laura Shechter. Composition in Blue. 1980. Oil on masonite. 13″ x 11″.
(Photo: eeva/inkeri)

I set realistic goals because I need nine hours of sleep a night. My husband and I aren't interested in a savings account, or a house in the suburbs. We haven't had a dinner party in three years, and it's hard to find a chair to sit on. But we have lots of energy and ideas.''

Most successful, mainstream artists do. They aren't discovered, suddenly thrust into the limelight. They work hard at it, learning as much about business dealing as about art making. And they persevere. Anna Dunwell went through hell during the three years her tapestry was in production. She got mugged and was blind for a month, vandals slashed the warp at the factory, and she had a hysterectomy and was bedridden for two-and-a-half months. "I just kept on going," she said in her gentle, energetic way. "A lot of women feel impotent; a lot of black women feel impotent; a lot of artists feel impotent. But it's a matter of wrapping your mind around life as it is, and keeping on doing it.''

## Choosing an Alternative Path

"Keeping on doing it" for some women means developing their own delivery systems. They want their work to get to the audience they intend it for—the public. They find that emotionally and financially, they can't afford to give up control. Besides, New York City galleries look imposing, the Kennedy Center is booked with antique theater pieces, and Random House is waiting for blockbusters to pull them out of a deficit. Women wonder, "How do we get art to *people*?''

In Washington, D.C. and Texas, two groups are answering that question. In Washington, **Roadwork**, a nonprofit cultural organization, gives women of diverse racial and ethnic heritages the chance to express their cultural perspectives. "Women are unique carriers of culture,'' said Director **Amy Horowitz**, "whether through weaving fabric, improvising music, or creating intricate philosophical thought.''

Roadwork's commitment to present a cross-cultural display of women's talent has grown out of their connection with Sweet Honey In The Rock, a quintet of black women who sing songs of liberation. "Sweet Honey has been one of Roadwork's teachers,'' Amy said. "That they've survived for a decade without diminishing the scope of their politics comes from their willingness to keep struggling with each other and with external issues. They've helped us know that when we speak of women's culture, we speak about issues facing women all over the world.''

Amy describes organizing a concert as a creative act that is similar to conceptualizing a song or a painting. "Except,'' she continued, "here the canvas is a living moment in history framed by the dynamic interaction between human beings. Concerts are vehicles for a diverse group of people to come together, to work and celebrate. Our goal is to encourage coalition building, and concerts are an excellent training ground for that.''

list of galleries they thought would be sympathetic to Laura's images. Then, Laura called for interviews. By the third appointment she had a dealer. She was twenty-five years old. "I've been making money at art for five or six years," Laura said, "supporting myself for three years, and earning half the household money for the last two."

In the middle of all this, Laura had a baby. She didn't sleep much for two years, but she painted four or five hours every day even though she was up with the baby every fifteen minutes. "A washerwoman with ten children still has to wash clothes for a living," Laura said. "Her children don't keep her from doing it because it is what she has to do. The same is true for me. It's very easy *not* to do art. You have to give up some things, no question about it. But you don't give up your work.

"I am ambitious, and I want to be successful, but that does not mean I sell out all my shows, or that my images are 'in,' " she continued. "Being successful means that when people think of still life realists, they think of Laura Shechter. I don't change my work to make that happen, but I'm always thinking clearly, trying to understand what's happening with curators, dealers, and collectors in the commercial art world."

Laura likes telling art school students around the country what she's learned. "An artist always has to be in control, and the way you get control is by having information. The art world is irrational, so I don't pay attention to trends. I do my work, understand who I am, and learn which galleries like my images. Art is more than creating something. Art is business."

Mary Beth, Pat, and Laura work hard to get their images seen by the public, juggling personal relationships, job changes, and children so they can continue to make art. **Shereen LaPlantz**, California basketmaker, has two additional tasks: convince the art establishment that baskets are art forms, *and* educate her audience. "Baskets aren't always containers to put things in," she said. "They are art objects in themselves. But people see and buy them as craft items. I even have to have a clause in my contracts that gallery owners won't display my baskets with plants in them."

Shereen has five-year, ten-year, and lifetime goals. Fourteen years after graduate school, she's right on schedule—two books (*Plaited Basketry: The Woven Form* and *The Mad Weave Book*), a basketry periodical, baskets in several large collections in Tennessee, California, and Kentucky. She is recognized as an authority on basketmaking, a regular speaker at international fiber conferences, and organizer of basket conferences in conjunction with art centers in Connecticut, California, and Chicago. For the future, she's hosting an international basketry exhibition and competition. She also wants the Museum of Modern Art to own one of her baskets. And, for her 80th birthday, she'll have shows the whole year long.

She is also realistic. "The plan is working, but it's long range," she said. "I'm a plodder. I don't move mountains daily. I keep on going.

**Rita Starpattern**, founder of **Women and Their Work** (WTW), an arts organization in Austin, believes women artists have something unique to say to the people of Texas. WTW sponsors statewide tours of traveling art exhibits, and lobbies the legislature for arts support. "Our history, our books, our songs, and our visual symbology are our culture," Rita said. "Women have always been responsible for creating some of this culture, and we need to credit them and encourage them to continue. WTW is changing cultural notions by integrating contemporary women's art with the larger community, showing work in parts of town where people don't go to galleries. We are always involved in a process of engagement among the makers of the art, the work itself, and the viewers."

**Ann Langdon** is committed to precisely this same dynamic between artists, their work, and audiences. She moved from Washington, D.C., to New Haven, Connecticut, and after multiple gallery rejections from New Haven's finest, she converted her studio above a hat store into Gnosis Gallery, a feminist gallery. For two years, until her rent skyrocketed, artists from all over the country participated in shows about women's fantasies, the Equal Rights Amendment, witches.

Accompanying each exhibit was a "Dialogue With the Artist" evening, which gave artists and non-artists a chance to talk. One of Ann's goals was to raise awareness of feminist art—its themes, sources, power to transform. In the "Dialogues," she accomplished that goal. She wanted to upgrade alternative space available to women artists, take a chance on women whose work wouldn't be shown elsewhere, and invite the community to experience images they might never see. "We can't validate women's perspective until we know what it is," she said. "I showed work by women who were in touch with themselves as women and were representing some aspect of that experience in their work."

**Katherine Faith Prior** is on the same track. She started Ephebi Gallery: Art for the 21st Century, because, "The commercial gallery system is philosophically and economically bad for artists, particularly women artists." She said, "Art is an important form of communication, and the commercial system doesn't care about that. Economically, dealers like artists to make art so dealers can make money. And the art world is conservative and western European male in its orientation. I just can't buy into those values."

How to represent a wide spectrum of artists then? How to show and sell their work to their advantage, not her own? Katherine works with twenty-three artists. They are women and men—blacks, Hispanics, Asians. She takes a small commission on sales and helps artists get exposure in museums and other places. Several times a year, she has a show at her home in Northwest Washington D.C. and invites collectors and other interested people to come. "I like showing work at home," she said, "because people who buy art want to live with

Ann Langdon. Untitled. 1980. Acrylic/enamel/plexiglass.

it, have it around. This setting is spiritually more satisfying than galleries and museums.''

**Pat Vecchione**, always the innovator, arrived at the Rhode Island School of Design, and found there wasn't enough gallery space for her students' sculpture. Undeterred, she set up a gallery, to scale, in a locker. It was called "OK Harry." "You opened the door, and saw this entire art display inside a small metal box," Pat said. "It had lights to scale and everything." A *Boston Globe* reporter wrote a hilarious review of the first show, and it has become an alternative gallery for serious work. People show there and are reviewed. "When you really need to get your ideas shown, and there's no space," Pat concluded, "there are always ways to do it."

Boston poet and teacher **Kathleen Spivack** knows that. She's been publishing poetry for years. Recently, she left Doubleday for Applewood, a small press, because "putting out a book is a joint creative endeavor, and I wanted an editor I could create with." She continued, "A lot of my work is regional, so I looked for a regional press that liked my work and would be committed to it. Going with Applewood Press was a decision to simplify. Besides, I can work small and local and be a lot happier in my heart."

Kathleen is impatient with women writers who wait for a big editor or a well-known press. "I know women who won't even try to publish unless they can get into *The New Yorker*," she added. "They're waiting for the patriarchal penis in the sky to give them permission to put their poem out. They will not give themselves just the plain pleasure and satisfaction that come from their own hearts. We must re-think our entire attitude about *big* being equal to *good*."

**Jane Barnes**, another Boston poet, was never burdened with myths of grandeur. She has always been content with the small scale. In 1974, she and six friends self-published *Dark Horse: A Poetry and Fiction Newspaper*. They contributed enough money to pay printing costs for the first issue, and sold copies on the street. They made enough money to publish again, and by issue number four, they had a National Endowment for the Arts grant and a list of subscribers. "The newspaper looked better all the time," Jane said. "The stories helped carry it, and the poetry got really good. Soon we were flooded by hundreds of submissions for each issue."

Several years later, Jane used what she had learned to publish a book of her poems. "No one ever gave me permission to run a poetry magazine," she said. "So when I wanted to publish a book of my poems, no one needed to give me permission for that either." She raised money from friends, found a printer in the Midwest, and distributed *Extremes* herself. "If I ever go to a publisher, they're going to have to offer me at least as good a deal as I can offer myself, because otherwise, I can do it alone."

Self-publishing makes Jane feel powerful, in control of her work. "When I go to the typewriter to write a short story," she explained, "I know that I can have it in print in a couple of months if I want to. If you don't think you can publish your work, it's a lot harder to write it. Virginia Woolf always knew she could publish, so she was free to write things like *The Waves*. She didn't need anyone to tell her it was forty years ahead of its time.

"Here's my life plan," she concluded. "I expect to live until I'm in my late eighties. By that time, I'll have published about a dozen novels, and a book of poems every three or four years. I have all my letters since age five, and about twenty journals. I might publish those too. I figure I'll publish forty or fifty books before I die. And you know what? That's no more expensive than getting a used car every couple of years."

Visual artist **Helen Redman** would concur. "I've stopped wasting time with galleries," she said. "Year after year, you do a show, haul it all out, hang it up, throw a party, take it down, and haul it away." The last time she delivered her slides to a San Francisco gallery owner, and waited for his reply, nothing happened. "Finally I realized the guy was a loser," she continued, "so depressed he was pathetic, and I thought, 'What can he do for me anyway?' "

Helen went to pick up her slides. "He got all whiney, and said, 'Wait a minute. I'll look at your work now.' I walked out. I am so disgusted at how these small people have dominated our lives. The whole art distribution system is a go-nowhere system. If you stay in a system like that, you're demeaned by it."

Sour grapes? Hardly. Helen has had twenty-two one-person shows over the last twenty-five years. She's taught at major universities and received honors and prizes from national foundations and arts commissions. Her paintings are part of permanent collections in France and the United States, and her portrait business reflects her very distinctive style. Still, she wants out of the mainstream. "All my art is based on people and is totally personal," she said, "so I have to make direct contact with the individuals who buy my work. I do extraordinarily well when I do that because I'm building bridges between my art and real people, instead of between it and museums."

It never occured to **Susan Boss** to do anything else. "Only five percent of the population can be counted as gallery-goers," she said. So she takes her art to the streets of western Massachusetts. A muralist, seam-stress, sculptor, teacher, and performance artist, Susan believes people are afraid of contemporary art, "hushed and nervous about how to react." She wants to draw people in close to her work and attract people who ordinarily wouldn't be interested. "I want that other ninety-five percent of the population."

To get them, she creates banners and murals for public places. For one project, she worked with twenty-seven prisoners at the Hampshire County House of Corrections. For another, she constructed wings to fit across her back, and covered them with fabric. She's worn butterfly wings for spring parades, red, white, and blue wings for Fourth of July celebrations, death wings for antinuclear marches. Amherst shops hire her, wing-clad, to roller skate around town advertising their stores.

"There isn't enough magic in the world," she said, "Art is one way to get it back."

## Art In the Open

You can almost hear Lucy Lippard clapping. "Art in the open," she wrote, "can be more intimate and accessible, closer to people's lives, than art seen in brutally hierarchical buildings...or in elegant, exclusive settings. Nature on some level is felt to belong to all of us. Art in nature or in the local community becomes more familiar, a part of daily life."[5]

Especially if it is concerned with the complexity of that daily life. At Gnosis Gallery one evening, a group of artists agreed that creating art could help control and diminish destructive forces. If individual artists kept centered and positive, and kept creating, they could help a life-giving future come. But one woman disagreed. "I'm not an artist," she said. "I spend most of my time working on political issues, and I'm very concerned about what you're saying; i.e., if you present a positive, self-centered, open vision in your art work, planetary destruction won't happen.

"I tell you, *we are in danger*," she continued. "And if every artist or typist or factory worker says, 'I'll just *believe* it will be all right,' it *won't* be all right. You don't have to criticize social reality in your art; you don't have to protest or picket. But you have to be *conscious* of the real world. Otherwise, nothing you do will make any difference at all."

**Saphira Linden** is artistic director of Theater Workshop Boston and one of the leaders of Boston's Sufi Center. She has established the Omega Arts Network for artists who are working towards a vision of a better world with works that are healing and transformational. She believes that artists can be the healers of our time by seeking truth; addressing issues like prejudice, pollution, health, and human values in a technological society; helping others understand their human potential; and by attuning to a purpose beyond ourselves.[6] "Today we live in a most challenging time in history," Saphira said. "We can become discouraged, blame everything around us and give up, or we can have the courage to call on that inexhaustible resource deep inside to create the kind of world we want to live in."

Lucy Lippard believes that energy can be found in the streets. For years now, she has worked non-stop to increase the connection between political action and art. She is a co-founder of *Heresies*, and works with New York's **PADD** (Political Art Documentation/Distribution Project) and the **Alliance for Cultural Democracy** (ACD). "I'm constantly combatting the image of an artist as somebody who's separate from everybody else, or a puppet of the dominant culture," Lucy said. "I'm interested in keeping 'the personal is political' idea, but I also want to know how 'the political is personal.' How are our own lives and personal relationships affected by what's happening in the world?"

**PADD** members want artists and social activists to combine social activism and personal creativity. And the organization holds public forums to discuss Hispanic art, education, intervention in Central America, peace encampments, and gentrification of New York's neighborhoods. It also initiates public art projects. To prepare for the 1984 election, PADD initiated a "State of Mind/State of the Union Outdoor Streetworks" project. Its purpose: to provide "an organized way for the New York City art community to convey their views on where we are in this critical moment of history, and where we should be going."

Artists were invited to address themselves and their work "in exhibitions and performances, streetworks and image-grams" which would "saturate the city with images aimed at stripping away the facade of mystification that Reagan and his supporters have so successfully built up around his policies." Encouraged to use *USA Today* and *New York Times* vending boxes, subway cars, and phone booths to display art, artists were also treated to a "Beginner's Graffiti-Propaganda Sheet: A How-To For the First Offender," which urged, "Put it where people can see it."

The **Alliance for Cultural Democracy** is just as innovative. A national liaison of progressive neighborhood arts groups, ACD is "committed to cultural democracy, which is a natural companion to political and economic democracy." Lucy explained. "When you gentrify a neighborhood, you take away people's community and culture, and, thereby, their right to cultural democracy, just as certainly as you take away their economic democracy. Cultural democracy embodies the idea of a multi-cultural society, an anti-melting pot society. It is fundamentally a feminist vision—a world in which everybody has a voice."

Women artists are helping people speak through art. In the process, myths about art making are dissolving. One at a time, bricks in the artist-on-a-pedestal are falling. Art is coming down to earth. Women are embracing their creativity, trusting their products, and taking responsibility for reaching their audiences.

## What Difference Does It Make?

Why do they bother? Because they want to change the world. "Artists are like the thousands of turtle eggs laid on the beach," said Myrna Shiras. "It's not our business to find out if we'll be a surviving turtle. Nature needs the diversity and the choice of all those turtle eggs so it can choose which ones are relevant, powerful, living. We don't see the end result of that choice, and that's hard on our egos, but our function is to be part of this great pool of ideas for culture to draw on. If we don't keep ideas alive, the next generation won't have any to choose from."

Artists are prophets. And art, in an indirect way, reveals the future. Mary Beth Edelson was using her body and moon cycles to explore women's reality long before any woman wrote a book about it. Images often come before words. "Artists look at a situation, analyze it, and see what lies inherent in it," said Faith Wilding, author of *By Our Own Hands*. "Then they shape something which makes the whole experience understandable. When we, the audience, see the final product, our hearts are opened up. Artists deal with what love is—the real life force—and how it can be conveyed. They are always remembering what's at the heart."

Artists are change agents. When we see Judy Chicago's blossoming vaginal images, we change our perception of female genitalia. When we call out missing Chilean women's names with Holly Near, we are connected to our sisters everywhere. When we read Virginia Woolf's *A Room of One's Own*, we want one. "Art is an encounter," said Sr. **Marian McAvoy**, president of the Sisters of Loretto. "It involves people in a whole way. We social activists try to change people's mentality and values by organizing, educating, and talking to them. But we are not changing them. It takes artists to change people's minds about Central America, or hopes for peace, or global awareness."

Art making requires a faith stance. We tell you about these forty women artists because *we* like them. They make a dent in our minds. We have faith that they'll make a dent in yours. But there is no way to be sure. "I don't write to change people's minds," said **Hollis Giammatteo**, Seattle writer, and member of a theater group that walked across the United States along the path of the White Train. "I'm not that direct about it. Probably the way I change people's minds is that I simply like what I'm doing so much that it's catching. When I'm true to my journey, I amaze myself with what kind of teacher I end up being." Every artist is a guide.

"Art is disarming," **Bonnie Sherk** declares. On election day in 1982, she hired an airplane to fly over the Bay Area in California towing the words "Be Disarming—Choose Life." She's made A New Patriotic Flag in red, white, and blue that says, "Be Disarming—Choose Life/Be Disarming—Choose Art/Be Disarming—Create." She does this because "traditional politics are divisive. They separate people. What we need is to show how we're connected and to create larger situations in which opposing points of view can be incorporated and understood as analogies. Art can do this because it is an integrated system, a wholistic way of creating positive connections between different cultural forms, belief systems, ways of being and feeling. As such, it is a new/old paradigm of transformation. Art is the most powerful human mechanism we have and we must harness its energy. Art is the true form of disarmament."

Feminist artists are the leaders. They dismantle walls that separate art from life, artists from each other, artists from craftspeople, artists from their audiences, artists from global, human problems. They insist that art and the creative process can change institutions and social structures, change hearts and minds, and transform the planet. They reject, out of hand, the stereotype of artist in garret, alone and poor, walking the streets with portfolio in hand. They take to the streets, rediscover performance and ritual, invite non-artists to participate in the magic of art making, and plaster images on billboards to protest political activities of their government.

And they shout, in unison, with members of Vermont's enchanting Bread and Puppet Theater, "Art soothes pain! Art wakes up sleepers! Art fights against war and stupidity! Art sings halleluja! Art is for kitchens! Art is like good bread! Art is like green trees! Art is like white clouds in blue sky! Art is not business! It does not belong to banks and fancy investors. Art is food. You can't eat it but it feeds you. Art has to be cheap and available to everybody. It needs to be everywhere because it is the inside of the world. Hurrah!''

# 8

# THE SKIN WE LIVE AND WORK IN

**B**efore beginning work on this book, we lived in a small house in northern Virginia surrounded by sixteen acres of farm land. In this suburban, yet rural setting, we harvested wildflowers, apples, persimmons, walnuts; grew vegetables; and planted peach trees. We shingled the house, built a greenhouse on the southeast side, claimed one room for quiet meditation and prayer. We settled in, made a space in which we and our friends felt comfortable and at home.

Then the surrounding land was sold. Day after day, we watched the meadow in our backyard turn into a multiple housing tract. First, men peeled off the grass, rolled and hauled it away to sell for turf. A road was cut, pavement laid, gutters formed. A sign appeared. "Woodcroft Estates," it said.

Men pounded sticks in the mud, tied them with pink, plastic tassles, threw down hay bales to keep the earth, bare of grass, from washing away. Our lot, the smallest in the "Estates," got its own flag-waving stakes. The peach trees blossomed forty feet outside our legal line.

Backhoes dug foundations, cement trucks lumbered through, hammers banged us awake in the early mornings. The new, two-story house thirty feet away blocked the early morning sun, and our greenhouse vegetables stretched to find the light. Suddenly, there was a next door, and neighbors.

We were sick at heart. No more nude bathing in the blue, plastic K-Mart swimming pool, no more picking wild violets in the meadow. We moved the garden, mowed the grass to a new neighbor's line, put in hedges. The peach trees were over the line, so we pruned them, spread manure around their tiny trunks, and when it was time for us to leave, presented them to the neighbors.

Edward Hall wrote *The Hidden Dimension* to explain the dynamics of space and our personal and cultural experiences of it. He concluded that human beings are "surrounded by a series of invisible bubbles which have measurable dimensions."[1] These "spatial envelopes" extend beyond our bodies. After six years of privacy and quiet, we felt choked when our "envelope" shrank from sixteen open acres to a 60' x 100' lot. The size of our house didn't change. It still looked the same. But we felt cramped when the space around us shriveled.

**Hadley Smith**, new age designer and human systems planner, wrote, "The external built environment is the largest, most graphic, most pervasive, and most tangible force in our lives. Likewise, and perhaps more significantly, interior space [inside of structures] is the most *intimate*. It is an internal, physical jacket as close and enveloping as our skins. It can be as functional and transcendent as our pulse, and it can trigger infinitesimal associations of who we are and who we could become."[2]

## How Space Affects Us

Space—visible and invisible—affects how we think, feel, behave. It can accentuate potential or destroy initiative. In Vancouver, British Columbia, and Chicago's South Side slums, we found examples to illustrate the positive and negative effects. Vancouver's **Community Alternatives Society** is an intentional community of adults and children. In the mid-1970s, founding members designed a living space to house forty-four community members in nine units called "pods." The pods include a kitchen, living/dining room area, and a bedroom for each adult and child over ten years of age.

An auto shop, darkroom, bike storage, and wood shop are in the basement. A room designed for children, but not used by them, has been converted into an office, piano practicing room, and place for teenagers to gather. Residents study quietly in the library and hold community gatherings in the large meeting room. The space is open, clean, well lit. Walkways are covered. Contained vegetable and flower gardens decorate the landscape. The whole environment supports and nurtures the residents.

"The building went through five designs," said Society member and former resident **Val** (last name withheld by request). "Our funding sources wanted to be sure the complex would resell if our community failed." The resident designers originally wanted five-, six-, and seven-bedroom pods, but the money lenders opted for three-, four-, and eight-bedroom units. Society members went along with the change, but realize now that three-, four-, and eight-unit pods are not quite right. "The eights are too big, and the threes and fours are too small," Val said.

Yet in spite of this, residents live in harmony; each pod works as an extended family; and people move from one pod to another as they wish and as arrangements can be made. Also, Society members have built a farmhouse on land outside Vancouver for women, men, and children who want a more rural setting. And since the opening of their house, they have designed two similar projects for the city. Their built environments have grown out of their social and political consciousness, and sustain the lives of persons living in them.

On the other hand, residents of Chicago's South Side housing projects are damaged by the city buildings they rent. "Psychologically, this environment does you in," said **Hattie Williams**, life-long resident of the South Side. "You start off with a sixteen-story building, like that one across the street. You've got ten apartments on each floor. Maybe I've got seven kids, the lady next door's got ten, another's got eleven. You're gonna have anywhere from seventy to a hundred kids on one floor. That floor has one small balcony with a chainlink fence in front of it. It's like living in a cage."

Studies show that overcrowding causes crime, sexual abuse, violence. Low-income housing is shoddily constructed and insufficiently maintained. High-rise projects jam together the most disenfranchised and impoverished, and contribute nothing to their well-being or health. Spaces created for the poor break their families, their culture, and their minds.

Hattie explained. "People turn on one another in these projects. Viciousness is what's going on now—child abuse with very young children, incest, a lot of sexual molestation. It is frightening. But I can tell you this," she added. "If the three of us were shut in this room for a week, like caged animals, we would turn into different people too."

Yet when residents try to control the violence, housing authority officials reject their efforts. For example, in one project building, three young women were raped. A group of male relatives formed a vigilante group, rode the elevator twenty-four hours a day for three weeks, and captured the suspect. "The women felt so good about the men taking this interest," Hattie said. "They got together and set up a small fund to support them. But before anything was established, Chicago Housing Authority guards came in and told the young men to get the elevators and go back to their apartments. 'We're here to protect CHA's property,' they said. 'Not you.'" South Side Chicagoans know that developers, contractors, and housing authorities care about buildings, not people.

---

Mary Frances Fenton. Solstice Circle Plan. 1982.

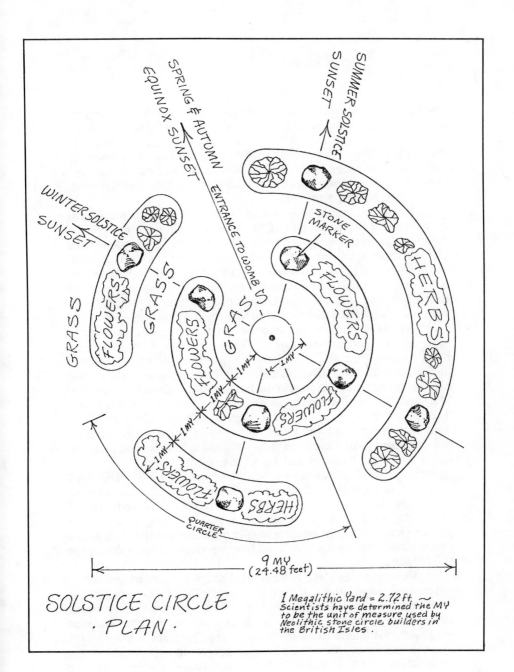

SUMMER SOLSTICE SUNSET

SPRING & AUTUMN EQUINOX SUNSET

ENTRANCE TO WOMB

WINTER SOLSTICE SUNSET

STONE MARKER

HERBS

FLOWERS

FLOWERS

GRASS

GRASS

GRASS

FLOWERS

FLOWERS

GRASS

1 MY

1 MY

1 MY

1 MY

1 MY

FLOWERS

FLOWERS

HERBS

QUARTER CIRCLE

9 MY
(24.48 feet)

# SOLSTICE CIRCLE
## · PLAN ·

1 Megalithic Yard = 2.72 ft.
Scientists have determined the MY
to be the unit of measure used by
Neolithic stone circle builders in
the British Isles.

## Male-Designed Space

The built environment is based on the availability and cost of building materials as well as on the convenience of zoning commissions and local tax collectors. Money controls the spaces around us, and men control the money. "Not only do they control it," said **Rebecca Peterson**, co-author of *New Space for Women*, "they also plan living spaces for a mythical family—mother who stays home with the kids, and father who leaves suburbia to go to work."

Yet Harry and Harriet Homeowner with their little lawn and children comprise only fifteen percent of the households in the United States. Another fifteen to twenty-three percent are headed by single women, half of whom are below the poverty line. The rest, seventy percent, live in households where both adults work[3]. Planners who design suburban houses with half-acre lawns and ten rooms, don't seem to care that Harry and Harriet can't mow lawns or scour three bathrooms every weekend. They're too busy working to meet their mortgage payments.

Neither do planners design interior, residential spaces that support the lives of the people living there. "The home is a domestic workplace. It isn't a country club," said Rebecca, professor at York University in Toronto, Canada. "But planners don't value home work, so they hide all work-related facilities in the basement, the carport, the kitchen. Male designers put doors on cupboards for the same reasons. They don't want to see the tools of the workplace. I keep the baby's clothes in open shelves because I don't want any 'secrets' in my house. And my laundry room is on the second floor next to the baby's room, because that's where my husband and I do the work."

Architect and educator **Leslie Weisman** believes, "The built environment transmits and embodies patriarchal beliefs about women, class structure, technology, and money." And she described a typical obstetrical ward as an example. "It is designed to treat birth as a pathological event," she said, "spatially organized for the convenience of the traditionally male doctor and unresponsive to the needs of the childbearing family.

"A woman giving birth is wheeled through a series of confusing, impersonal, labyrinthian spaces that isolate her from those giving emotional support," Leslie continued. "First, she sweats it out in the labor room, strapped to a bed and fetal monitor while her husband sits in nervous ignorance in a waiting room. Then she is transported to a delivery room where the physician breezes in and out like a star on stage. After the birth, she is taken to a recovery room while her baby is whisked off to a nursery someplace else. Finally in a post-partum ward, she sees her husband and baby again. Because she has been anesthetized and cut, she is groggy and in pain."

Not only are spaces inconveniently designed for users, they are also dangerous. Toxic building materials leak excessive doses of formaldehyde, asbestos, lead, phenols, urethane, chlorine, and hydrocarbons into home and work places. And people are getting sick. But contractors and designers are slow to respond to health hazards, and they continue to buy and use polluting products. "As home and work environments become more threatening," Rebecca said, "women will become more engaged in environmental planning and design. They will start to ask, 'What kind of spaces are we living in? What kind of spaces do we *want* to live in? How do our living, working, and playing spaces restrain or enable our goals for the future?' "

## Working and Teaching Processes

Hadley Smith insists that women and men designers have a moral obligation to address these questions. She suggests two approaches. First, architects and teachers must reexamine hierarchical working and teaching processes, and secondly, because they know how people and structures interrelate, they must design spaces with people in mind.[4] To address the matter of working processes, **Joan Sprague**, with five other women architects and planners, including Magda Brosio and Marie Kennedy, formed the **Open Design Office** in Cambridge, Massachusetts. They wanted to see if an architecture and design office could function wholistically.

The alternatively structured office was open for six years. No member took any profit, and all income was distributed as hourly payment for work. Members set their own schedules, consulted with other members if they needed help, and were responsible for making final decisions about their projects. Office policy and questions of management were taken up at weekly meetings, and all questions were decided by consensus. "It wasn't a collective," Joan said, "but it was not hierarchically structured. We recognized differences in each person's expertise and experience.

"Architecture schools paint a picture of architects as heros," Joan said. "Many architectural offices are structured with a slave class at the bottom working for the hero at the top. This myth is very destructive to creativity. The Open Design Office was our way of testing an alternative."

**The Women's School of Planning and Architecture** (WSPA) was another. It addressed Hadley's question of alternative teaching processes. Co-founded in 1974 by Joan and six other women architects, planners, and design educators, WSPA gave women (who are still a minority in those professions) a chance to teach each other what they were learning about women and space. It also offered them a break from professional isolation. **Leslie Weisman** was one co-founder. "We were a peer group," she said. "We didn't know each other very well, but we trusted each other's need to create a forum in which we could

Swan Orchid House.

Patricia Johanson.

explore, with other women, the relationships between design, planning, architecture, and feminism.''

Instinctively, the seven women applied design principles to the first event—a two-week, around-the-clock, live-in experience. They put in seed money, formed a partnership, developed a curriculum based on their interests, and sent out publicity. ''We looked at several small campuses where we could rent facilities for our summer sessions,'' said Leslie, ''the more neutral and the less architecturally 'fancy,' the better. We wanted a blank canvas, a space we could transform into our own by our presence.'' For the next seven years, women from around the world met in Maine, Colorado, Rhode Island, Connecticut, California, and Washington, D.C.

During the first session in Biddeford, Maine, each co-founder taught a core course: Leslie and Phyllis Birkby developed methods for a feminist analysis of the man-made environment. Joan Sprague and Marie Kennedy discussed architects' roles and the Open Design Office; Katrin Adam organized a carpentry workshop to teach how various tools related to different construction methods and how each was used. Ellen Perry Berkeley dealt with the politics of community development, and Bobbie Sue Hood had her ''students'' re-plan and re-design the campus so that inside/outside and public/private space were continuous instead of segregated. ''Each course had one or two closed sessions,'' said Leslie, ''one session in tandem with every other course, and one session open to the entire 'school.' Every participant had some involvement with everyone else and with the entire curriculum. Workshops and sessions were added and moved constantly, like choreography. Yet, our calendar was extremely structured, a wonderful cacophony of events that never collided.''

Do women design spaces differently from men? Leslie thinks so, because women's values about space are different. During her WSPA classes, she and Phyllis asked students to draw their environmental fantasies. ''There was great diversity,'' Leslie said, ''but we discovered certain patterns of shared values, aspirations, experiences. For example, the environmental models focused on the development of people, not the development of technology. Energy was renewable, and the built forms recyclable. Space was movable and flexible, responding to the moods of those who used it. Environments were human in scale, not monumental. Many drawings expressed sensitivity to bodily senses— the quality of natural sunlight; the sounds of water, wind and animals; the fragrance of flowers and cooking. We seemed to say, 'Environments that support people's autonomy, empowerment, and comfort are ideal and paramount.' ''

Every summer, women left WSPA experiences encouraged and affirmed, ready to take up Hadley's second challenge to design spaces

Patricia Johanson. Swan Orchid House. 1974. Ink and charcoal. 24" x 45". (Photo: Eric Pollitzer). Patricia Johanson's gardens are often macrocosmic projections in stone and earth of very small organisms— bacteria, lichens, leaves, plants, butterflies, lizards. This illustration is from Ellen H. Johnson's collection, Oberlin, Ohio.

with people in mind. Leslie went on to apply feminist architectural values to natural childbirth center designs. They were a far cry from the obstetrical ghettos in most hospitals. In her centers, birth is a biological event, an experience to be shared and celebrated, requiring skilled assistance, but little technological intervention. "The birth room is furnished like a bedroom," she said. "Couples bring their own plants, linens, photos, or anything else they want. This room attaches to a lounge, kitchen, and bathroom to form a 'birthing suite.' During labor, the woman may walk around, talk to those present, eat and drink, or rest privately in the birth room. After the birth, the couple can shower together, even get into bed together with their newborn. Family and friends can share a meal. Within eight to twelve hours, the mother and infant will be ready to go home, where they are visited by the birth center staff."

## Designing Spaces with People in Mind

**Barbara Chenicek and Rita Schiltz,** interior designers and Dominican nuns, design sacred space. Like Leslie, they believe space has the capacity to open awareness, and free people to experience the holy. They define sacred space as "that space in which the holy is sensed." Barbara explained, "Sacred space is clear and simle, inviting and peaceful, whose structure and light bring about a deep feeling of being home."

From INAI Studio, their workplace in Adrian, Michigan, Rita and Barbara conceive designs that convert ineffectual "period" churches into startlingly simple spaces. Their work is characterized by simplicity of form and use of natural materials—wood and clay, iron and glass. Their multiple award-winning Dominican Chapel of the Plains in Great Bend, Kansas, is a testament to their design ideas.

But to them, sacred space is not confined to church space. When a coalition of eight national Catholic women's groups held their first conference in November, 1983, they asked Barbara and Rita to create an environment within the setting of the meeting site—the Holiday Inn ballroom in Chicago. "Ever try to make a spiritual statement in such a setting?" Rita asked. "It was quite a challenge!"

And challenge it was. Over 1300 women would attend *Woman Church Speaks*, and the organizing task force wanted each one to feel her own source of leadership and power. "They wanted a multi-focused environment that shifted power away from a given podium," Barbara said. "They wanted to keep leadership among the conferees."

"So we designed modular environmental units that changed with each session," Barbara continued. "Lighting was created and designed throughout the space for the actual circumstances of each event. Ritual

Barbara Chenicek and Rita Schiltz. Harvest Sanctuary of Central Liturgical Space. Dominican Chapel of the Plains. Great Bend, Kansas. (Photo: Thomas Treuter)

and symbol—marvelously non-verbal—were entered into by all. All was bi-lingual, multi-aged, multi-racial, and international. It was an unforgettable experience!''

Unlike Barbara and Rita, the women at **Bloodroot Restaurant/Bookstore** in Bridgeport, Connecticut aren't trained architects or designers, but they have created a sacred space of sorts with people definitely in mind. Their restaurant overlooks the Long Island Sound and is surrounded by vegetable, herb, and flower gardens. Inside, a cozy blend of furnishings, good food, and a well-lit bookstore invite and relax the visitor. When Mary Clare visited, she sat by a large, interior window and watched **Selma, Noel,** and **Betsy** prepare meals, arrange plates with care, cut salad vegetables, ice a cake, and cook pasta. ''We're offering a feminist place here,'' Selma said. ''A place to listen to women's music, read women's books, see pictures of women, have good food, be in a women's space.''

Bloodroot is home and vision for the four women who built it. Their work has spiritual roots, firmly centered in the earth and growing things. The menu changes with the seasons, giving a sense of connection with the food growing outside. Mary Clare visited in the winter, and was offered sturdy casseroles and vegetables, home baked bread, fresh salads, and good, sweet desserts. Their cookbook, *The Political Palate*, describes their commitment to a wholistic aesthetic of food and cooking and place. ''We are working for a women's space,'' wrote Selma in the ''Women Working Together'' issue of *Heresies*, ''a place that is and will be the expression of our and other women's dreams. We all feel passionately that Bloodroot is our lover, our creation, larger than ourselves. There seems no other world we are nourished in, or even feel at ease in.''[6]

## Women's Spaces

In addition to designing environments with people in mind, women planners and architects go one step further. They help ordinary people design their own spaces. Since 1981, architects **Katrin Adam** and **Barbara Marks** have worked with six Hispanic urban homesteaders to redesign a five-floor apartment building on New York's Lower East Side. To get the architecturally inexperienced women started, Katrin and Barbara began with a series of exercises. ''In the first exercise, we asked simple questions,'' said Katrin. ''Questions like 'Who is going to live on which floor?' and 'How will you relate to each other?' and 'Do you want to share any space, or rent any apartments?' We used different colored blocks to represent the floors of the building. The women worked with the blocks until they knew what combinations they wanted.'' They decided to use the first floor as a community room and an apartment for a handicapped or elderly person. They wanted two efficiencies on the second floor, and single apartments on the other three floors.

For the second exercise, the women measured their apartments. "We told them to notice sunlight, street noise, window placement," Barbara said. "We wanted them to know exactly how much space they were working with, and what it looked like. No abstractions, no guesses."

Next, the women drew floor plans. One woman wanted to wake up with the sun, so her bedroom was the back. Another wanted her bedroom in the front. Two women were going to share an apartment, so they discussed privacy needs. The floor plans were conventional, but each was different, because each woman was different. "We worked with colored papers," Barbara added. "Each color represented a purpose—kitchen, bedroom, storage, living room, etc. We cut out bits of paper for furniture, and put them in place. The women told each other why they arranged things in a certain way. We talked about communal and private space, how walls separate, the function of doorways. It was an excellent process for all of us."

Katrin and Barbara would like to see community design centers where "architects, trained in sociology and related disciplines, involve people in their own housing. We need to work with people about spatial ideas," Katrin said. "Men design homes for women, and they don't understand what we need. They have no idea what's involved in child care, for example. If women learned what worked for them spatially, they would radically change the whole concept of residential structures."

## Integrated Environments

Women want their spaces to meet human needs—safety, diversity, warmth. As we create such spaces we notice that they are functional, flexible, and integrated. They overlap between public and private environments—children and animals in office settings, for example. We are tired of everything having its place. "To have a totally integrated society," Katrin said, "everybody needs to be fulfilled, and fulfillment, at this moment in history, takes place in the public sector, in the workplace. Private sector work is not recognized as valuable. But women, who combine the public and private, want the parts to be related."

Several women we met have made the connection. In Grand Rapids, Michigan, **Kit Dorsey** and **Mary Zuiderveen**'s house is a center for art openings, monthly music making, and women's community activities. They have studio space on the second floor and performance space on the first. They started their Wimmin's Gallery For Art when they couldn't find a decent place in town to exhibit a photography show. "The available spaces were cheap, dark, basement-type places," Mary said, "or high rent places with a lot of light. We decided to hang the show at home, and it was such a success, we did it again."

Friends and, sometimes, strangers attend art openings. Once a neighborhood woman wandered in. "She looked around at the art, very

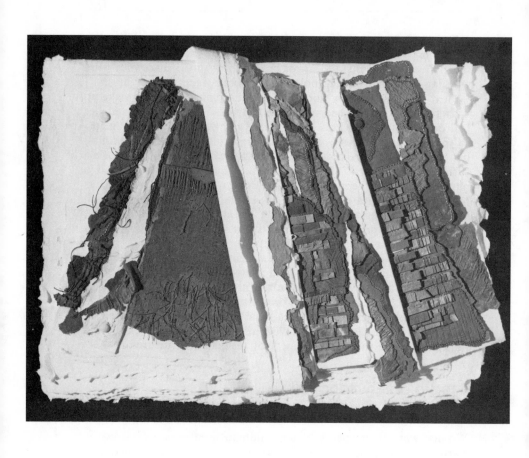

pleased and excited," Kit said, "and exclaimed, 'I didn't know we had something like this right here on our block!' "

Benefits abound for Kit and Mary. They get to know artists, talk with them about their work, wake up in the mornings with women's images all over their house. The artists, on the other hand, have a warm, hospitable space in which to work and show, and everybody has a lot of fun.

**Colleen Sterling** and **Laura Catanzaro** experimented with their Cambridge, Massachusetts apartment in much the same way. For a time, Studio Epona was "home, work space, and gallery," said Laura. The apartment, one of several lofts created in an old synagogue, has windows on two sides. Colleen and Laura left most of the space open, and built portable panels for hanging art. Their first showing was the traveling art exhibit we carried on our trip, to which they invited local artists to contribute work. Poets read poems, filmmakers showed films, comediennes made us laugh, artists told each other what they were doing and why. Two hundred women attended the home-based, women's arts festival. "Because this was also our house," Laura said, "there was an intimacy about the whole arrangement that contributed to its success."

Colleen added, "Of course, we felt vulnerable when we opened our home to let strangers in, but we were committed to make the space available to women. Besides, eating breakfast with art around was wonderful."

The blending of home/private and art gallery/public is just the sort of crossover we women seek in our environments. We like mixing and matching functions. When we prepared the interior of our Chevy van for our one year tour of the United States and Canada, we had a chance to try out some of these principles. Linda Donald, friend and architect, said, "Make a list of everything you're taking. Bring it to me, and we'll design storage and working spaces." One two-burner Coleman stove, one large ice chest, one portable typewriter, four twelve-inch file boxes for three-by-five cards, one sixteen-inch lantern, three blankets, two winter coats, four pairs of jeans each. We made a list.

Then we designed the space: a new storage bin in back for clothes; a padded shelf along the sides for dry food goods and toiletries; a split front bin for blankets, moped helmets, and coats on one side and the traveling art exhibit on the other; a hinged door for desk space; a small closet for hanging clothes. When we packed, everything fit.

We made door pockets for road maps, overhead pockets for wallets, pencils, pads of paper, toll tickets. On side walls, we pasted pictures of family and friends, and in front of the bed, we pinned a photograph of the Earth taken from outer space—to give us perspective. We designed and sewed a screened porch to extend six feet beyond the van's

Myrna Shiras. Unbound Pages. Stitched relief painting. 31″ x 38″ x 4″.
(Photo: Janice Felgar)

sliding door, attached with velcro. When it was open, we doubled the amount of covered, living space.

Before leaving, we road tested the design. Mary Clare came back from camping with her mother and said, "We need towel racks." Soon, they were screwed onto closet doors. We took a short trip together and said, "We need more privacy." We hung a piece of cloth from the ceiling's center to be rolled up during the day and let down at night. Only visual space was changed, but it gave us the privacy we needed.

In our vehicle, we created a working *and* living space. We slept on the bed at night and used it as a desktop the next day. Towels hung over a bulletin board covered with notes about upcoming appointments. And, as we went, we made room for talismen given by Willow in Massachusetts, Jean and Ruth Mountaingrove in Oregon, Peggy Feerick in New Mexico, Gail Fairchild in Seattle, Daphne Shuttleworth in Washington, D.C., Sue Williams ("Rainbow") in Florida, and Vicki Hovde in Maryland. Our public lives as project directors blended with our private lives as two women involved in a long and stressful and exciting venture. All the while, the space served every function well.

## Women-Owned Spaces

**Joan Sprague**, trained in comprehensive planning and design, has always been interested in multi-functional spaces. Now she works through the Women's Institute for Housing and Economic Development to help social service agencies and women's centers develop housing and businesses for low-income heads-of-households. The Institute was formed in 1981 by Joan, attorney Barbara Brower, and a bank community investment officer. The Institute's booklet, *A Development Primer,* explains the housing and business development process, and its relation to women's needs.

In Pittsfield, Massachusetts, Joan helped women put theory into practice. The Women's Service Center approached the city and proposed to rehabilitate four vacant schools in the area. The women wanted to establish an integrated home setting with apartments, child care facilities, jobs and job training for single heads of households. The Institute helped prepare the design and development package.

Had the Women's Service Center been chosen as the developers, they would have provided emergency apartments for women in transition, as well as apartments for long-term occupancy by single heads of households. Several large apartments would have been set aside for home day care providers, and office/business spaces would have brought job opportunities to women in the building.

But Pittsfield's mayor and city council responded to property abutters' distrust of housing for single parents and awarded the schools to private developers. One of the schools will be converted to thirty-one luxury apartments. The Women's Center acquired a smaller, tax-foreclosed structure.

Joan believes women must influence environmental development. "The vast majority of women are unaware that they can own and manage property," she said, "so they need support of others or organizations. Otherwise, they are continually displaced. My dream is to get women and women's groups to own pieces of the world, and to make those pieces beautiful and comfortable and humane."

And safe. Lesbians often feel vulnerable in a homophobic world, and sometimes they create women-only places to feel safe in. We met women in two lesbian communities who have established environments over which they have total control. In St. Augustine, Florida, women own **Pagoda** , consisting of ten small cottages and two larger buildings on the beach. A common kitchen, meeting and ritual space, and theater/performance space complement the small houses. "I had never been in a women-only space until I came here," said **Sue Williams** (who also calls herself "Rainbow"). "The first time I came here, I was ecstatic. I still am. It's like being in heaven. There are good nurturing women in every cottage, and I feel constantly sustained by this environment."

Pagoda is a membership organization, and permanent residents of the cottages are joined by transient members who visit from time to time. This latter group participates in Pagoda's life for a variety of reasons, but one member said simply, "I can come here, have my own space, and also be with other women. It is important for me to know this space is here, even if I don't choose to live here right now."

A few hundred miles north, members of **Atlanta's Lesbian Feminist Alliance** (ALFA) feel the same way about their ALFA house. It is a visible center for an invisible, underground community. "If we didn't have this house,"said **Elizabeth** (last name withheld on request), "communication between Alliance members would be much harder than it is now. We'd have no place to store our archives, files, library. We would be much more scattered. We need our own space, and we need to have control over it."

Ten ALFA members hold keys to the rented duplex in northeast Atlanta. The house is buzzing every night with meetings, workshops, parties. Some members just hang out—use the library or practice the piano or shoot pool in the basement. Atlanta's Feminist Chorus has practiced there; a group of socialist feminists used to meet there; and a racism consciousness raising group now meets at the house. **Judy** (last name withheld on request) summed up the feeling. "It is a women-only space where we can be ourselves," she said. "Our homes are not always women-only, so the ALFA house is the one place we can go and just be with women. It feels great to have this house. It's vital to our survival."

Whether or not our ideal spaces are exclusive or inclusive, the business of space is women's business. For too long, the lots we live on have been sliced into smaller and smaller bits, our homes and bodies staked and surveyed to fit a plan we knew nothing about. For too long, men have designed, built, and paid for walled rooms; poorly lit offices; long,

vacuous passageways; hospital waiting rooms without windows. For too long we have been unconscious of how environments are constraining *and* liberating. What is built affects us.

*"One of the most important tasks of the women's movement,"* wrote Leslie Weisman, *"is to make visible the full meaning of our experience and to reinterpret and restructure the built environment in those terms* (our emphasis). We will not create fully supportive, life-enhancing environments until our society values those aspects of human experience that have been devalued through the oppression of women, and we must work with each other to achieve this."[7] Katrin and Barbara teach women on the Lower East Side, Joan helps women's centers around the country, Hadley urges a new style of teaching, and Rebecca pushes women to think about the spaces they want. We are all learning.

R. Buckminster Fuller used to say that humane and sensitive environments would make us tolerant and loving people. He was right. When we notice the effects of our environments—whether spacious or crowded, urban or rural, high-rise or ground level—we understand the inherent, invisible values in our culture. And *then*, we are ready to change those values so the "skin" we live and work in fits us like a glove.

JEB (Joan E. Biren). Building the Boardwalk for the Differently-Abled Resource Area at the Michigan Music Festival. 1983. Photograph.

# PART III:
# WOMEN HEAL

# 9

# THE FEET OF THE EARTH ARE MY FEET

The natural world is inexorably routine. Bodies wear out and die like flowers, darkness follows light, rivers flow down, trees grow up, new birth emerges from decay. There is no controlling this process. It just goes on and on. The human animal comes into this universe in a certain time and place. We are neither the center, nor the beginning, nor the end. We are only one manifestation of life.

In the face of the enormity of nature and its indifference to us, we feel impermanent, insignificant. Time bound and short lived, we seek to master instead of join. We concoct religions that tell us to subdue the earth, repress the flesh. God above is holy, we learn; we below are spoiled. We fabricate power grids to explain the world. In *Patriarchy as a Conceptual Trap*, **Elizabeth Dodson Gray** described one such construct:

> In this view of reality, nature consists of "inanimate" material such as rocks and dirt—substances without "spirit." Plants are below animals because they don't move; animals are defined as subhuman. Children are subordinate to their parents, women are the property of men, and men sit on top of the heap, lower only than God who occupies the pinnacle.[1] This vertical view of reality is a lie, a construct created to justify patriarcal subordination and control. We live in a circle, not along a line.

159

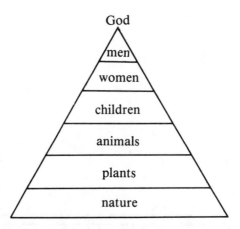

When allegiance to this pyramidal construct prevails, destruction results. If the earth's abundance is ours to manage, we can waste it. If our lives are more valuable than other life forms, we can use and abuse them. If we want something, we can take it. When we are separate from, we dominate, and domination leads to violence.

We violate the planet. We pollute and cover up, excavate and refill. There are places on Earth where brown gullies washed by rain form moonscape topography, where deserts creep into forests. In some areas, most nutrients are gone from the ground; the earth just props up plants. Acid rain is killing lakes and forests, yet gaseous smokestacks continue to belch. Poisons seep through soil and destroy drinking water. The planet, source of raw materials and food, is treated like a giant wastebasket into which we toss tin cans, tupperware bowls, and worn out polyester shirts.

We violate other life forms. On one hand, we domesticate and love animals. Sometimes domestication is non-violent, like milking cows, or riding horses. Household pets are loved and regarded by most owners, and are often the only link urban dwellers have to the natural world. But domestication turns into violation when we project human characteristics and needs onto other species. Cats dancing to and fro on TV commercials are good, ludicrous examples. Animal hairdressers, clothiers, hospitals, and cemeteries are others.

We also eat, hunt, and study animals. Supermarket chickens start off as day-old chicks in windowless sheds. They stand on wire mesh their whole lives, and sometimes, the flesh of their feet grows around the wires. Calves, living in darkness and deprived of iron, develop diseased livers and produce pale veal. In some laboratory experiments, scientists give animals electric shocks without anesthetics. Drugged, given cancer, made alcoholic and insomniac, animals bear the brunt of human experimentation, subjected to substances they instinctively avoid.

"The human race ought to quietly pack up its tents and slip away," said **Sally Gearhart**, author of *The Wanderground: Stories of the Hill Women*. "Right now, cease to have children, cease to exist as a species. We are the only animals to have fouled our own nest so thoroughly that neither we nor anybody else can live in it. What would the planet lose except a lot of devastation if it lost us?"

In a 1981 speech, she answered that question. "We might note a lot of rejoicing in the stockyards and the zoos of the world," she said. "Imagine the singing of the trees, the rumble of relief from the hills and the valleys, and the joy of the fresh winds in the waters."[2]

Human beings don't sit on top of a conceptual heap. There is no hierarchy, no pyramid of order. All forms of life—trees, flowers, sheep, human babies, crows—move in random and purposeful ways, roaming, feeding, dying, crossing each others' paths. The earth sustains them all, and we are part of nature, not separate from it.

## Kinship with the Earth

Many women are dismantling pyramidal constructs, are developing what Sally calls "we-feeling"—empathy for, and identification with, the earth and animals. "We-feeling" means that injury to anyone is injury to all. Sally insists that "women, particularly feminist women, particularly lesbian feminist women, are the vehicles for this return to empathy. Men must let go of the 'big gun/big man code' " she said, "and of the individualism that makes them unable to see beyond the self. Their part, this time, is to follow women's lead."

We met women they could follow. Women who, through some event, comprehend the oneness of all life and honor their bond with nature. Sally described her experience. "I became an environmentalist from the inside out," she said. "For three years, I had pain attacks whenever I drove by laboratories or slaughter houses, and the attacks continued when I went on sabbatical to Northern California." There a neighboring farmer was neglecting several horses, and Sally confronted him. "I went on a campaign against that guy," she said. "I brought photographers out to take pictures, and finally, the farmer got scared and did something about the horses."

The intensity of her response surprised her; she thought she might be too sensitive. But other events convinced her of the reasonableness of her feelings. One day, she burst into tears in the grocery store when she passed the meat counter ("I saw a pig when I looked at the pork roasts."). When a neighbor began to slaughter hogs, Sally couldn't stand hearing the dying animals scream. "I didn't mind the blood and gore," she said. "I'd seen animals killed all my life. But somehow, it just seemed like such an unconscionable thing to do." That year, Sally stopped eating meat.

"In the future, we will have to look at the ways we eat," she concluded. "The whole question of meat eating hinges on whether or

not we will eat our own flesh, and cannibalism is still our biggest taboo. We have destroyed all our predators and are no longer preyed upon. If we were food for something else, we would have a very different idea about our lives, our relationships to each other and to other animals."

Sally understands her connection to nature more deeply today than ever before. **Ruth and Jean Mountaingrove**, editors of *Womanspirit* magazine, share her knowledge and work to preserve and respectfully use their land in Oregon. Their buildings sit on natural contours and inclines, they heat with wood, and eat organic vegetables from their garden. Jean spades sawdust and kitchen wastes into the fertile garden soil. "I feel religious about my relationship to the land," she said. "I am involved in my compost heap. I don't want to waste resources, so saving sawdust and compost is healing Mother Earth. To me, it is a religious act."

**Gloria Anzaldúa's** awareness began as a child. "When I was four or five, my mother would put a chair by the sink so I could wash the dishes," she said. "Out the window, I could see a gnarled mesquite tree and a windmill. The roots of the tree went down into the earth, and the windmill went up into the sky.

"I knew the wind and the tree had something to tell me in different languages," she continued. "The cycles would come—dust and tumbleweed, rain. I remember my father always waiting for rain. The tree produced pods which we fed to livestock in bad times. The natural processes were real and alive, and sometimes I paid more attention to them than I did to my mother and father.

"But when I grew up, I thought it was just superstition," Gloria said. "I repressed my sense of the physical world so I would be acceptable. But when I used drugs, it opened up for me. When I was high, I could see the physical world again, but more than that, I could see worlds behind the physical. When that happened, I knew I had seen it all before, out the kitchen window."

## Working with Nature

Environmental artists often work with what is "natural." They adjust to weather conditions, topography, animals, and seasonal changes as they create. They focus on the rhythms of nature and become aware of the interdependence between themselves and other life forms. **Marsha Hewitt**, an environmental sculptor in Boston, is one of them. During a retreat at Yaddo, an art center in upstate New York, Marsha combined place, earth materials, mythology, ritual, and unexpected events in an outdoor piece called "Autumn Ritual." She wanted to commemorate the passing of the harvest season, and she located the piece in a nearby cornfield. "The field was surrounded by trees," Marsha said. "The

Teri Carsten. Vermont 1981. Photograph.

brown cornstalks were dead and dry, just the right expression of autumn.'' She built three goddesses out of corn husks, and cut down enough corn to make a circle for them to stand in. Then she arranged a pyre in the middle of the circle.

But one day, she found all the corn cut down. Her three figures remained, but the space had been cleared by a farmer come to harvest. Surrounding trees, previously invisible, formed the new periphery. Marsha had to change her sculpture, respond to the new space. First she dug a spiral trench and filled it with water. Then, she made masks and hung them from low tree branches, and dressed the goddesses with gauze and leaves. One night at full moon, she invited friends to the site, and the northern lights came out, filling the sky like a huge pink cloud. ''It was really incredible,'' Marsha said, ''like a wonderful omen.''

As the ritual evolved she realized it needed an ending, and she decided to sacrifice one of the goddesses. ''People started telling me stories of ancient cultures where virgins were sacrificed,'' Marsha said, ''but I didn't want to deal with that aspect of what I had made. I only wanted the white purity, the goodness of the thing, not the bloody, sacrificial side. But I couldn't deny it. The whole idea of death and decay and rebirth and life—that cycle—was at the core of what I was doing. So I went ahead and burned one of the goddesses to finish the piece.''

**Bonnie Sherk**, a New York City performance and environmental artist, has explored her kinship with animals on several occasions, but her first awareness came in 1971 during her ''Public Lunch'' performance at the San Francisco Zoo. At feeding time she entered a cage the same way the lions and tigers did, paced back and forth, and finally sat down to a formally set table. Then she ate a full course, catered dinner. Tigers and lions were eating raw meat in adjacent cages, and a white rat was in a cage in her cage.

During the performance, Bonnie climbed a ladder to the upper platform of her cage and lay down to rest. The neighboring tiger got up, walked across his cage, and stared at her. ''At that point,'' she said, ''I started wondering what he was thinking. What kinds of invisible, psychological, emotional things were going on in his head? In many ways, that moment led me to focus on the invisible spaces in other animals and myself, and between us.''

She brought the white rat back to her studio to live, later naming it Guru Rat. Soon there were two rabbits named The Lady Doe and Buck, a pig named Pigme, chickens, a rooster, other rats, fish, and two doves. ''They weren't pets,'' she said. ''Pets are animals of compromise, meant to echo human behavior. Animals, like people, are more interesting when they're able to be themselves, make choices, and behave as they wish. The animals were my teachers. I learned about life, art, whole systems, and natural processes.

Marsha Hewitt. Autumn Ritual. 1981. Environmental sculpture at Yaddo.
80' x 200'.

"We were all architects and performers," Bonnie concluded. "Free of cages, we built structures and communicated. The chickens communicated with each other and with the rabbits and the rats. There was communication on many levels and in many combinations. I learned about racism and sexism, about power and territory, about human beings in relation to other species, about the complexity of animal languages."

"I have a thread of hope," said Sally Gearhart, "that if women were in charge *and* the system we now have was gone, we would make something better of our relationship to the earth and other species. I believe that biologically women would do it differently." As women acknowledge the connection between themselves and nature, they *are* doing it differently. And with a commitment that is impressive. **Baba Copper**, one of the founders of California's Heraseed, a woman's land coop, put it succinctly. "I am a city woman," she told Elana Freedom in an interview. "I've been a city woman all my life. But I feel passionately that women must reconnect to the earth and learn the lessons we have forgotten. Our bodies are the manifestations of life forces. We must be connected emotionally, psychically, intellectually, and every other way to the life forces of nature itself."[3]

## Protecting the Earth

Alert to the connection between themselves and nature, women understand that their task is to defend, preserve, and protect other living beings that have no voice. But cultural attitudes toward nature are ingrained and unconscious. As "civilized" beings walking the earth with shoes on our feet, and standing under rain with umbrellas over our heads, we often miss nature's lessons of survival and adaptation. To pry loose awareness in others, women teachers resort to various tools. **Mary Appelhoff** uses worms.

Twenty years ago, she read Rachel Carson's *Silent Spring*, took it seriously, and looked for something to do to reverse environmental abuse. Ten years later, she answered an ad in *Organic Gardening Magazine* to "Raise Worms for Fun and Profit," and was soon the proud owner of two pounds of worms. For the last ten years, Mary, a biologist, has researched the simple technology of vermicomposting—the use of earthworms to transform household garbage into rich fertilizer.

"I am developing a consciousness about limited resources on earth," Mary said in Kalamazoo, Michigan. "Our society has developed consumptive, exploitive, and destructive mechanisms. But maybe women can change those mechanisms because we didn't set them up, and don't have a stake in their continuation. We've got to treat every bit of our environment as something that is ours, not something we can haul off and dump next door. Worms are my vehicle to stop the movement towards entropy, and restore a life-giving flow to the earth."

Over the years, Mary has demonstrated worm composting to over sixteen thousand people at energy fairs, technology demonstrations, arts festivals. Her recently published book, *Worms Eat My Garbage*, describes how to set up a household system. "After you determine how many pounds of household garbage you create every week, set up a box with shredded cardboard or peat moss for bedding," Mary said. "Wet it down and add a couple of handfuls of soil, the worms, and garbage. It doesn't smell like you thought it would, and before you know it you have black, earthy-smelling humus you can use to grow house and garden plants. It's the ultimate in being responsible for yourself."

Mary doesn't stop with kitchen wastes. She's interested in composting garbage by the ton. "I've visited large scale, solid waste disposal sites, and they work," she said. "In San Jose, city officials dumped sludge in a three acre sewage lagoon. When the water evaporated, they bulldozed the sludge into windrows, put worms on the windrows, and the worms reduced the volume. The castings were removed and sold to the public. San Jose has a limited number of acres for sewage disposal, so officials need a plan that involves recycling. With worms, they can develop a market for the castings, re-use the space, and fill fewer lagoons.

"Unfortunately," Mary concluded, "the powers that be prefer the so-called 'high tech' way to solve problems. Engineers seem to get scared when they think of biological organisms. But we have to think differently about waste. It isn't something you can just let someone else deal with. We have to clean up after ourselves."

## Learning From the Earth

Being responsible for ourselves is respectful of natural systems, and women like Mary are teaching us how to be more so. **Maureen Newton** is an outdoor education teacher, and her goal is to help other women learn from the natural world by living in it. Her programs are recreational—day-long and weekend trips to learn rock climbing, canoeing, rafting, caving, kyacking, hiking, and backpacking. But when she taught at Hollins College in Roanoke, Virginia, Maureen's favorite event was the month-long trip during semester break. "When students know they have to survive in the desert environment of Big Bend National Park in Texas, they pay attention," Maureen said. "And they learn a lot. One year, my students had to deal with an electrical storm, hail, and flash floods—all in three days, and all alone. They learned skills, of course, but mostly they learned self-sufficiency and self-confidence."

Maureen always feels like a student in nature. "When I'm in the wilderness, I am not in control," she said. "The physical environment is the content *and* the teacher. When I'm in the wilderness, I go by nature's rules."

Which are? "Well, for example, if you're rock climbing," she said, "you have to remember four points: (1) Breathe. When people are afraid, they don't breathe. (2) Maintain a three-point contact with the rock—two feet/one hand, or two hands/one foot. (3) Be intentional about your moves and don't expend a lot of energy looking for a foothold or handhold that's not apparent. Often, you have to reach blindly, but if a hold isn't there, you must look somewhere else. (4) Don't over-extend yourself. Don't get an arm so far out that no blood can get to it, or you'll start to tremble.

"If you think about it, these are lessons for living, as well as rock climbing," Maureen continued. "Learning this way makes me realize I can do anything. Nothing is an obstacle. At the same time, I have to choose my struggles, and ask, 'Is it worth it? What do I want?' I become very realistic about what's important and what's not. At the heart, being outdoors teaches me two things: how to control my life, *and* that there are some things I can't have any control over. It teaches me to be both confident and humble."

Learning from the earth takes another form at the Wright-Ingraham Institute in Colorado. Ten years ago, architect **Elizabeth Wright Ingraham** founded the Institute for graduate students to participate in land-based, wholistic education. She acquired 640 acres of Colorado grasslands for what would come to be the Richard T. Parker Center for Advanced Study and Research, and designed the curriculum and working space. "At the end of the 1960s, I had to turn my attention to effective social change," she said. "So I called together a group of scientists, humanitarians, artists, and academics from all over the country to see where there was a gap. The biggest one seemed to be in education, with specialization creating a lot of fragmentation, and with no clear synthesis happening anywhere.

"Educational institutions systematically kill creativity in young people," she continued, "and at this time, with tremendously complex problems to be solved in the world, we need creativity and integrated thought more than ever before. Here, we use the environment—land, air, sea, water—to reference everything that is known. For example, if you want to understand the key principles of how to go about learning history, instead of just reading a book, you can look at the area around you—both the physical and the human-built—and reconstruct history from what you see. This is a very important discovery, and we're starting to document it with almost every discipline. Eventually this concept will revolutionize education."

At the Center, nature is the teacher. The land surrounding the school lies in a semiarid environment at the nexus of mountains and plains. A slow-moving plains stream ties the Center to a larger river basin. Weather can be extreme, with twelve to eighteen inches of rain determining the amount and kind of vegetation. And grasses that hold soil and prevent erosion indicate human presence, as do nearby metropolitan areas. During a speech at the University of Massachusetts in Amherst, Elizabeth said, "It was a place where the linkages and interfaces of natural and human-built systems could be clearly observed and studied; limits could be explored; questions could be formed."[4]

Every summer during the Center's nine-week core course, students study the environment to learn history or geography or mathematics or language. They live at the field laboratory and meet for six to eight hours of intensive seminars each day. They spend hours in the field doing research, using field equipment like telescopes and surveying equipment. First they learn firefighting and first aid skills. Then they study physics—principles of energy and entropy—and the chemistry of air, water, and soil. They move on to earth and life sciences—geology, grasslands and stream ecology.

Next the students explore the role of human beings on the land, including economics, law, and politics. Food production, labor management, and local and global political systems are taught. Anthropologists provide a broad evolutionary perspective, leading students into the fields of planning, engineering, and architecture, using local forms for historical perspective. Finally linguists talk about language as a vehicle for synthesis of the learning.

Learning is intense. Teachers say that they can teach as much biology in three days in the field as they can in three months in the classroom. And students' abilities to handle new knowledge improve exponentially in the nine weeks. Discussion and activities involving paleontology, geography, mathematics, art, and philosophy bridge gaps between traditional disciplines.[5]

At Amherst, Elizabeth gave an example of this integrative approach. "On one occasion," Elizabeth said, "faculty members gathered in the field to discuss what appeared to be a trivial topic—the meaning of a barbed wire fence. A philosopher saw the fence as a way of including or excluding involvement; a biologist saw it as a roosting place for birds, observing how non-indigenous plants had been introduced to the area by seeds dropped by birds perched on the fence; a lawyer saw ownership defined; a physicist illustrated the short span of human civilization by using the barbs on the wire to simulate segments of historic time; a hydrologist saw the fence as a barrier to the flow of water, noting that vegetation on one side was more diverse; an historian explained how the invention of barbed wire had revolutionized land use in the West.[6]

"The environment has proved to be an excellent paradigm for an integrative approach," Elizabeth concluded, "comprising, as it does, everything that impacts the individual; i.e., people, plants, animals, habitats, soil, food, water, and air. Its characteristics can be studied scientifically, historically, and poetically. In summary, the environment itself has the necessary physical, legal, and literary dimensions for teaching the dynamics of complex systems."[7]

## The Earth Is Home

Nobody has to be a guru to learn from the earth and its creatures. Mary Appelhoff studies worms, Maureen Newton treks through forests, and Elizabeth Wright Ingraham teaches from environmental systems. All of them strive to protect the earth from further ravaging and to learn her lessons. Artists, because they work on non-verbal and non-rational levels, can also help us remember the lessons.

Since the early 1970s, **Betsy Damon** has done a series of planetary healing performances on the streets of New York City. Sometimes she uses bags of sand, and sometimes she uses rocks. During one performance, she spread dirt on the sidewalk, and invited participants and friends to lie down and put stones on their bodies. At the end of the performance, Betsy asked everyone to make a specific commitment to the earth's survival. "When you lie with stones on your body," she said, "it is very healing. They are full of the innate power of the planet, like tight bundles of survival energy."

In cities, the environment is artificially controlled and monitored, and evidence of nature is scanty, at best. Yet **Bonnie Sherk**, like Betsy, also chooses urban settings for her art. When she lived in San Francisco, she convinced city officials to let her convert four unused acres underneath three interlocking freeways into a nature environment, and called the place "The Farm."

The Farm consists of a farmhouse; theater; school; library; darkroom; herb, vegetable, and flower gardens. Programs include training in animal care, a pre-school, summer day camp, training in landscape horticulture and agriculture for teenagers, and a drop-in program for children after school during which they help with indoor chores and animal care. One visitor described it as "a place where acrobats, actors, activists, artists, dancers, poets, kids, clowns, rabbits, rosebushes, flowers, vegetables, children, chickens, cats, dogs, old people, young people, middle-aged people, workers, ecologists, cooks, gardeners, dreamers, and doers all hang out and somehow hang together—creating a lively and wonderful environment in two warehouses and on some land by the side of a freeway."[8]

"The Farm is at a crossroads of several multicultural neighborhoods," Bonnie said, "and when I was there, we changed the environment and the programming to relate to different cultures. For example, there were Hispanic people in an area adjoining The Farm, so I got benches from Mexico, and developed programs from that cultural base. I even wanted to get a Japanese farmhouse and have programs related to that.

"The Farm exists on several levels at once," she continued. "It demonstrates the multicultural and multigenerational interconnect-

Betsey Damon. 7,000 Year Old Woman. 1977. Prince Street, New York City. (Photo: Su Friedrich)

edness. It also connects people with plants and animals, and creates a balance between technological and non-mechanized forms. And all these layers of interconnection—animals, people, programs—create a life-scale sculpture as well as a unique series of community gatherings.''

In New York City since 1980, Bonnie hopes to convert Bryant Park into A Living Library (ALL). An elegant, formal park at 42nd Street and Fifth Avenue, Bryant Park is a midtown headquarters for drug dealers. ''There's no real constituency there,'' Bonnie said. ''A Living Library will create new constituencies by making the park an educational, ecological, and aesthetic resource.''

The Library will catalog and label, in different scales, languages, and visual modes, the existing life forms in Bryant Park—human, plant, animal, and mineral. International garden beds will be planted, representing various cultural styles and sources of food. There will be banners and flags, large scale paper-mâché plants, insect and animal emblems. Workshops in gardening and programs of live and audiotaped animal songs and dances will be interspersed with human activity.

''A Living Library would not only create an environmental performance sculpture,'' Bonnie said, ''but would create opportunities for experiential learning, create an ecological awareness in the heart of New York City, and demonstrate how art, mixed with community involvement and good will, can transform and maintain an environment.

''I'm interested in evolution,'' she concluded. ''The Farm and A Living Library are learning places. People need to remember their relationship to the earth before they can move into the future. In the future, we will see greater communication not only between people, but between different species, and a greater sense of balance between the human animal and other life forms.''

Women are proclaiming the integration of all life. They are studying Colorado grasslands, and creating city parks that incorporate food, plants, history, words, cultures, trees, and animals. They are living in the wilderness, and lying with stones on sidewalks. They are abandoning attitudes towards nature that restrict and destroy.

Round and brown, hard as ice and hot at heart, the earth is home, source, sustainer, provider. During our trip around the United States and Canada, we drove across 30,000 miles of North America. Standing at the Grand Canyon's South Rim, walking along Glacier National Park's Highline Trail, or swimming in the Shenandoah River, we were awed by the variety, majesty, and permanence of the place, and our presence in it. Gradually we came to understand this old Navaho prayer:

''It is lovely indeed, it is lovely indeed. I, I am the spirit within the earth. The feet of the earth are my feet. The legs of the earth are my legs. The bodily strength of the earth is my strength. The

Bonnie Sherk. Schematic Plan for A Living Library. 1983. Hand colored drawing. 24″ x 36″.

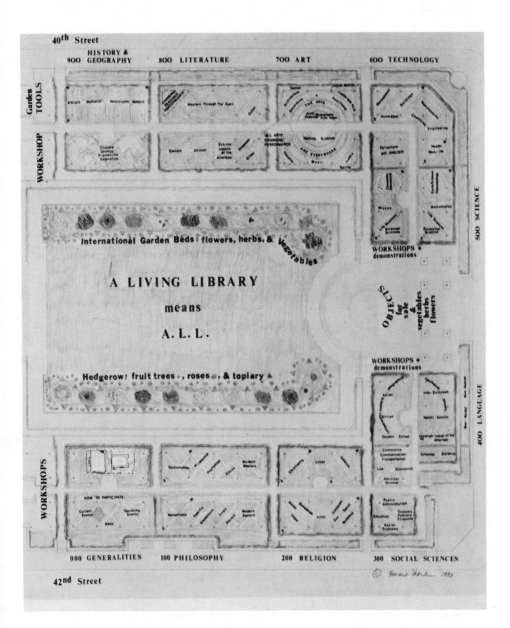

A LIVING LIBRARY

means

A. L. L.

thoughts of the earth are my thoughts. The voice of the earth is my voice. The feather of the earth is my feather. All that belongs to the earth belongs to me. All that surrounds the earth surrounds me. I, I am the sacred words of the earth. It is lovely indeed, it is lovely indeed."

# 10

# REWRITING THE SOCIAL CONTRACT

**E**very day, newspaper stories report the vicious oppression of one group or another:

• Teenage boys in Maine stone and drown a gay man. Homosexuals are oppressed.

• The President fights to eliminate school lunch subsidies and a program to feed infants and nursing mothers. The poor and vulnerable are oppressed.

• A gang of men rape a woman in a Massachusetts bar while other men cheer. Women are oppressed.

• Fearful whites throw bricks and garbage into an apartment rented by a young black couple in Chicago. Neighbors say they just don't want "those kind of people" in their community. People of color are oppressed.

• Persons in wheelchairs are denied access to public events because buildings housing the events don't have ramps and elevators. People who are blind, deaf, unable to walk or talk or control their muscles are oppressed.

• A major insurance company denies a 65-year-old widow her husband's pension. She is left with a Social Security check of $325 a month. Older people are oppressed.

•A Vancouver lesbian is ostracized from her Chinese community because she has a woman lover, discriminated against by blacks and whites because she is Chinese, and threatened on the streets because she is a woman. Oppression on the basis of race, gender, and sexual orientation is often interlocked.

Oppression occurs when any deviation from the norm is seen as unwanted or threatening. This norm reflects the characteristics of the dominant group in the culture. For example, white, affluent, middle-aged, heterosexual, educated males are dominant in a patriarchal society like the United States, so all "Others"—women, people of color, homosexuals, the poor, young, and older members of the society—are less valued. Rank is assigned, taboos are created, pariahs and fringe groups are given names. All of the "Others" are subtly or blatantly reminded of their "place"—"Jews can't join this country club," "Blacks can't live in this neighborhood," "Children belong to their parents," "Queers can't have civil rights." "Others" are never equal.

Attitudes like these solidify and turn into governmental policy, employment practices, laws and court decisions. Adequate health care is often denied to the old, the poor, the uneducated. Most schools perpetuate sex-role stereotyping, authoritarianism, and competition; and inner-city schools, filled with children of color, are notoriously poor. In a racist or sexist or homophobic society, all institutions participate in the oppression of groups different from the norm. And they do it daily, in every realm—from personal interactions to Supreme Court decisions.

Women know this reality intimately, not only as the group called women, but as women of color, as poor women, as old women, as poorly educated women, as differently abled women. Violence and discrimination aren't news to them. So it is no surprise that they are on the front lines, working to erase phony, hand-me-down attitudes, *and* to dismantle established institutions which fortify them.

Women begin this work where they usually begin everything else—with themselves. They examine their own self-hatred and prejudice, seeking to dispel their fears of difference. As they honor their own cultural, religious, and ethnic heritages, they marry the "other" in themselves. **Gloria Anzaldúa**, one editor of *This Bridge Called My Back: Writings by Radical Women of Color*, described the process for women of color, but it fits all women. "We knew we were different, set apart, exiled from what is considered 'normal,' white-right," she wrote. "And as we internalized this exile, we came to see the alien within us and too often, as a result, we split apart from ourselves and each other. Forever after we have been in search of that self, that 'other' and each other."

As women re-member themselves, they begin to see the inherent desirability of difference. They broaden, reach out, build coalitions, and consciously swell their communities to include people unlike

Faedra Kosh. The Mind of Gaia #2. 1984. Painting.

themselves. Montana's **Judy Smith** is one of them. "I don't want to live in a totally homogenous world," she said. "That would be very boring. I want to live in a world with lots of different kinds of people."

"I've done a lot of thinking and reading about how human beings create the category of 'Other,' " Judy continued. "I used to question whether or not this behavior was inevitable, but now I've pretty much concluded that it is. It is so prevalent, and it crosses race, class, and cultural lines. If we have to have the category of 'Other,' I'll accept it. But if we do, we have to answer the question: How shall we treat the 'Other?' "

It may take a lifetime to answer this question, to unravel the twists and turns of racism, sexism, ageism, classism, and every other unspeakable system of oppression. But women have begun. They understand the consequences of "other thinking" because in a patriarchal system they are "other than." But they are also discovering the value of difference, and the power that comes from diversity. Rewriting the social contract will take more than a few lessons in sentence structure. It will require a whole rethinking of how human beings deal with difference. Women in every region are sharpening their pencils and refilling their pens.

## OVERCOMING OPPRESSION BASED ON GENDER

After Dustin Hoffman's movie performance as a woman in *Tootsie*, high school teachers had a heyday assigning students sex-change compositions. A teacher friend asked her senior English students to write essays describing how they'd spend one day as members of the opposite sex. The young women had all the fun. As men they felt powerful; they took advantage of social privileges suddenly available to them; they frolicked in male bodies. Their essays surged with originality and verve.

The young men were miserable. They moaned and groaned, squirmed in their seats. As women they fretted about their make-up and hairdos, carried on trivial conversations about men. Confined to dull jobs, dull housework, or dull dates, their lackluster lives were boring. Their essays, devoid of invention, sagged and dragged.

Young people like these carry sexist stereotypes around in their bookbags. Despite years of feminist energy, to them being born male looks better than being born female. And it still is. *Playboy* cartoons of big-breasted, dumb broads and Madison Avenue's detergent salesladies don't mirror strong, able-bodied, independent women. They reflect objects on a misogynic assembly line—bodies to be ogled, brains to be washed. Those twelfth-grade women, free to be men, only had an hour's reprieve from the inhibitions imposed by society's hatred of women.

## Women-Hating

Feminist activist **Sonia Johnson** argues that misogyny is the basis for all separations—environmental abuse, racism, colonialism, war. "The oppression of women is the archetype upon which all other oppressions are modeled," she said when she announced her 1984 candidacy for President of the United States. "Historically, before men conquered neighboring tribes, they had already raped and subdued women. In learning to dominate women, they developed a conquistador mentality: 'If it is reasonable and justifiable and necessary for us to rule women,' they surmised, 'it follows that it is justifiable and reasonable and necessary for one nation to rule another, for the strong to rule the weak, for people of one color to rule people of another color, for the rich to rule the poor.' "

Newspaper and television reports confirm that misogyny is *international*. Some Chinese parents, restricted to one child, drown girl babies. They want sons. Many Puerto Rican women are sterilized without informed consent. Clitoridectomies (the excising of the clitoris and other parts of a woman's genitalia) are regularly performed on pubescent African girls. Women around the world are denied civil rights and traded as property ("Who *gives this woman* to marry this man?").

Labor statistics prove that misogyny is *economic*. Women are the world's poorest citizens. In the United States, government programs to help women are regularly sacrificed on the altar of militarism. Overseas, foreign aid money dangles just beyond the grasp of women who need it. Meanwhile, pornography, a business that objectifies, dehumanizes, and humiliates women, takes in six billion dollars a year.

Older women are the poorest of the poor. "The average yearly income for older women in 1982 was something like $4,500," said **Tish Sommers**, founder and president of the Older Women's League. "If you're a woman of color, God help you. A black woman living alone has an average income of only $2,000 a year. Only eighteen percent of women receive pensions. For the sixty percent of older women living alone, Social Security is practically their only income."

Misogyny is *violent*. One out of every three women in the United States is raped in her lifetime, and fifty percent of them are under eighteen years of age; twenty-five percent are under twelve. One out of every two wives has been beaten by her husband. One out of every four female children is sexually abused during childhood, usually by close family members or friends. Eighty percent of the women who work outside the home report being sexually harassed on the job.[2] Steelworker **Denise Winebrenner** is one of these statistics. She was repairing a crane at U.S. Steel's Pittsburgh plant one day when her foreman came behind her and snapped her bra. Startled, she dropped an inspection plate that was holding the crane assembly, and a co-worker narrowly escaped injury.

Denise was furious. "It scared the shit out of me," she said. "I twirled around, took my helmet off, and hit the man as hard as I could in the knee. He screamed and threatened me with suspension. I said, 'You better not suspend me, because not only will I have your job, but I will also phone your wife and tell her what you do when we work all night.' After that, he filed a lot of poor workmanship notices on me, but every time he did it, I filed a grievance and beat him. Finally we signed a truce and he got off my back."

In Basin, Montana, a small town tucked between high Rocky Mountain ridges, many town residents turned against the sixteen lesbians living there because **Marilyn Sternberg**, one of them, ran for the school board. She wanted a seat on the school board because she thought her son was being discriminated against in school. A local minister was appalled. He organized a reactionary group called "Concerned Citizens Against Homosexuals" and asked Marilyn to withdraw her candidacy. She refused, and the group went to work.

They stated that all lesbians were child molesters who should be "cast out" and shunned until they moved out of town. "Lesbians worship Satan," they declared. "Therefore, they had no civil rights and should be prevented from buying land." Marilyn lost the election, and by 1985, only five lesbians remained in Basin. "It just was too hard to overcome such focused hatred and negativity," Marilyn said, "I myself have moved to another part of the state."

"To be born female on a patriarchal planet is to be born behind enemy lines," Sonia Johnson declared. "War is the only appropriate word for women's lives."

## Empowering Victims of Hatred

War produces casualties of all kinds—shattered minds and spirits, as well as battered bodies. Part of the work of confronting misogyny is to heal and empower victims of physical violence. An entire industry has arisen to do the job. Women from the front lines with black eyes, burned arms, broken legs, and split vaginas arrive daily on the doorsteps of battered women's shelters. There, the "Red Cross" for the physically abused write handbooks, advise women about legal rights, organize Take Back the Night marches, teach self-defense classes, offer emotional support, and make safe places for these refugees. Thousands of women have joined this army of healers. The reason seems clear: many women have been hurt, violated, or wounded in some way, and they are eager to help the most visible casualties.

When the victims strike their abusers out of desperation and rage and are charged with serious crimes, their supporters stand by. In Colorado, **Lenore Walker**, psychologist and author of *The Battered Woman*, works to keep these victims out of prison. "At least half of

Deborah Kruger. Crosses to Bear (detail). 1984. Collage.

my cases are public defender cases," she said. "The attorney asks the judge for an expert witness, and I am called to testify. I use this position to educate the court, the lawyers, the jurors, and the community about the effects of violence against women."

After Lenore meets the accused and listens to her story, she encourages local news reporters to learn the facts of the case. She persuades local attorneys to contact local feminist groups, and offers to give benefit presentations for the shelter or a training session for shelter volunteers. Always, she uses the case to make visible the prevalence of violence against women, and to alert the community that service organizations can help. "It's a wholistic way of working," Lenore continued. "At the trial, I am the expert, so I have authority in the case. By pulling in other groups, I share that power, and they get validated, too."

Lenore has devoted ten years to research on battered women, and she sees no end in sight. "Some women have sold their souls for relationships with men," she said. "They have sold their ability to grow and be who they are. It's the ultimate betrayal when they find they don't even own their own bodies. Philosophically, battering is the same as rape, incest, and child abuse. Rapists are the shock troops to keep women in their place; batterers are the home guard."

Whatever we call the perpetrators—conquistadors, misogynists, or the home guard; fathers, lovers, or husbands—brutality exists somewhere in many women's lives. Rape crisis centers are outposts for victims of physical violence, and the **Coal Employment Project** (CEP), in Oak Ridge, Tennessee and Dumfries, Virginia, serves as a sentry for women miners, often victims of sexual harassment, discriminatory policies, and hazardous working conditions.

Founded by women who forced coal companies to hire women, CEP now works to protect those women. In the beginning, sexual harassment, from peepholes in women's lavatories to direct solicitation—was commonplace. So was inadequate equipment. Gloves, hats, and shoes were too big, and women injured themselves frequently. "Miners have to handle big tools and work in very difficult conditions," said **Betty Jean Hall**, CEP's legal counsel. "Most women miners didn't have gloves or hardhats that fit. They were stuffing handkerchiefs and scarves inside their hardhats, and when they couldn't find small enough steel-toed boots, they'd wear seven or eight pairs of socks inside them.'" Yet when miners complained to foremen, they were laughed at.

CEP began to offer workshops and give legal advice to women, and has become more influential with coal companies and unions as the number of women miners has grown. Today CEP sustains local support groups, arranges national conferences for women miners, publishes a monthly newsletter, sponsors foreign exchanges for women miners, and continues to struggle with the coal union for women's issues like maternity/paternity benefits.

**Tish Sommers** works on behalf of older women, obvious victims of economic violence, to teach and empower, to prod and enlighten. When

Tish was divorced at age fifty-seven, with no medical insurance (she was a "high-risk" patient because of an earlier mastectomy), she was transformed from a homemaker to a policymaker. "I couldn't get any health coverage after my divorce," she said. "I had a graduate degree in psychology and Hispanic studies, but it wasn't any help to a woman my age just entering the job market. I wondered if there were other women like me."

There were millions. And before long Tish had named them "Displaced Homemakers"—women who because of divorce or widowhood were forcibly ejected from their jobs as homemakers. Before long, Displaced Homemaker legislation was popping up in state capitals around the country, generating programs to help women move from dependency to self-sufficiency.

Eventually, Tish left Displaced Homemakers, by then a National, grassroots organization, and formed the Older Women's League. To build that organization, she focused on women not traditionally involved in politics. "OWL members may not be active members of the National Organization for Women or the League of Women Voters," Tish said, "but they still have a stake in economic independence."

OWL chose three issues to get them that independence—equitable and available health insurance, fair pension laws, and Social Security reform. "I'm constantly looking for cracks in the system," Tish continued. "The health insurance issue is a very small one that can bring to light an invisible problem of women—four million women between ages 45 and 65 are simply not covered. Neither the aging nor the women's movements were addressing this issue, and it was an issue OWL could develop state by state. Besides, it had great potential for educating women. Unless we get organized, we will never change national policies that affect our lives."

Women like Lenore, Betty Jean, and Tish are protecting the health and rights of women abused by patriarchy because nobody else will. Women are society's caretakers, and we have to take care of each other too. But these and other women are not merely nursemaids. They are re-constituting the institutions that form society by their demands for equal status for women. Their newly created organizations challenge laws, and their lawsuits redefine justice. Some women work within existing structures; others challenge and confront those structures from the outside. All are committed to reclaiming society for themselves and all outlawed "Others."

## Re-Forming Institutions

Women are the minority in most institutions, so if they seek to change those institutions from the inside, their first task is to learn the rules of the game. Denise Winebrenner couldn't accomplish anything at the steel mill, for example, unless she learned to work with men. "We women, new in the mill, didn't attack the men all the time," she said. "It was a change for them just as much as it was a change for us. Imagine—you work thirty-five years in one place with all men, and all of a sudden here comes this twenty-five-year-old woman on your job.

"You have to decide what's important and what's not," she concluded. "So I didn't get bent out of shape if the millwright I was apprenticed to called me 'girl.' He was fifty-nine and had daughters my age. But I would get upset if he didn't show me my job, or if I asked a question and got a lot of shit. In the mill, you work in a crew, and your life depends on everyone in the unit doing their job. Somebody could really get hurt or killed if I didn't know my job. Working all this out takes time, but I have a lot of patience."

**Claudine Schneider** is learning to work it out in the United States Congress where she is a Republican Member of the Democrat-run House of Representatives. She understands patience very well. "I'm in the minority on two counts—as a woman and as a Republican," she said. "If I am going to accomplish good things, which is why I ran for Congress, I have to build coalitions with powerful Members.

"Anybody can have a good idea, a brilliant concept," she added, "but moving that idea into action is very difficult. I've always been interested in diplomacy, and it's a challenge to bring people of different points of view together, to point out areas of agreement. Where there is polarization, there is stagnation; but where there is commonality, you can move ahead and get things done."

Women who infiltrate male-dominated institutions and use male tactics to "get ahead" are often suspected of personal aggrandizement. For some women, this characterization is true, but others maintain their values as women. They seek power so they can help other women. Congresswoman **Lindy Boggs**, a Representative from New Orleans, is a good example.

Lindy helped form the Congresswomen's Caucus to create a visible voting block from which to educate male Members about women's issues. "It's very difficult for men to put themselves in women's shoes," Lindy said, "especially when they don't understand the problems. Once when he was head of the Federal Reserve, Arthur Burns asked me, 'Lindy, do women *really* have a hard time getting credit?' That unawareness is fairly typical, and men have resisted full awareness for too long. But sensitivity among men to women's issues has increased dramatically in the last twelve years."

One day during a subcommittee meeting, Members were writing an amendment prohibiting credit discrimination for small business loans because of age, race, and veteran status. Lindy noticed the omission of women. "I ran into a side room and made fifty copies of the amendment, adding sex and marital status," she continued. "When I handed my changes to the Members, I said, 'I'm certain it's an oversight, but if we're going to list all other categories, we need to include women as well.' 'Of course,' they all said. 'Yes, we had just forgotten.' That amendment passed the committee, the House, and became law."

Today Lindy sits on the powerful House Appropriations Committee, but she can vividly recall the days when no woman served on important budgetary committees. She and other women of the Congresswomen's Caucus changed that tradition as soon as they established their group. Democratic women went to their leadership and the Republicans went to theirs. "We said, 'Congress needs a greater sensitivity to women's issues,' " Lindy reported. " 'We cannot separate women from their families; we cannot separate almost half of the work force from the economy; we cannot separate women's issues from any part of our national or international life. Unless there is some sensitivity on each of the truly important committees, the women of this country cannot be served.' " They won their case, and Lindy claims, "It is *the* most significant change in Congress over the last decade."

Why? "Because women Members of Congress are the surrogate representatives for all women—a large portion of whom are not represented by women," Lindy added. "It is up to us to bring their concerns before Congress. We've formed the Congresswomen's Caucus, gotten seats on every important committee, are building coalitions with Members, and are raising consciousness about women's issues. I'd say we are making progress. Today when I'm not at a hearing, my male colleagues ask my questions. That is remarkable in itself."

What difference do women make in national politics? "Women are the humanizers of law, politics, and government," Lindy concluded, "and my hope is that we women will never lose the womanly qualities we have when we come to the political arena and the public sector. Because if we do, we won't add anything new."

## Confronting Policies

Some women infiltrate and change institutions from the inside; others are more effective as confronters from the edges. **Sonia Johnson** is one of these women. As a Mormon, she favored passage of the Equal Rights Amendment, and was excommunicated from the church because of her position. She wrote *From Housewife to Heretic* about that experience. After her struggle to pass the ERA failed, members of the Citizens Party urged her to seek their nomination for President of the United States.

She was hesitant but finally made the effort "because the imbalance of power between men and women in this country and the world is dangerous and potentially lethal," she said in her press announcement. "Men with their monopoly on power are not just nudging us, they are hurtling us toward planetary annihilation. To restore the balance necessary for survival, women's voices must be heard and attended to in the decision-making councils of the world. Only in a massive global revolution in the status of women is there hope for the survival of the planet and the human species. Such a revolution would signal the death of the conquistador mentality—the rapist mind—which is destroying us all."

She won the nomination but lost the election. Still, she made her point. "Patriarchy has so deadened the world, so destroyed it," she said, "that the planet is gasping, almost expired. We've got no good air; we're turning blue. In a time when everything is almost dead, any evidence of life looks outrageous. If I can be bizarre enough to run for President, I'm hoping more women will run for something else. Being out on the edge is my way of making the world safe for moderates. It helps women feel not as terrified to move. We have to do what opens up for us to do—the more outrageous, the better."

**Phyllis Jane Rose** and **Martha Boesing** use theater the way Sonia uses the podium. Their company, **At the Foot of the Mountain,** is America's oldest, continuously producing, professional, feminist theater. "Mainstream theater is rooted in upper-class, white, male views of the universe," said Phyllis, currently the executive director. "But they never name this, so they are dangerous. Our struggle is to name what is true about who we are and what we believe as women."

Politically, At the Foot of the Mountain's goals are to revolt against misogyny, racism, and related violations of the human spirit; to renew hope; and to celebrate the healing power of women. Their plays expose the raw bones of prostitution, addiction, marriage, nuclear war. "For example, in our play about prostitution," explained Martha, former artistic director and playwright, "we got to know some of the prostitutes here in Minneapolis, but the play was ultimately about how we've all been trained to sell ourselves, and how our spirituality and sexuality have been divorced through the process of prostitution."

Artistically, their plays come out of their lives, values, and visions. They use ritual and improvisation techniques, and respect the discipline necessary to make theater a catalyst for social change. "The acting style we're looking for is 'super realism,' " Martha concluded. "We're not so much interested in people acting, as in people telling their stories, telling the emotional truth. That is a very female approach to the world. We work to knock down the mimicking and get to what is real."

Whether they confront or reform, effective women carry self-respect and positive images of womanhood in their pocketbooks, bookbags, and backpacks. They don't see themselves as victims; they don't consent to falsehoods about women's inadequacies. These women are strong because they believe in themselves.

At the Foot of the Mountain Theater. Ismene says goodbye to her sister Antigone. from "Antigone Too: Rites of Love and Defiance." play by Martha Boesing. Premiere Performance, August 4, 1983. (Photo: Chris Parker)

## Overcoming Self-Hatred

Sonia Johnson is commited to helping women overcome negative self-images. Every activity she engages in promotes it. She knows that unless we change our minds, oppressive social structures will remain entrenched. During a three-day gathering in the summer of 1983, she called women together to be strengthened and encouraged. "We women were despairing," Sonia said. "We needed to get together, and we needed new processes to invigorate our spirits." At the meeting, she introduced three processes—visioning the future, examining self-hatred, and hearing into being.

Visioning came first. Sonia asked women to construct wholistic images of a feminist future. "If we can't envision the specific, the concrete," she said, "there is no hope." Over one hundred fifty women, including Mary Clare, sat in small groups and recorded their dreams on long sheets of newsprint.

But women crippled with self-hatred can't create their dreams, so on the second day, Sonia asked participants "to feel how hurt we are, how negative we feel about ourselves and other women because of our conditioning, and to contradict these feelings by forcefully affirming how wonderful, beautiful, intelligent, and independent we are." Participants examined woman-hating, woman-loving, and self-affirmation in small, caring groups.

Finally, women at Sonia's gathering practiced "hearing into being." Each woman had three half-hour sessions to talk without interruption. Speakers didn't have to talk, but they couldn't pass. Confidentiality was assured. Some women sat in silence; others spoke non-stop. Talkers didn't perform or defend their ideas because listeners listened. Nobody argued, challenged, doubted. Mary Clare loved the process. She had time to be outrageous, say how she and others could change the world, time to name her gifts, confess her fears. Because she was heard, she took herself and her ideas seriously.

Women's aim is to create a new society where it is not unusual for a woman to be listened to. They want to live in a world where the oppression of women does not exist. And they are using their money, minds, talent, and bodies to make this dream come true. They are erasing messages of inferiority, envisioning the future, growing stronger. They do it first for themselves, then for the life of the planet; and, secondarily for their sons and nephews and male cousins, who when asked to imagine being women, may someday rejoice in the assignment, and feel the great pride that being female means.

---

Helen Redman. In the Palm of Our Hand. 1983. Oil Painting. 50″ x 34″.

## OVERCOMING OPPRESSION BASED ON RACE

**Diane Sands**, a feminist organizer, grew up on the Fort Peck Reservation
in Eastern Montana. The Missouri River meandered through Frazer,
"civilization" the whites called it, carrying silt from eroding Rockies
two hundred miles west. The heat in summer was enough to send her
family clamoring for cool mountain breezes; winter temperatures well
below zero were routine. Not many people lived on the arid plains.
Sheep and cattle and farms of ten thousand acres were common.

On the reservation, Diane's father was the school principal in Frazer
and Brockton, so Diane's friends were children of the Sioux and
Assiniboine tribes. Early on, she witnessed racism. "Indians drew their
drinking water from polluted wells," she said. "We had clean wells,
but the whites had no interest in developing a common water system.
They just said, 'The only good Indian is a dead Indian.' My Indian
friends lived in little log houses, some without windows or heat. The
kids slept on the floor. On cold winter nights, when it was sixty below
outside, children died from the cold."

Slowly, Indian children dropped out of school. "In first grade, there
were four Indians for every white kid," Diane continued. "But by high
school, if there was one left in your class, you were lucky. They were
run out by the teachers in subtle and not so subtle ways." By the time
she was old enough to menstruate, Diane Sands had seen the effects
of racism—inadequate housing and health care, discriminatory
education, poverty. She knew nonwhites in Montana were born on the
bottom.

Obviously, racism isn't confined to one of the United States. Its
poison spills into every region, institution, mind. In Montana, the native
American children and Diane cultivated their respective social positions.
Diane learned that her traditions were superior, that she was smarter,
that her life was more valuable than the lives of her Assiniboine
classmates. Her Sioux friends learned that their customs were archaic,
their history irrelevant, their future bleak. These subliminal messages
reverberated during every exchange between Diane and the Indian
children, and they destroyed any promise of equality.

Furthermore, Diane had power. As part of the dominant group, her
values prevailed on the reservation. Local laws, customs, and rituals
reflected her belief system. Organizations, schools, and environmental
decisions benefitted her well-being. Her water was pure, her teachers
expected her to excel, her doctors treated her sicknesses immediately
and with care. In the racist system, privilege was awarded simply because
she was white.

Diane Sands remembers hearing racist slurs and hate-filled innuendos
directed toward others. **Yolanda Tarango**, an Hispanic, remembers
receiving them. To survive, Yolanda tried to assimilate into Anglo
culture. She was rejected and betrayed by those she emulated. She then
raged against blatant racism, unjust social institutions, and feelings of

inferiority. Finally, she embraced her Mexican culture and committed her life to her people.

"I'm a Chicana," she began, "the fifth generation to grow up on the same land. My mother told us to call ourselves Spanish-American, but I never did. I called myself Mexican. When I went to school, I spoke only two or three words of English, but I was raised at a time when assimilation was the only option, so I quickly learned my new, adopted language. Even though there was an Hispanic school in El Paso, the Anglo school was next door, so I went there. I had to learn English to survive. Years later I remember being proud when I didn't know how to speak Spanish anymore.

"When I was in the third grade," Yolanda said, "the parish changed its boundaries, and all Hispanics had to leave the Anglo school or pay higher tuition. I left. This was a real blessing to my self-concept, because the message I had been getting at the Anglo school was that I was inferior—at the bottom—and I internalized the message. But in the Hispanic school, I finished on top of my class and began to think of myself as a leader.

"After high school, I joined an Irish-Anglo religious order," she continued. "I could have joined a Mexican group, but I didn't know if I could handle the cultural differences at their novitiate in Mexico. I was, after all, an American. But I ended up struggling with the cultural differences in the Irish-Anglo group, which were many times greater. The internalized oppressor always tells you, 'White is right.' It is so deeply ingrained, that I struggle with it even now.

"Anyway, convent life was another violent cross-cultural experience. There were fourteen women in my class—one black, three Hispanics, and several white women from New Orleans. Some of the whites really had a problem with the black woman, and she left after two weeks. She and I were close, and I internalized all that happened to her, thinking, 'If they say all that about her, they must feel the same way about me too.' That was my first consciousness of racism.

"Meanwhile, the two other Hispanics and I never admitted to each other that we were Hispanic," she said. "We were trying to make it, to forget who we were. The white women believed their Southern accents were the norm, and took to mimicking me whenever I stood up to talk. After that, I'd go to class and sit and listen. I became withdrawn, and my self-confidence was practically destroyed. All my energy was going toward fading out and fitting in. It was, without a doubt, the most destructive period of my life."

In 1968, Yolanda went to Dallas to work at a mental health center. But perceptive co-workers saw how angry she was and knew she couldn't help others until she helped herself. "They challenged me to look at who I was," Yolanda said, "to claim myself and my heritage.

"As I healed myself, I helped form Las Hermañas, an organization for Hispanic sisters," she continued. "We couldn't even conduct the first meeting in Spanish because none of us could speak it well enough. Most of us were working in suburban areas with Anglos. We started

telling our stories to each other. Most of us had not claimed our identity and were considered successful only because we were passing as whites. We began a whole campaign to affirm ourselves and our people, to return to our culture, and to create our theology out of our Hispanic experience. We felt a lot of anger; many women left their orders. Those of us who stayed dealt with our anger outside our communities. I am just beginning to challenge my community now."

Today, Yolanda Tarango is director of pastoral education at San Antonio's Mexican American Cultural Center. She has reclaimed her past, embraced her culture. "My call is *for* my people and comes *from* my people," she said. "Any revolution in the Catholic Church will come from Hispanic people. The Catholic Church is not a white church with a large brown population. It must also be an Hispanic church, and this must be reflected in the liturgy and hierarchy. At this time, our numbers have been discovered, and the official church is making all kinds of efforts to minister to us, which may mean to subvert and recolonize us. It's critical that we claim our church. A community needs its own theologians and leaders. I work with marginated people on the grass roots level because I believe they are the seeds of a new church," she concluded. "I want to use my theological background to explore the signs and symbols of Hispanic people."

## Looking to Each Other

Women of color, oppressed by sexism and racism, have looked to each other to affirm cultural and racial identities. "In the 1970s, we concentrated on ourselves," **Gloria Anzaldúa** explained. "It was an era of focusing. We had to get a sense of who we were, where we came from. We learned that we couldn't separate ourselves from our race. We couldn't cut ourselves off from our brothers and sisters because the family unit was our unit of survival.

"The 1980s is an era of linkages," she continued. "Even though third world women are getting strong and vocal, we aren't exclusive. Just as we can't cut ourselves off from our own families, neither can we withdraw from white men and women. That's why the mestiza, the mulatta, the half-breed, mixed breed, and lesbian (and woman) of color are the bridge between the white world and the indigenous world."

On the opposite shore, white women are beginning similar work. Many were raised on homogeneity—segregated neighborhoods, all-white softball teams. Tonto taught two Indian words, "Kemo Sabbe," and parents read *Little Black Sambo* at bedtime. History books encouraged arrogance—white men "discovered" the New World; Mexicans fought to keep us from "our land"; and warlike Indians tried to stop "our conquest" of the West. Brainwashed by junior high school, whites thought their pink ancestors were the saviors of the world. "We

Jay Goldspinner. Breastplate—Love/Anger. Papier-mâché.

must admit our conditioning to the lie of white superiority," said **Terry Wolverton**, Los Angeles artist, "before we can move on."

To shake loose the truth, Terry asked other white women to form an anti-racist group. "Eliminating racism means exposing and unlearning the lie," she continued, "*and* dismantling the institutions that keep the lie intact. Our group discovered ways we denied our racism or hid it by trying to 'appear' non-racist. Many of us had resorted to guilt and helplessness. But eventually, we saw that we could be anti-racist *while* we unlearned our racism, that we didn't have to wait until we were 'pure' to take a stand. Racism permeates every facet of the culture. It is entrenched, potent, pervasive, intractable, crippling to us all. To think we can broaden our horizons without dealing with it is to try and lay a white gauzy sheet over a stinking swamp and pass across the mud."

Nowhere in America has that sheet been more cleverly used than in the South where it masks faces in angry mobs and masquerades as manners. **Mab Segrest**, lesbian writer and former editor of *Feminary*, grew up in the South during the Civil Rights Movement. "It was very traumatic to grow up white and lesbian in Alabama," she said. "I remember being very confused, as if I were on the wrong side. I identified more with black people than with white people, wanted to be on their side, but didn't know how to get there."

How could she have known how to get there? Surrounded by burning crosses, signs over water fountains, and black mammies in every white kitchen, Mab, like other sensitive whites, lived in a schizophrenic society. The "right" side was the "wrong" side, and there were no bridges across the chasm.

As an adult, Mab has begun to come to terms with her experience. She reads books, writes articles, talks with white and black women. At a workshop on racism, she began affirming the liberation tradition in the South. "Part of the lie about any oppression is that there has not been resistance to it," she said. "Part of the lie about racism is that white people never resisted it. Even though resistance to slavery and civil rights have been talked about in black terms, whites were involved, too. I'm hooking into that tradition, and claiming it."

On June 12, 1983, Mab attended a peace march in New York City. As a member of Necessary Bread, an affinity group for anti-nuclear resisters, Mab walked in support of those being arrested. "We had decided to do a slow trance walk toward the policemen," she said. "Right in the middle of that walk, I had a sense of being in Selma. I could hear the dogs, see the cops. It was like Martin Luther King was there. I had always wanted to be part of the Selma march, but I was only fourteen at the time. The New York march took me back there somehow. I was finally on the right side."

Mab isn't going to leave the South any time soon. In spite of its racist history, she chooses to stay. "We have this load of pain here, and certain things restimulate it," she concluded. "Staying could mean I'm stuck in old patterns or I'm masochistic, but I don't see it that way. If I can find my way out of the pain, I can go. To find my way out, I'm going to have to stay around here for awhile.''

## Building Alliances

White women like Mab, Terry, and Diane are unlearning lies taught in elementary schools and climbing off pedestals of privilege. Women of color like Yolanda and Gloria are remembering who they are and joining with their sisters to edit best-selling anthologies, organize conferences, form publishing houses. Both groups are building bases from which to form alliances. "Every person needs to know he or she can be an ally for an oppressed person or group," said **Carole Johnson**, co-director of **Equity Institute**. "Guilt and shame don't help anybody."

Carole and her partner **Joan Lester** help oppressors and oppressed work through feelings of guilt and anger so they can be allies. Their clients included western Massachusetts police departments, corporations, school systems, anti-nuclear groups, and reproductive rights organizations. During their workshops, participants talk openly about their experiences of oppression. "Our process works because people get a chance to talk without being blamed or threatened," Carole added. "By laying down ground rules—confidentiality, no zapping with jokes, treating each other with respect—we help people find their voices, name their fears.

"Our main goal is to create the concept of allies," she concluded. "White males, especially, say, 'No matter who I am as a person, or what my politics are, I'm always blamed.' We show how people who aren't targeted for any specific oppression may benefit in the short run, but not in the long run. Everyone has a stake, and it's not just 'poor them.' Oppression hurts everyone, and we want everybody to take part in overcoming it."

There is plenty to overcome. Joan and Carole use charts to show the interconnectedness of all oppressions. Even though an agency may hire them to work on one oppression, like heterosexism, (a current project with school systems) Joan and Carole always talk about all oppressions. "They're all interchangeable parts," Joan said, "based on deviation from the norm. In patriarchy, the norm is maleness, whiteness, education, youth. We ask people to look at their individual histories and messages about race, sex, class and age, and see how those attitudes are translated into social institutions. Finally, we get them to look at their own institutions so they can begin to be change agents within them."

A white woman who participated in Equity's first workshop went to a housing conference a few weeks later, and practiced what Joan and Carole had taught. She was one of a hundred white women in attendance; there were two black women. During the symposium, a speaker made a racist remark. The white woman stood, interrupted, and said she was offended by the comment. Before she knew it, other women in the audience were also involved. Afterwards, one of the black women approached her and said, "That's the first time a white woman ever stood up for me. I always have to do it myself." "The white woman felt strong enough to interrupt," Joan said. "She practiced what we teach: speak up, not because you think something offends 'them,' but because something offends *you*."

Reaching across the miles of historical prejudice and fear takes courage, and women building alliances between cultures and races are demonstrating that courage. They are interrupting; they are telling each other stories. Eradicating racism is not as simple as storytelling, but speaking and listening to each other is clearly a way to begin. Yolanda Tarango took a risk when she told her story. She neither knew us, nor knew what we would make of it, but she told us anyway. "I have told you my story," she said, "because that's how I build sisterhood. If I don't reveal myself, you will judge me by your old stereotypes. So I want to speak about who I am, good and bad. But if my part is to tell you who I am, your part is to tell me who you are. In addition, you have to reach out to women unlike you, women who do not speak your language, and share stories, too."

## CELEBRATING OTHERNESS

"How do we treat the 'Other'?" Judy Smith asked. And women of all shades, classes, ages, and abilities are stretching their minds to answer. They aren't willing to blend in or acquiesce to what is offered. They see value in "otherness," affirm that difference is a source of power.

**Joan E. Biren**, Washington, D.C. photographer, is a lesbian who chooses to be "other than." She acknowledged her lesbianism to herself and her lover when she was in college, and came out of the closet several years after graduation. She's never gone back in, nor is she likely to. She is convinced that the only way "others" will be accepted is for them to be visible. No more hiding, no more pretending to pass.

She remembers the loneliness of the closet, of feeling "less than" in college. "I knew you didn't go around being a lesbian in a visible, public way because bad things would happen to you," she said. "I never knew what, but I was careful. I felt terrible isolation, like I was the only one, different in a way that wasn't good, that there was something strange, wrong, and sinful about me."

With shame and fear implanted in her mind, Joan, who also calls herself JEB, looked for ways to make lesbianism visible. In 1979 she published *Eye to Eye: Portraits of Lesbians*, a book packed with her photographs of women who love other women. "This is the book I wanted all my life," she said. "A book with the word 'Lesbian' on the cover and pictures of lesbians on every page. I wanted to show us in all our diversity—different colors, abilities, ages, alone, together, working, and resting."

But Joan's book is not only a celebration of lesbianism; it is also a celebration of "otherness." "My politics are about *being* in a different way," she continued. "Lesbians are not just women who are like everybody else, only we do something else in bed. We are different. We are women figuring out how to be 'other than' in a society that has no tolerance for deviance. Therefore if we can see what we look like, have a visual image of lesbians, we can more easily be ourselves. I don't want to be absorbed into the mainstream. I want everything to change."

The brave and thoughtful women here are unraveling the most insidious, malicious, and destructive forces in our society. As part of a species that hates its own members, these women battle real, daily, and ever-present demons. Their victories are miniscule, infrequent, personal. Yet these few women, representing thousands more, are our sisters on the front lines, literally fighting to save us all from species-inflicted destruction. Gloria Anzaldúa, in her foreword to the second edition of *This Bridge Called My Back*, has written their/our chorus for the victory march.

> We have come to realize that we are not alone in our struggles nor separate nor autonomous but that we—white black straight queer female male—are connected and interdependent. We are each accountable for what is happening down the street, south of the border or across the sea. And those of us who have more of anything: brains, physical strength, political power, spiritual energies, are learning to share them with those that don't have....
>
> Mujeres, a no dejar que el peligro del viaje y la immensidad del territorio nos asuste—a mirar hacía adelante y a abrir paso en el monte. (*Women, let's not let the danger of the journey and the vastness of the territory scare us—let's look forward and open paths in these woods.*) Caminante, no hay puentes, se hace puentes al andar. (*Voyager, there are no bridges, one builds them as one walks.*)[3]

# 11

## WAGING PEACE

In December 1980, **Frances Crowe** met a Russian woman who feared nuclear war as much as she did. Tatyana Mamanova was one of four Soviet women exiled because they dared to publish a hand-typed feminist magazine. Several of the women were married to dissidents, and Tatyana's husband had refused to serve in Afghanistan. *Ms.* magazine sponsored a United States lecture tour for the women, and Robin Morgan, author of *Sisterhood Is Global* and *Anatomy of Freedom*, accompanied Tatyana to western Massachusetts. Frances and several women leaders were invited to have breakfast with Tatyana on the morning of her Amherst College speech.

Frances was happy to meet Tatyana. She wondered how a woman from the "other side" saw the world. To find out, and to tell Tatyana what American women were thinking, Frances suggested that each guest say something about the issue she thought was primary for women. One woman talked about job discrimination; another mentioned child care; and another said that women must have reproductive rights. When it was Tatyana's turn, everyone was eager to hear her perspective. She said, "The nuclear arms race." Frances was ecstatic. For decades, she had worked for peace, for understanding between citizens of the USSR and the United States. And here was a Russian woman who shared her belief that nuclear weapons were the single greatest threat to life.

That night, Frances sat in the front row of the Red Room at Amherst College for Tatyana's speech. When the question and answer period began, Frances stood and asked again, "What is the most important issue facing women today?" Again Tatyana said, "The nuclear arms race." The next day, Frances sent a copy of Tatyana's lecture schedule to the national office of the American Friends Service Committee. "I suggested that somebody attend every lecture," Frances said, "and stand and ask, 'What is the most important issue facing women today?' I knew Tatyana would give the same answer, and we needed to hear it again and again."

## Thinking The Unthinkable

Violence permeates our culture. Weapons mania grips leaders of every nation. MX missiles are planted in deserts like tulips, and laser warships hurl through space like fastballs. Vigilantes patrol neighborhoods with loaded pistols, and men rape women and children in their homes. Imperialistic nations vie for dominance in the third world, and the United States government routinely dishonors treaties between itself and native American peoples.

Alice Walker, author of *The Color Purple*, speaking at an anti-nuclear rally said, "When I have considered the enormity of the white man's crimes against humanity. Against women. Against every living person of color. Against the poor. Against my mother and my father. Against me...When I consider that he is, they are, a real and present threat to my life and the life of my daughter, my people, I think—in perfect harmony with my sister of long ago: *Let the earth marinate in poisons. Let the bombs cover the ground like rain. For nothing short of total destruction will ever teach them anything.*"[1]

Men talk glibly about surviving nuclear rain. Civil defense planners plot evacuation routes for major target areas. The post office issues forms to fill out and file in case a nuclear war forces you to evacuate. Magazine editors feature stories about annihilation that include circular maps of vaporized inner cities, burned suburbs, and irradiated farms. "Nuclear winter" scenarios describe survivors coping with contaminated food and water, festering injuries, and darkness. Movie star Jason Robards wanders bleary-eyed through rubble "The Day After" a nuclear exchange between Moscow and Kansas City.

Can ordinary vocabulary and syntax describe something so extraordinary as the death of all culture and history and nature? Can videotaped "docudramas" capture the smell of one hundred thousand burning bodies? We lounge on couches with our feet propped up, read holocaust articles sandwiched between comic strips and gossip columns, and watch end-of-the-world movies advertised by McDonald's. We are thinking the unthinkable.

What to do in the face of this madness? Do we seek revenge? Curse the war mongers? Alice Walker considers that tack, then retreats. In

the end, she argues for life. "Life is better than death," she said, "if only because it is less boring, and because it has fresh peaches in it. I intend to protect my home...But if by some miracle, and all our struggle, the earth is spared, only justice to every living thing (and everything is alive) will save humankind. And we are not saved yet."[2]

Justice is not a passive notion. It requires diligence, perseverance, awareness, work. We can't be innocent readers, paralyzed by military mania, and bring about justice in the world. Joanna Macy would suggest that the only way to action is through our feelings of terror and rage. Author of *Despair and Personal Power in the Nuclear Age*, she helps people cope with the dread that surfaces when they put down the Sunday paper and let the reality of nuclear annihilation sink in. "Despair is the loss of the assumption that the species will inevitably pull through," Joanna writes. "It represents a genuine accession to the possibility that this planetary experiment will fail, the curtain rung down, the show over."[3]

Her workshops are for people like Mary Clare who wrote in her journal several years ago, "I am sick for the race, ashamed and sick. Why do we want to self-destruct? I and all other life are held hostage by men who have the power to kill us. They are foolish, boastful, and deluded men, out of touch with themselves, living in fantasy. It goes on and nothing improves—presidents elected, economic crises, people hungry, war here, war there. We are on a downward spiral, and I weep over the typewriter, 'bitter tears.' Bitter tears for the children—Amanda and the unborn baby inside Mickey, Damien and Bryan and Melissa and Heather and Anne and Cathy and Serena and Liz and Allison. What a waste! What a waste! It overwhelms me, and I can't move."

These feelings are not popular. In a society where "have a nice day" is the most common salutation between friends and strangers, where yellow smiling faces adorn car windows and school notebooks, despair is hardly tolerated. If Mary Clare started crying "bitter tears" in the middle of conversations, she wouldn't get many invitations to tea.

Nobody likes pain, anguish, and fear; but Joanna insists that we can't act until we experience it. In her view, despair isn't craziness; it is an appropriate response to the daily news. It represents an understanding of the unity of all life, and a sensitivity to the serious threat to that life. When we drop our defenses and let grief and apprehension surface, we are released from paralysis, and connected to all life. "Through our despair," she writes, "something more profound and pervasive comes to light. It is our interconnectedness, our inter-existence. Beyond our pain and because of our pain, we awaken into that....Despair work, experienced in this fashion, is consciousness-raising in the truest sense of that term. It increases our awareness, not only of the perils that face us, but also of the promise inherent in the human heart."[4]

Susan Boss. No-Nukes Wings. 1981. Mixed media. (Photo: George Dimock)

## Acting For Peace

Justice and interconnectedness are hard won. They don't grow in a garden of war toys. They rest in a soil of peace. **Frances Crowe** has committed her life to enriching that ground, year by year. She interrupts people to talk about peace. She wades into crowds at shopping centers, stalks cars waiting for stoplights to change, and threads her way through assembled audiences at lectures to hand out pamphlets. She sets up tables on Northampton, Massachusetts' Main Street, hires performers, such as jugglers, to stand nearby, and leaflets bystanders who stop to watch.

Whenever she rides the bus to Boston, she takes along anti-war literature and passes out half of it to riders. "Would you like something to read on the trip?" she asks. On the way home, she strolls up and down the aisle giving away the rest. "Never has there been a society with more freedom, whose people use it less," she said. "Very few people take advantage of freedom in this democracy, because they don't take themselves seriously enough. They walk around like zombies, afraid to step out of their paper doll roles."

Her role is confronter, nay-sayer to war and domination. "I bring up subjects that people don't want to think about," she said. "For example, maybe the oil of Iran or the resources of South Africa, or the cheap labor of Latin America, Asia, and Africa aren't ours. In the case of war, maybe there are alternatives to killing people. Maybe we would be stronger and more secure if we had a stronger economy. Maybe we would feel more secure if we used civilian, nonviolent resistance instead of weapons."

Her civil disobedience record is comprehensive and on-going. Wherever there is injustice, Frances is nearby. She scaled the fence at Seneca Falls Peace Encampment in 1983, painted THOU SHALT NOT KILL on a Trident nuclear missile stored at a Rhode Island military base in 1984, and went to jail both times. She has signed and promotes the Pledge of Resistance, in which she promises to resist nonviolently if the United States government escalates its military activity in Nicaragua, El Salvador, or Cuba. "I'm doing all this," she said, "because I *have* to do it. I feel deeply compelled. I don't seem to have a choice. I'm a Quaker, so I believe a life force keeps good alive. So we don't have to do it all, but we must constantly affirm that good."

Frances disobeys her government when it makes war machines. She refuses to conspire with death-loving forces. This stubbornness is typical of women who wage peace. They refuse to cooperate with what is; they will not "go along." They use different strategies to educate and catalyze public response—demonstrations in the streets, peace camps, fasting, art. Everywhere, over and over again, they stand together saying "No."

Arlene Hartman. :Epitaph for Later. 1984. Charcoal and masking tape on paper. 30" x 22".

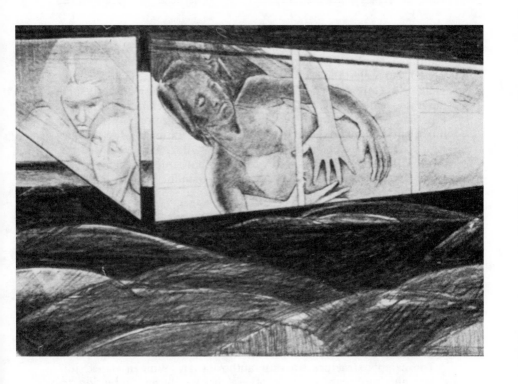

Peace camps are a recent phenomenon. They started in 1981 in England when a group of women and children, largely Welsh, set up camp at Greenham Common Air Force Base, seventy miles west of London, to protest the planned deployment of ninety-six, United States-built, cruise missiles. The camp grew in spite of evictions, arrests, and miserable living conditions, and on one day in December 1982, thirty thousand women from all over the world converged on Greenham to link arms and surround the base in a "celebration of life." They wrapped themselves around the nine-mile radius, and decorated the fence with symbols of life—baby clothes, photographs of loved ones, letters. They wove the word PEACE in the chainlink and lit candles in the evening. The next morning, four thousand women, in a massive demonstration of non-cooperation, sat down in roadways and blockaded the base.[5]

The Women's Encampment for A Future of Peace and Justice started a year-and-a-half later in upstate New York, near the Seneca Army Depot, receiving station for the cruise missiles bound for Europe. **Sandra Boston**, a western Massachusetts peace activist, was there. "We wanted a women-only encampment," Sandra said, "because if anyone was going to stop these weapons, it was going to be women. The best-intentioned men in the world are still hooked into patriarchal privilege, and women, who are outside that system, have nothing to lose by going against the law."

The camp's structure was non-authoritarian. Women signed job charts and took care of each others' needs. By an "intention to cooperate," they created a community that functioned well, though decision making was sometimes hard. Once a local man brought an American flag to the camp and told the women that if they didn't fly it, he would tell the media they were communists. "We didn't need any extra stories about how alien we were," Sandra said. "But seven hundred women were living on the land by then, and no one was in charge to say 'Yes' or 'No.' Seven hundred people have a lot of opinions, and it took us a day and a half to reach consensus. But we did: everyone who wanted to could make a flag out of a pillow case, and we would fly them all. The next day the front looked like a clothesline with fifty flags flapping in the breeze. This experience was an example of the nonviolence we advocated—there was no *one* right way: we allowed for difference, but pulled together to make a statement."

As the camp grew, press coverage increased. But media stories centered on lifestyle—lesbianism, witchcraft, and nakedness—instead of on nuclear weapons. To draw attention to peace, the women resorted to creative surprises. For example, a water tower stood inside the Depot with a baffling message painted on it—"Mission First, People Always." Women at the camp decided to change it. One night, two women scaled the fence, climbed the eighty foot tower, and with one standing on the other's shoulders, painted out the first part of the slogan. Undetected, they climbed down and returned to the camp. The next morning they called a press conference. "The military police didn't even know why we were there," Sandra said. "Neither did the press, but we got a good turnout. When everybody was present, we just looked at the water tower and pointed. It read, 'People Always.'

"Here we were," Sandra continued, "up to two thousand women living in a little farm town of two hundred and fifty people. We were breaking every rule of patriarchy. We were proud to be with women, and didn't care what men thought about it. We had cast off our naiveté (they will take care of us), and our conditioning (we must mind, be good, do as we're told), and we had begun to confront. Like constantly goading mosquitos, we were drawing attention to America's commitment to a first strike capability. It was a transforming experience for all who went there."

And for all who watched. The presence of confrontive peacekeepers transformed Seneca citizens as well as protesters. "The local people did everything they could think of to get us to leave," Sandra concluded. "But we didn't. When they gave up and listened, there were some significant turnarounds. One officer at the Depot resigned, and came to the Encampment with a case of Sprite to thank us for helping him realize what his life was about. And a preacher came by one Sunday to read us a prayer he had said at church that morning, asking God to support the women working for justice.

"We live in a violent culture," Sandra concluded, "so nonviolence is cultural revolution. It isn't just another way to be nice. It is a strategy for political change and a personal lifestyle. I'm a cultural worker and a revolutionary. I'm not interested in reform; I want a new society to live in. I take responsibility for that society; I won't let somebody else dish it out to me, or settle for less."

Peace camp women don't work for justice abstractly. They go to the places of injustice and pitch their tents on the ground. They breathe the same air, feel the same sunshine, rain, and cold as people working in weapons plants. And they don't stop with Greenham and Seneca. Other encampments exist in Minnesota, Arizona, Wisconsin, at the Silence One Silo near Great Falls, Montana, and at Puget Sound, across from the Boeing plant near Seattle. In every case, women have put their bodies next to death machines, and insisted on peace.

In Seattle, writer **Hollis Giammatteo**, who knew about the Puget Sound camp and dealt daily with her despair, finally decided to act. She and eight other women agreed to walk across the United States alongside the trackline of the Nuclear Train. From Amarillo, Texas, the Train, also called the "Death Train," carries bombs to Trident submarines in Bangor, Washington, and to the Naval Weapons Station in Charleston, South Carolina. "On The Line" walkers started in Washington, and spent a year getting to Charleston. Hollis walked for six of the twelve months.

Organizers stated their commitment in a brochure. "We walk in the spirit of nonviolence to serve as messengers and to bear witness along the tracks of the Nuclear Train. We walk in full knowledge that this may be our last walk, for we are a species threatened with annihilation through use of nuclear weapons. We are forced to take action. Living on the brink of annihilation is intolerable. We choose resistance. We choose to connect with the heart of the American people. We choose to respect and honor all life. In so doing, we take our power in creating a world free of war and all weapons.''

They climbed the Rockies, and walked across the plains. Through Caldwell, Idaho; Alva, Oklahoma; Monett, Missouri; and Tupelo, Mississippi, they followed the tracks. They wore out sneakers, slept in garages and sheds, drank milkshakes and lemonade given by friendly townspeople. They listened to teenagers, conservative churchgoers, farmers, lone war resisters, and isolated feminists like the owner of the Emma Chase Cafe in Cottonwood Falls, Kansas. They held vigils whenever the train went by, and occasionally talked with the train's engineer. They encountered fear and apathy and despair and numbness, prejudice and violence and poverty and hope.

They also brought their own bag of tricks in two hand-pulled, specially built carts—films about Nagasaki and Hiroshima survivors; bits and songs from the Tiny Grace Theater's play, ''Hurry Up Please, It's Time;'' materials for despair/empowerment workshops; information about tax resistance, nuclear-free zones, feminism, civil disobedience, racism. During the evenings, they sat with townspeople, made connections between defense spending and inflation, poverty and unemployment, and raised questions about the country's priorities.

Hollis walked for 2,700 miles to say ''No. I am giving my permission when I stand by,'' she wrote in the trip journal, ''letting the fences go up or the gates come down; letting the corporations churn out products we do not need; letting the advertisers tell us why we need them; letting the dollars seduce us, and the chemicals kill us; letting the doors close, so we can formulate our prejudice and dogmas to keep distant from the information of our breaking hearts, for so much, it seems, needs doing.''[6]

And is being done. Fence climbers and walkers are joined by artists in Canada and the United States who confront militaristic policies with creativity. **Wilma Needham**, visual artist and teacher at the Nova Scotia School of Art and Design, is a member of NAAGS (Never Again Affinity Group). The group's actions are varied and timely. In 1983, Nova Scotia's federal officer in charge of emergency measures announced a war game plan to house 329 government officials (318 men and 11 women) in the bunker at Debert Military Base, forty miles outside Halifax, in case of nuclear attack. The plan was absurd, and NAAGS spoofed it.

They created ''Debert Debunkers Lottery,'' a street performance, printed tickets, and passed them out on the street. Lottery prizes included front row seats at Ground Zero, supplies of cyanide for the whole family, and seats in the Camp Debert bunker. During the draw, the master of ceremonies, Bob Bunker, interviewed a series of nuclear fools—Hope Fool, Blind Fool, Capitalist Fool, Nurturing Fool—people who believed in the bunker mentality.

"Debert Debunkers" was followed by "The Continuity of People Programme," a counter-proposal to the government's bunker plan. "We proposed," Wilma said, "through a detailed 'white paper' with photos, to fill the bunkers with a sperm bank (appropriately screened genetic material, of course), and women of child-bearing age. It got lots of media attention and smiles."

During one Christmas season, NAAGS members went to shopping malls and sang new words to old carols. "While we sang," Wilma continued, "we gave out pamphlets entitled 'Who Made Your Christmas Presents?' with information about companies like Litton, Tandy, and Union Carbide. They make toys *and* MX-missile components. It wasn't a cheery note, but it was an important addition to the true message of Christmas—'Peace.' "

To commemorate the dropping of the atomic bomb on Hiroshima, they produced a solemn choral work which was performed in five locations in Halifax, capital of Nova Scotia. The piece was called "Ghost People of Hiroshima." Black mourning costumes and white face were appropriate to tell the story of bomb victims and also those who mine uranium, process radioactive ore, test warheads, and transport and store missiles. "This piece still makes me cry," said Wilma.

NAAGS' last and most recent piece was a cookbook/press action by LOHA (Ladies of Halifax Auxiliary). Members compiled recipes for the *New Ways to Cook with Toxic and Radioactive Wastes* cookbook, including "Radium Waffles" sent in by Mrs. U.R. Mort, and "Tritium Tarts" from Mrs. A. Lepreau, Jr., from Downwind, Nova Scotia. Wilma signed off, "We must move with the future!"

Five feminist artists in Los Angeles share Wilma's despair and determination. They have performed collaboratively as the **Sisters of Survival** since 1980 when Cheri Gaulke and Nancy Angelo did a performance called "The Passion." They dress like nuns in rainbow-colored gowns. "We decided to adopt the nun image as a metaphor for sisterhood," Cheri said, "and the rainbow imagery is intended to evoke hope, humor, and a celebration of diversity."

In 1981, Cheri, Nancy, Jerri Allyn, Anne Gauldin, and Sue Maberry began "End of the Rainbow," a three-part project dealing with nuclear war. The first phase was local: together with peace activists and other Los Angeles artists, they organized "Target LA," a huge anti-nuclear arts festival. For the second part of the project, they toured Europe and gave performances in the streets. "Europeans were really calling out to Americans for help," Cheri said. "They didn't want cruise and Pershing missiles deployed on their continent, and we wanted to show our support for their resistance."

While in Europe, the "Sisters" collected art from artists in England, Amsterdam, West Germany, and Malta, and for the third phase of

"End of the Rainbow," they developed a traveling exhibit for the United States. "We wanted to take responsibility as Americans for the nuclear threat," Cheri concluded, "and raise consciousness within our own country."

Crusaders like Frances, campers like Sandra, and artists like Hollis, Wilma, and Sisters of Survival are joined by fasters. Fasting is one of the oldest and most effective forms of nonviolent disobedience, and on August 6, 1983, **Dorothy Grenada** and ten German, Spanish, French, Japanese, and United States citizens began an open-ended Fast for Life. Their goal was simple: when enough people and institutions pressured their governments to end the nuclear arms race, the Fast would end.

The eight fasters encouraged limited support fasts, letter-writing campaigns, work stoppages. They hoped for a massive demonstration against the arms race. "We have to make peace as seriously as they make war," Dorothy said. "It's not enough to sign a petition or go to a march. The American peace movement has got to get more sacrificial and stop being comfortable. We've got to put our lives on the line, take some risks. We can't have business as usual. We have the power to make change, and we must make it because governments aren't going to. The crisis we live in won't go away."

Gandhi, who was influenced by the British suffragette movement's policy of nonviolent resistance and fasting, used fasts effectively in India's struggle for independence from Britain. But fasting has not been widely used in North America's peace movement. As a civil disobedience method which is also a religious/political tool, it steers clear of criminal justice systems. Dorothy and her companions were careful not to use it as blackmail. "Our fast is not a hunger strike," she said. "We aren't saying, 'Meet our demands or we'll die.' Instead, we are saying, 'We want you to look at our truth. If your truth does not meet our truth, then let us die. If it speaks to you, then act.' In that sense, it is non-coercive. We take the suffering on ourselves. And because fasting does not inflict suffering on others, it can really shake people."

We interviewed Dorothy before the fast began and asked about her commitment to the peace movement. "I gave up my work with Hispanic people, and I'm basically ignoring the women's movement," she said. "I've been criticized by third world people because of this, but I don't feel guilty anymore. The arms race is the most dangerous symptom of a racist country. The arms race is the most evil manifestation of the patriarchy. So I don't think I've abandoned my people who are Chicanos and women. It is particularly appropriate that third world people are involved in the peace movement because we're all going to be the same color when the bomb goes off."

We asked Dorothy about fasting to death. "I don't want to die," she said, "I love life. But I'm preparing myself by praying and being as honest as possible with myself as I can be. I am an ordinary woman.

Sisters of Survival. Pictured l. to r.: Cheri Gaulke, Anne Gauldin, Sue Maberry. (Photo: Joyce Dallal)

I am no more special than the child or mother being shot in El Salvador. I am a representative of those people because they are my family. So far, this fast feels right inside.''

The fast began. Three fasting centers were established in Bonn, West Germany; Paris, France; and Oakland, California. The eleven fasters were assisted throughout by medical teams and friends. By the fourth week, media attention was building. Newspapers and television stations in Japan were treating it seriously; in Germany, it was receiving top story status. The press in Northern California was also increasingly involved in the story, and United States coverage was broadening. In addition to press coverage, peace activists from around the world were writing letters of support and pledging to increase their efforts to stop the arms race.

Then in early September, a Soviet Union war plane shot down a Korean Airlines passenger jet flying two hundred miles off course above the USSR. International attention shifted to the new event. In the meantime, the fasters' bodies were deteriorating. In Bonn, Didier Mainguy ended his fast on the thirtieth day, and Charles Gray, Dorothy's husband, went into the hospital for saline infusions. Dorothy and several others were dehydrated, and had to be given fluids intravenously. On September 14, 1983, the ten remaining fasters mutually consented to end their fast, forty days after it began.

Dorothy and Charles spent many months after the fast preparing a report on its history and the activity it generated. During the forty days, citizens of twenty-four countries had begun support fasts. In Canada, Karen Harrison continued to fast for twenty-three days beyond September 14, and brought attention to the testing of cruise missiles in Canada. Almost three thousand people, including children, wrote letters to the fasters before, during, and after the fast. Eleven-year-old Robert Snowden was one. "Dear Fasters for Peace," he wrote on September 16. "I admire what you did for peace. I also hope you won't have to do it again. I hope they spend more money on food and schools instead of military arms. I hope you proved your point and a change is made."[7]

Has change been made? Are these walkers, pamphleteers, and fasters idealistic women engaged in ineffectual actions? Sandra Boston asks herself these questions all the time. "Women at Seneca didn't stop the first strike weapons from being shipped," she said. "They are in Europe now. So what difference did we make? Was our water tower action only one of a number of symbolic gestures? Are we destined to a lifetime of symbolic gestures? But maybe symbolic gestures cause change that we can't see. Maybe real change doesn't have to do with whether or not the world is rid of first strike weapons. If not them, there will be something else. Maybe change happens in people's hearts—a growing consciousness of global community, of personal responsibility to act. So it ends up being a matter of faith: I act even when I don't see the results.

"My own journey has been from unawareness to assuming responsibility for my world," she concluded, "by understanding that the forces that oppress me have that power only because I cooperate with them. These forces seem impenetrable—the Pentagon, the multinationals. They seem to have the world parceled out and under control. But I challenge them because they don't create justice. I take my cooperation away, and I encourage others to do the same. We can make change when large numbers of us act in unity."

Women, in unison, are moving through despair to action, confronting the manifestations of violence in the world—angry international posturing, war games, rape. We want to end violence on planet Earth once and for all. We want reverberating international threats to cease. We want neighborhood squabbles that turn into bloodbaths to stop. We want human behavior to reflect caring instead of fear. We want violence to be socially unacceptable. We want peace to be the norm.

## Teaching Peace

Among us, peace teachers are emerging. **Judy Smith** and colleagues at the University of Montana are writing articles about peace habits; mediators Janet Rifkin and Susan Carpenter are resolving individual and organizational conflicts; Sandra Boston is teaching nonviolence training when confrontation is either desired or can't be avoided. For these women, and others like them, making peace is not only a matter of opposing militarism. It is a habit of mind.

In Montana, Judy Smith, Sheila Smith, and Leslie Burgess adopted the concept of "peace habits" from another Montanan, Jeanette Rankin, the first woman elected to the United States Congress. "She was the only Member of Congress to vote against both world wars," wrote Judy, Sheila, and Leslie in *Peace Habits*, "and she was always proud that the first vote cast by a woman in Congress was a vote for peace."[8] Rankin believed women understood and practiced peace habits more than men, and should teach these habits to others.

Judy, in a class at the University in Missoula, explored the connection between feminism and peace. She began with two premises. "First, feminism and peace are not separate concerns," Judy and the other women wrote. "As long as male values are dominant (the old 'I win—you lose' competition where physical force is the bottom line), war will be the technology used to resolve conflict. Peace is only possible when women are empowered and female values ('I win—you win' cooperation and concern for relationship) are respected and used to negotiate conflict. The second premise was that the possibility of achieving peace has to be understood and practiced first at the level of personal relationship with self and others, and then can be applied to larger systems of human activity."[9]

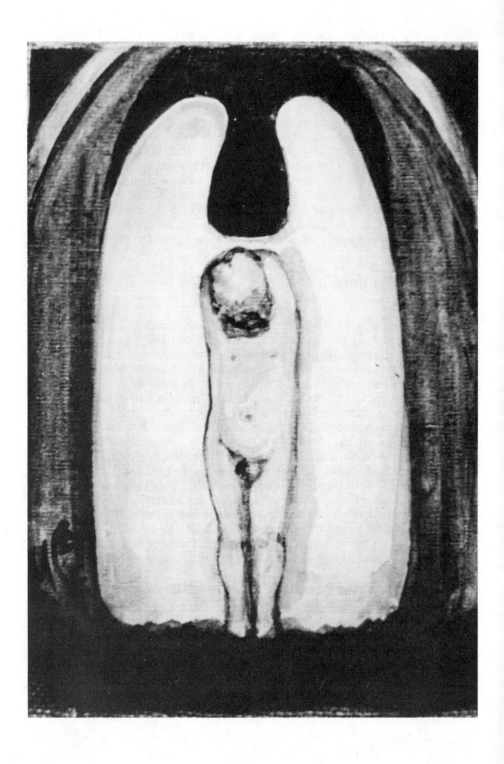

"Peace habits" can be practiced and learned until they become automatic.

- Neutralize "otherness." Put yourself in situations where you are in the minority, where you are "other than." Learn to appreciate diversity. Define commonality, in addition to difference, and resist polarization by not devaluing a person or group because you disagree with them.

- Broaden the arena for caring. Teach children to care for pets and smaller children. Involve men in child care. Spend time with someone who is sick, differently abled, older.

- Reduce threat. Make sure that everyone's needs for survival, safety, and security are met. When everyone has an equal share, no one wants to take from another. Notice how the accumulation of material things by some results in the material deprivation of others.

- Promote empowerment, especially in women. Aim to redistribute power so everyone has an equal amount. Take courses in leadership development and group process; learn assertive communications skills so you cannot be easily violated. Develop self-esteem, and practice these skills in families, schools, with friends, in support groups and institutions.[10]

"We can never achieve a world without conflict," concluded the authors of *Peace Habits*, "but we can recognize a world where conflict is resolved by peaceful means, where every life is valued. The future of humankind, and perhaps of our planet, depends on creating a new set of relationships as the basis of our existence. We believe that women, that feminists in particular, will be the ones to implement peace—by educating the world's people to practice peace habits. Peace is our work."[11]

**Janet Rifkin**, director of the Mediation Project at the University of Massachusetts in Amherst, is one of the workers. She left law practice because "it was a hierarchy run by men. It consisted of making futile arguments to them on behalf of people I wasn't even sure I wanted to represent, and waiting for them to accept my point of view," she said. "I felt like I was talking to my father all the time, and I didn't want to do it anymore."

Janet began teaching legal studies at the University, got bored with theory about law and justice, and looked for a practical application of conflict resolution. Mediation looked like a good possibility. "Law is a male modality," she said. "It is hierarchical and authoritarian. Mediation is no panacea. It wouldn't have stopped a Hitler, for instance. But the process of people sitting down together, deciding what their problem is, and figuring out how to solve it peaceably is better than any other process we've got right now."

Marvel Cox. Guardian Angel. 1979. Painting.

To develop the Mediation Project, (the first for a university), Janet interested the administration, got a small foundation grant, hired a group of community mediators from Dorchester, Massachusetts, to train her staff, and opened the doors for business. Individuals walked in with roommate, noise, and property problems. Parents called with out-of-control children. A group of low-income housing residents asked the Mediation Project staff to help them work with the mayor's office. They wanted better access to city services. "In the beginning, none of us knew what we were doing," Janet said. "We were flying by the seat of our pants, opening ourselves to every possibility."

And something magic was happening. "The most powerful thing about mediation is that you take control over your life," she continued. "When people talk with each other, the success rate for resolving conflict is extraordinarily high. People say it changes their lives. Our biggest challenge is getting more cases, because people don't come to mediation voluntarily. We live in such a litigious society that we would rather deal indirectly with problems. The idea of sitting down with a third party, a community member, and talking about an issue is uncommon and scary."

Janet is trying to make it more common and less scary. One way to do that is to train local people and university students to be mediators. So far, over one hundred people have learned the skills, and now work as mediators for the Project. "People wonder why our mediators do this work for nothing," Janet said. "It's not an ego thing; they believe in the process. It's different from therapy. A therapist has a certain set of filters or theories when she hears a problem described. A mediator doesn't. She doesn't interpret, only helps people come to agreement. It doesn't matter what the agreement says. A mediator may think the agreement stinks or the relationship between people is horrible, but it doesn't matter. She only wants them to resolve the conflict without violence and do it outside the courts."

Janet is excited by mediation, but also skeptical. Ultimately she wants to unearth the underlying roots of violence, and she's not sure mediation training will do it. "I'm sure all these people will use their skills in good ways," she concluded. "Lawyers will not simply be litigators; they will also be conciliators. Therapists and ministers will use it. But sometimes I wonder if it will really make a difference. Will it just be used for disputes between neighbors and relatives, and not have a dramatic impact on policy making or resource use? Will this whole conflict resolution mode change the distribution of power in a patriarchal system?"

Two thousand miles west, in Boulder, Colorado, **Susan Carpenter** got a chance to answer Janet's questions. ROMCOE, the organization she co-directs, works with industry people, government representatives, and environmentalists who are in conflict about environmental issues. So far, all three groups have seen the benefit in non-litigous resolution. "Pragmatic business people like chief executive officers are recognizing that they spend far too much on legal fees," Susan said. "When they 'win,' they haven't won anything, and they've got bad public relations in the process. They are fascinated with the notion of sitting down and working out problems. 'Do you really think we can do it?' they ask. The three groups don't have to love each other, and they don't. But by working through a carefully managed process, they can jointly solve their problems.''

The Metropolitan Water Roundtable Project (MWRP) was one success story. Thirty-one parties, including six mayors, four county commissioners, numerous environmentalists, the Denver Water Board, and farmers were locked in battle over the use of water flowing off Denver's Rocky Mountain west slope. "There was tremendous animosity," Susan said. "Suburbanites on well water hated city dwellers on Denver's city system; skiers on the west slope feared Denver would take water from their communities; agricultural users on the plains worried that water would never get past Denver to reach their farms. Twelve lawsuits were on the table when we began."

Susan and her colleagues didn't start with water issues. "Part of conflict management is getting down to the nitty-gritty issues," she explained, "but the other part is building relationships, overcoming stereotypes and misperceptions. In conflict management, you have to improve communication first."

Members of the Roundtable spent the first two sessions developing a code of conduct and ground rules: decisions would be made by consensus, and participants would only speak for and about themselves to the rest. "These meetings were fruitful, and members began to experience agreement. Next, the thirty-one participants identified their interests. "Positions and interests are the heart of the matter," Susan said. "Positions are statements like 'I want a dam,' or 'I don't want a dam.' Interests are things like 'I want to preserve wildlife,' or 'I want protection against floods,' or 'I need water for my crops.' When you get people off their positions and onto their interests, they see that though the positions are different, the interests may not be mutually exclusive."

On the basis of interests, the group divided into four task groups, and began to study the water issue. After months of study, they reported back with options and began to negotiate. "By then, the parties had enormous respect for each other," Susan said. "They had worked with people they had neither had previous access to, nor any relationship with. And though the process took time, it was shorter than litigation and much more satisfying. Everyone was generally pleased. They felt this was how business should be conducted, and most of them wanted to acquire more skills in conflict management.

Sandra Boston applies peace habits to civil disobedience actions, not just to interpersonal or community conflicts. At her nonviolence training workshops, she stresses three points. "When you confront an opponent," she said, "you first seek to understand what the other person wants you to understand. This is more than active listening. It is taking in the experience of the other—not just what they are feeling, but why. Secondly, look for areas of agreement. Noticing common interests is a way of joining with the person. And thirdly, when differences emerge, question the other person about their position; don't keep explaining yours over and over. Ask why they believe nuclear weapons are the best protection for their children. Ask them if they believe we could survive without them. You can lead people to the cracks in their logic, and they can lead you to yours.''

Sandra practiced this respectful process at the Seneca peace camp. "When townspeople came to harass us," she said, "the local sheriff said he couldn't guarantee our safety. So a small group of us agreed to be buffers between them and the women climbing the fence. One day I started talking to the man who was one of the most feared of our opposition. In the course of our conversation, I found out that his son had resisted the Vietnam draft, and spent time in jail for it. He was mad because when we were arrested, we all gave the name 'Jane Doe' instead of our real names.

"I explained that we didn't want to cooperate with the legal system or give the state the right to punish us," Sandra continued. "But to him, it looked like we were avoiding responsibility in a way that his son hadn't. Gradually, I found myself being persuaded by the humanness of his story, and as I listened and really heard him, he changed too. His voice softened; his body language shifted. The threat between us was gone, and we had a genuine dialogue about our lives."

The techniques that Sandra, Janet, and Susan teach can be applied throughout the culture. "We are a heterogeneous society," said Susan. "We have experienced conflict every day since we were born. In our families or communities, something is always going on. It is assumed that we know how to handle it, but none of us handles it well. And we have no classes, no teachers.

"I envision conflict management springing up all over," she concluded. "A state governor establishes an Office of Conflict Management to train state employees; a National Peace Academy has regional campuses to train citizens in peacemaking; and internationally, countries are encouraged to identify mutual interests like security or sovereignty. Eventually, conflict management becomes a household term."

## Imaging Peace

**Elise Boulding** does everything she can to encourage such envisioning. Like Frances Crowe, she has been doing peace work for decades. A Quaker and author of many books including, *The Underside of History: A View of Women Through Time*, she served on President Carter's National Peace Academy Commission, laid the groundwork for a program in Conflict Resolution Studies at Dartmouth while she chaired the sociology department there, and developed with Warren Ziegler a process for Imaging A World Without Weapons. "I go back and forth between three corners," she said. "Having people visualize the future so they are empowered in the present, helping people understand our present processes of negotiating conflicts, and exploring our relationships to society and to the universe through spirituality."

Elise is a relentless pursuer of peace, and she strives to help others clarify their images of the future. "In almost all civilizations, there has been some vision of the world as a 'peaceful garden,' " she said, "but we have lost this. No wonder our strategies get stale! We try the same old things with no sense of what the criteria are for nearing a goal because there is no real visualization of the goal itself. Only when we can visualize a world without weapons can we find a path to it."

Elise explained the imaging process. "I start with childhood memories," she said, "because going into the future requires the same kind of thinking that going into the past requires. Then I ask participants to imagine themselves thirty years in the future, and tell them there are no weapons there. As they imagine that world, I urge them to make their fantasies graphic and detailed—see faces, smell smells, feel the roughness or smoothness of objects. I ask what kind of families, agriculture, work, and government exist in their future world without weapons. When each person has a clear idea, they write it down and tell others about it. For the last step, I ask people to move back to the present, a few years at a time, and see what has to be done to create the vision. When people work backwards, they create a future history and know what steps to take to make their vision real."

Elise explained her vision in an interview for the *Valley Women's Voice*, "If all we can do is go around telling everybody there's a terrible threat, people will simply become paralyzed and not be able to work creatively," she said. "You can't scare people into peacemaking. And there's no fairy godmother for the planet who will make the bomb disappear. But it may recede gradually, like a setting sun. One day, it will simply fall below the horizon and be irrelevant because we will know so many other ways to deal with our need for security, our need to feel that we have a just and good and fair society and a fair share between societies. The bomb will simply disappear out of sight because it will be of no use."[12]

Sandra Boston saw a scene in a movie once that made a lasting impression. A man was picketing the White House in the middle of the night, carrying a placard about stopping war. Nobody was there to see him except a night watchman who walked over to the man and said, "You know, you aren't going to change the world." The protester kept on marching but said, "I'm trying to keep the world from changing me."

Women peacekeepers crusade against a world of violence. They protest, disobey, and refuse to cooperate with generals, Pentagon strategists, and Provincial evacuation plans. They are practicing peace habits, saying "No" to war and warmaking. And they are doing this peacefully. They reject the violent tools handed down to them, turn away from destructive methods. Instead, they set their minds on worlds without weapons, mediation, respect for opponents, tolerance for difference. They embrace the whole, seek to reduce threat, plaster cities with handouts proclaiming victory over violence.

Of course, they have miles to go before they sleep. Like Sisyphus, they push against a stone so heavy, so primeval, so indefatigable, that they wonder if they are making any progress at all. It is hard to tell. War plans continue; citizens kill and maim each other. Yet the women persist. In the face of insurmountable odds, they choose life, insist on it, rally and cry for it, rage and wail for it.

"What is the most important issue facing women today?" Frances asked.

And thousands of women answer, "That life prevail."

Rosie Thompson. Oracle #6. 1984. Mixed media (straw, bones, ribbons, paint, rocks, nylon, cement fragments, bamboo). 42" x 16"x 12". (Photo: Richard Faughn)

# SOLSTICE

*This year goes down and never will return*
*unless we beat on drums and kindle fires—*
*candle and evergreen—unless we learn*
*to scare away our darkening desires.*
*We could succumb still, welcoming this night,*
*laugh in the chill, singing as we hold,*
*embrace in darkness, drink to the end of light,*
*then plunge into the chasm of the cold.*

*But we evade the darkness once more, when*
*clamber to the surface of our days,*
*there to be suspended once again*
*like ash upon the tension of those rays:*
*thin sunshine. So we beat the solstice drums.*
*Scatter, darkness. This way daybreak comes.*

Ellin E. Carter

# AFTERWORD

# A MOVEMENT OF WOMEN

The Future Is Female.

I stared at the flyer shocked at the thought: the future *will* be female. As the idea resonated through me, something streamed down my body. The future will *also* be female—not just male as it's been for the past two thousand years, as it is in the present.

*Chingoa*!

The responsibility of rising from the dirt, legitimizing that marginated being called woman, "the abysmal part of bodily man," seemed to me a certainty on that day in 1981, as certain as the crick in my neck from staring up at the flyer tacked on a wall at Oscar Wilde bookstore in the West Village. An idea I had been wrestling with in my writing began to take shape, to solidify. *Madre*!

But as the years went by, the doubts came, and the ranks of men, and women, putting down the women's movements swelled. The voices I'd heard during the last four years as I travelled cross-country doing gigs—reading my poems and stories, doing workshops, promoting *This Bridge Called My Back*—contained a counter-thread: The times are bad, dead. Women aren't doing political-spiritual work like in the 70s. Our movement's laying low, in stasis, decaying. It's going through repression, depression, backlash. We're suffering from divisionary tactics, from reactionary contraction, from a plague in our gay cities.

Along side the soprano and alto voices, I heard the deeper tenor and bass of the American media, corporate-owned and male, cackle with glee: Let's undermine the women libbers like we did the Black, Chicano, and Native movements; let's set them at each other's throats. Put a bunch of women together—Jews, Blacks, mixed bloods, yellow skins—and stay clear of their screeches and claws. Look at their movement shuffling, crawling on all fours, its lifeblood draining away like the others, death rattling in its throat. Didn't we tell you it wouldn't last, they say, making bereavement noises.

*Mintieron.*

They lied, *mijita*. Open this book. Bear witness to the truth. The slick suited vultures will have to feed on other dead not us. They lied. The movement has never stopped, has only changed its rhythm, trekked across plateaus, climbed over peaks, slid down abysses. Moving always. Going. *This Way Daybreak Comes* throws off that boot. Our throats now partially free, we shout sing film tape paint write laugh dance act out alternative responses, make up our own anthems.

We act.

We act, *'manita*, even when we sit in meditation (as so many of the women in this book do) silently connecting to our Source, *la Tierra Madre*. Our feet solidly on the ground, we patiently work on ourselves, undoing society's conditioning. But the women from the pages of this book do not stop there. These *carnalas* of the soul do not concern themselves solely with "working on" themselves. Nor do the political activists disdain things of the psyche and the spirit. This integration of the three, one flesh, one movement, lays to rest the painful splits of the past ten years, buries the flak I and others like me got from the activists who saw meditation and ritual, part of our daily lives, as "escaping" from the real world. And the so-called spiritual (how I dislike the word, it's trendy and fast becoming meaningless) people, oblivious to the political oppression of those less cultured or monied than themselves, looking down their holier-than-thou noses at our less enlightened mortals. *Gracias a diosa*, women such as these are committed to making changes in both internal and external landscapes.

A persistent chord weaves in and out of each chapter of *This Way Daybreak Comes*. What is it that I hear?

The sound of hands clasping, linking. An invisible link of hands. A few missing, yes—but not as many as male America would have us believe. Hands opening.

Hands coaxing, demanding of entrenched heartless institutions—family, business, education—that they treat woman fairly, humanly. Hands forming fists, flailing the walls when pleas avail nothing.

I hear a movement of hands doing ground-root work. Woman, alone, in groups, in whole *pueblos*, no longer feeling impotent. Woman responding, taking care of each other, the taking care a constant no matter how busy she is scrambling, getting through the living. Woman looking for the crack in the system, infiltrating. Woman sinking her teeth into the patriarchal arm, thigh. Woman with the patience of the marginated, the perseverance of the turtle, woman who won't let go until the monster reforms or bleeds to death. Woman who wants to change *norte america*, who has already begun to change the world.

Casting the coins. Coming up with responsibility.

Responsibility, I read in one of my I Ching books, casting the coins when feeling guilty for putting off the writing of this afterword—my first and I not sure I could do it well. Responsibility is the ability to respond. And that is what *This Way Daybreak Comes* is all about: Woman responding to harassment, to indignity, to starvation of the soul, to terror, and above all, to love—the human hand, woman's hand, reaching out, to touch, to comfort. The love of woman for woman, for anything alive.

Responding.

Woman, developing techniques for listening to Self and others, teaching methods for resolving conflict. Woman changing the way she relates to other women, to children, to men, to her environment; woman pushing at the boundaries of love, redefining family. Some of the women in *This Way Daybreak Comes* attempt to change the world by working their home turfs. A Native woman stays in the state of Montana, influencing and changing the lot of women there. A white woman works within the South Carolina political system, nudging it toward a more respectful stance on women's issues. A Black woman remains in South Chicago, surrounded by twenty-story project buildings where children are raped and abandoned, staying and mobilizing the neighborhood to halt the urban rot. From one end of the country to the other, women appear in this book, small town women city women old young white colored Jew, *mujeres fuertonas*, *chingonas*, ordinary common folk for the most part, with a smattering of movement "stars." Here are women with hands outstretched, pulling a sister up from the bloody pool on the floor, wheelchair, cockroach-and-rat-teeming tenement room

One movement.

"One mind. We felt yoked," Annie, the storyteller, told me talking about how she and Mary Clare struggled to put together the millions of fragments of stories from the words of the thousand women they interviewed. Though the particulars of each woman's *responding* differs, though their values, political views, and color of their skins differ, though some pull in different directions, there is a common movement: The reaching out to heal.

And though I have some criticisms of *This Way Daybreak Comes* (not enough voices from Native, disabled, lesbians working against AIDS, the absence of voices from the radical sexual fronts; the format—letting each woman speak, presenting fewer but fuller oral histories would have added more meat, variety, and poetry to the book; its pace and style), it documents the vital things women are doing. It charts women's attitudes, values, hopes for the future, visions. The strength, endurance, and perseverance of Mary Clare's and Annie's four years of single-focused work—a litany of hurts, a litany of patience, a litany of triumphs—crosses color class cultural borders. It deals with "otherness" and "differences" in new ways and affirms that difference can be a source of power.

*...if my part is to tell you who I am, your part is to tell me who you are. You have to reach out to women unlike you, women who do not speak your language, and tell them your stories, too.*
—Yolanda Tarango

When I read the last page, closed the covers, Yolanda's voice and the voices of the other women in *This Way Daybreak Comes* left me thirsting for more pieces of their stories, their whole stories, more stories, *otra vez*.

And that idea that I'd been wrestling with, whose images had kept me going through the hard times, sprang fully fleshed from *la Tierra Madre:* People's view of reality, their perceptions would change, revolve 180 degrees or perhaps a complete 360 degrees—but *only when their beliefs about woman changed.* A massive planetary revolution in attitudes, beliefs, in the very nature of "reality" awaits us somewhere in the present. For the future is now and female. Woman is the catalyst, the agent for change. They lied *mijita*, we are a movement of women moving toward daybreak, even when we're keeping still.

Gloria E. Anzaldúa
Brooklyn, NY
agosto 1985

## Notes

1. A quote from one of Jung's books, can't recall which.
2. Gloria Anzaldúa and Cherrie Moraga, editors, *This Bridge Called My Back: Writings By Radical Women of Color* (NY: Kitchen Table Women of Color Press, 1983).

*Madre* means mother. Used here it's like saying *Jesus*.
*Chingoa* is a Mexican word for damn.
*Mintieron* means they lied.
*Mijita* is an endearment which literally means my dear daughter.
*Manita* is short for hermanita which means little sister.
*Carnalas* signifies a deep kinship though not a blood kinship.
*Gracias a diosa* means thank Godwoman.
*Pueblos* means many things: towns, nations, group of peoples.
*Mujeres fuertonas, chingonas* means strong women, powerful.
*Otra vez* means once more.

# ABOUT THE AUTHORS

# ANNIE CHEATHAM

Annie Cheatham is the former director of the Congressional Clearinghouse on the Future. During her seven years working in Congress, she arranged meetings between leading futurists and Members of Congress, and developed a trend analysis program for Congressional staff. She also edited a widely-read newsletter, "What's Next," and served as liaison between members of the futures community and policy makers. She was born and educated in North Carolina, lived for three years in Taiwan, and has traveled extensively. This is her first book.

# MARY CLARE POWELL

Mary Clare Powell is a writer and visual artist. She has shown her work in Washington, D.C., taught college-level photography, and published *The Widow*, a collaborative book about her mother's experience of being alone and aging. She believes creativity is the most potent tool available for personal and social transformation, and she enjoys teaching and sharing the creative process. She was born and educated in Maryland, also lived in Taiwan, and has traveled around the world.

# HOW TO CONTACT
# THE AUTHORS

If you are not in this book, it doesn't mean you shouldn't be. We could neither meet most of the women we had names for, nor include all those we did interview. If you want to keep in touch with us, receive our mailings, or find these women and others, send letters to:

Institute for Women and the Future
P.O. Box 1081
Northampton, MA 01061

# PUBLISHER'S NOTE

I especially like this book because it lets me know about the tremendous range of constructive and innovative work that women all over the United States and Canada are doing. Women are using the energy of their lives to experiment with new possibilities, and in the process, they are creating the potential for a better future. Because Mary Clare Powell and Annie Cheatham have focussed on the positive aspect of each woman's contribution and because they have opened up their minds and hearts to as wide a variety of women's voices as they possibly could, this book is an inspiration.

Within the context of our present historical situation, despair for the future may be realistic. Yet as I read the pages of *This Way Daybreak Comes,* I gain energy and hope. Look at all the exciting things these women are doing! If they can contribute to the future, so can I.

Nina Huizinga
New Society Publishers

# NOTES

Part I: Women Relate

*Chapter 1: The Wise Woman Inside*

1. Betty Dodson, *Selflove and Orgasm* (New York: PO Box 1933, Murray Hill Station, 1983), p. 42.
2. Jacqueline Livingston, "1983 Calendar—The Backside" (327 North Albany Street, Ithaca, NY 14850).
3. *Ibid.*
4. Billie Potts, *Witches Heal: Lesbian Herbal Self-Sufficiency* (Bearsville, New York: Hecuba's Daughters, 1981), p. 3.
5. Starhawk, *Dreaming the Dark: Magic, Sex, and Politics* (Boston: Beacon Press, 1982), p. 4.
6. *Ibid.*, p. 3.
7. *Ibid.*, p. 13.
8. *Ibid.*, p. 155.

*Chapter 2: Making Love*

1. Mary Daly, *Gyn/Ecology: The Metaethics of Radical Feminism* (Boston: Beacon Press, 1978), p. 3.
2. Carson McCullers, "A Member of the Wedding," *Critics' Choice:*

*New York Drama Critics' Circle Prize Plays, 1935-55* New York: Hawthorn Books, Inc., 1955), p. 471.
3. Mary Clare Powell, *The Widow* (Washington, D.C.: Anaconda Press, 1981), p. 24.
4. astra, "coming out celibate," *Celibate Woman Journal* (July, 1982), Vol. 1, No. 1, pp. 3-4.

*Chapter 3: New Kin*

1. Clarissa Atkinson, "American Families and 'The American Family': Myths and Realities," *Harvard Divinity Bulletin* (December 1981-January 1982), p. 10-11.
2. Barbara Vojejdo, "Single, Black Mother's Woes are Explored," *Washington Post*, May 6, 1984, p. B3.
3. Karen Lindsey, *Friends as Family* (Boston: Beacon Press, 1981), p. 9.
4. Margaret Mead in an address to the Congressional Clearinghouse on the Future, Washington, D.C., February, 1977.
5. James Mitchell, ed., *The Random House Encyclopedia*, revised edition (New York: Random House, 1983), p. 303.
6. *Ibid.*

*Chapter 4: The Grass is Greener Here*

1. Maryat Lee, "Indigenous Theater: Plays Without Actors," *Coevolution Quarterly* (Fall 1984), No. 43, p. 104.
2. *Ibid.*, p. 107.
3. "A Successful Art Product with a Social Impact," *La Comunidad: Design, Development, and Self-Determination in Hispanic Communities* (Partners for Livable Press, Washington, D.C., 1982), p. 15.
4. *Ibid.*, p. 16.
5. *Ibid.*, p. 25.
6. *Ibid.*, p. 24.
7. *Ibid.*, p. 20.
8. *Ibid.*, p. 24.

*Chapter 5: Meeting At the International Well*

1. Catherine Menninger, "Soviet American Media Exchange 1984: A Report," California Committee of Print and Broadcast Journalists, pp. 5-9.
2. Martha Stuart, "Village Solutions Make Global Community," *InterMedia* (September 1981), Volume 9, Number 5, pp. 35-36.
3. Menninger, p. 17.

## Part II: Women Create

### Chapter 6: How Do You Phone The Women's Movement?

1. Martha Stuart, "Village Solutions Make Global Community," *Intermedia* (September 1981), Vol. 9, Number 5, p. 34.
2. *Ibid.*

### Chapter 7: Be Disarming—Create

1. Lucy Lippard, *Overlay* (New York: Pantheon Books, 1983), p. 10.
2. *Ibid.*, p. 5.
3. *Ibid.*, p. 6.
4. Dorothy Seiberling, "A New Kind of Quilt," *New York Times Magazine*, October 3, 1982, p. 48.
5. Lippard, p. 13.
6. Saphira Linden Bair, "Transformational Theater," *The Omega Arts Network Newsletter*, p. 33.

### Chapter 8: The Skin We Live and Work In

'1. Edward Hall, *The Hidden Dimension* (New York: Doubleday and Company, Inc., 1966), p. 129.
2. Hadley Smith, "Future Trends and the Designer: New Options and Obligations," *Journal of Interior Design* (Spring 1979), p. 12.
3. "Alternative Investment from the Women's Institute for Housing and Economic Development, Inc.," *Insight* (Fall 1983), No. 4, p. 4.
4. Smith, p. 7.
5. William Ronco, *Jobs: How People Create Their Own* (Boston: Beacon Press, 1977), p. 213.
6. Betsy Beavan, Selma Miriam, Pat Shea, Samm Stockwell, "Bloodroot: Four Views of One Women's Business," *Heresies #7* (Spring 1979), Vol. 2, No. 3, p. 65.
7. Leslie Weisman, "Women's Environmental Rights: A Manifesto," *Heresies #11* (1981), Vol. 3, Number 3, p. 8.

## Part III: Women Heal

### Chapter 9: The Feet of the Earth Are My Feet

1. Elizabeth Dodson Gray, *Patriarchy As A Conceptual Trap* (Wellesley, Mass: Roundtable Press, 1982), p. 83.
2. Sally Gearhart, "Female Futures in Women's Science Fiction," *Future, Technology and Woman: Proceedings of the Conference* (March 6-8, 1981), San Diego State University, pp. 41-42.
3. Baba Copper from an undated interview with Elana Freedom, Durham, N.C.

4. Elizabeth Wright Ingraham, "Knowledge as a Manageable Resource in Educational Systems," presented at the symposium, "The Optimum Utilization of Knowledge," University of Massachusetts at Amherst, November 5-8, 1981, p. 6.
5. *Ibid.*, pp. 10-11.
6. *Ibid.*, p. 12.
7. 1983 Bulletin, Wright-Ingraham Institute (1228 Terrace Road, Colorado Springs, CO 80904, 1983), p. 3.
8. Molly Raunells, a statement about Crossroads Community (The Farm) from Bonnie Sherk's collage, "An Alternative to Alternative Art Spaces," 1979.

*Chapter 10: Rewriting the Social Contract*

1. Gloria Anzaldúa, ed., *This Bridge Called My Back: Writings by Radical Women of Color* (New York: Kitchen Table: Women of Color Press, 1981, 1983), p. 169.
2. Sr. Theresa Kane, "1984 New Year Message From Theresa Kane: A Pastoral on Women" (Silver Spring, MD: Mercy Center Washington, January, 1984), p. 1.
3. Anzaldúa, from the Foreword to the Second Edition of *Bridge*.

*Chapter 11: Waging Peace*

1. Alice Walker, "Only Justice Can Stop a Curse," *Home Girls: A Black Feminist Anthology*, ed. Barbara Smith (New York: Kitchen Table: Women of Color Press, 1983), p. 354.
2. *Ibid.*, p. 355.
3. Joanna Macy, "Despair Work," *Evolutionary Blues* (Arcata, California 95521), Issue #1, p. 37.
4. *Ibid.,* p. 47.
5. "They Will Not Be Moved," *Nuclear Times* (May 1983), p. 20.
6. Hollis Giammatteo, "Alone Together," *Journal of the Walk* #3 (August-September 1984), p. 5.
7. Dorothy Grenada and Charles Gray, "International Fast For Life" (Fast for Life Resource Center, 4848 East 14th Street, Oakland, CA 94601, May 1984), flyleaf.
8. Judy Smith, Sheila Smith, Leslie Burgess, "Peace Habits: A Feminist Tool for Achieving Peace" (self-published, 315 South 4th Street East, Missoula, MT 59801, 1983), p. 2.
9. *Ibid.*, p. 23.
10. *Ibid.*, pp. 4-16.
11. *Ibid.*, p. 21.
12. Phyllis Rodin interview with Elise Boulding, "Imagining Peace," *Valley Women's Voice* (University of Massachusetts at Amherst, April 1984), p. 6.

Authors' Note: All material in quotation marks and not footnoted was taken from taped interviews.

"Solstice" is collected in *I Name Myself Daughter and It Is Good: Poems of the Spirit,* edited by Margaret Honton, (Sophia Books, 1719 Eddystone Avenue, Columbus, Ohio 43224, 1981), p. 132.

# LIST OF ILLUSTRATIONS

43        Charlotte Robinson (designer and cutter). Daphne Shuttleworth, Ruth Corning (assistants). Wenda F. Van Weise (silkscreen). Bonnie Persinger (piecing). Betty Guy, Gena Simpson, Lena Behme (assistants for piecing). Signature Quilt #1. from "The Artist and The Quilt" Exhibit. 1983.

47        Olivia Bernard Wilson. Tree Figures. 1983. Plaster, Gauze, Wood, Wire. 10".

51        Deborah Jones. Bark Mask #5. 1978. Wood, Bark, Ailanthus with flax fiber. 10" x 8" x 3". (Photo: Elizabeth Liaquer)

55        Colleen Sterling. Inner Space. 1978. Watercolor on Paper, Cut-out and raised on foamcore, mounted in shadow box. 12" x 15".

58        Arlene Hartman. Soul Compressions. 1984. Graphite on Basinwerk. 5" x 38".

65        Janet Braun-Reinitz. Empty Bed of Roses IV—Geometry Quilt. 1981. Colored Pencil on Paper. 27" x 39".

67        Judith Baca. The Great Wall of Los Angeles—Detail Olympic Section. 1983. (Photo: Gia Roland)

74        Helen Redman. In the Palm of Our Hand. 1983. Oil Painting. 50" x 34".

78        Mariagnese K. Catteneo. Installation I (Lesley Collage). 1985. Cheesecloth and Acrylic. 120" x 120" x 120". (Photo: Nora Charleston)

83        Elizabeth Vail. Orange Kimono. Full Kimono is 7'x 8½'.

87        Anita Segalman. Rodomishl. (detail) 1983. Silk, barbed wire, wood. (Photo: Douglas Parker)

88        Shereen LaPlantz. Untitled. Basket—plaited, sewn, and knotted flat paper fiber split, half round and round reed, sewn with waxed linen. 9" x 17" x 17".

95        Ann Taylor Gibson. Earth/Sea Ritual Pouches. 1984. Mixed Media—hand made paper, ribbon, thread stone, shells. 12" x 16".

96        Menucha. Sisters of Lilith. 1981. Papercut. 24" x 36".

105        Heather Howarth. Saturn Cycle. Oilstick craypas on paper.

106        Laura Catanzaro. Amazon. Mixed Media on Plywood. 1980.

111        Kathy Schilling. Peppers. Embroidery sculpture.

112        Nancy Dahlstrom. When is the Time to Take Off the Bindings? Rape Journal Drawing. 1982.

118        Nelleke Langhout-Nix. Phases of the Moon. (detail) Mixed media wall hanging. 80″ x 62″. 1978. (Photo: Roger Schreiber)

123        Mischief Mime (Top: Barbara Anger, Bottom: Anne Rhodes) (Photo: Connie Saltenstall)

124        Pat Vecchione. Ice Environment From a Future Time. (detail) Polyester resin.

126        Laura Shechter. Composition in Blue. 1980. Oil on masonite. 13″ x 11″. (Photo: eeva/inkeri)

130        Ann Langdon. Untitled. 1980. Acrylic/enamel/plexiglass.

140        Mary Frances Fenton. Solstice Circle Plan. 1982.

145        Patricia Johanson. Swan Orchid House. 1974. Ink and charcoal. 24″ x 45″. (Photo: Eric Pollitzer). Patricia Johanson's gardens are often macrocosmic projections in stone and earth of very small organisms— bacteria, lichens, leaves, plants, butterflies, lizards.

146        Barbara Chenicek and Rita Schiltz. Harvest Sanctuary of Central Liturgical Space. Dominican Chapel of the Plains. Great Bend, Kansas. (Photo: Thomas Treuter)

151        Myrna Shiras. Unbound Pages. Stitched relief painting. 31″ x 38″ x 4″. (Photo: Janice Felgar)

155        JEB (Joan E. Biren). Building the Boardwalk for the Differently-Abled Resource Area at the Michigan Music Festival. 1983. Photograph.

163        Teri Carsten. Vermont 1981. Photograph.

164        Marsha Hewitt. Autumn Ritual. 1981. Environmental sculpture at Yaddo. 80′ x 200′.

171        Betsey Damon. 7,000 Year Old Woman. 1977. Prince Street, New York City. (Photo: Su Friedrich)

172        Bonnie Sherk. Schematic Plan for A Living Library. 1983. Hand colored drawing. 24″ x 36″.

177        Faedra Kosh. The Mind of Gaia #2. 1984. Painting.

181        Deborah Kruger. Crosses to Bear (detail). 1984. Collage.

186        At the Foot of the Mountain Theater. Ismene says goodbye to her sister Antigone. from "Antigone Too: Rites of Love and Defiance." play by Martha Boesing. Premiere Performance, August 4, 1983. (Photo: Chris Parker)

188        Helen Redman. In the Palm of Our Hand. 1983. Oil Painting. 50″ x 34″.

193        Jay Goldspinner. Breastplate—Love/Anger. Papier-mâché.

201        Susan Boss. No-Nukes Wings. 1981. Mixed media. (Photo: George Dimock)

202        Arlene Hartman. :Epitaph for Later. 1984. Charcoal and masking tape on paper. 30″ x 22″.

209        Sisters of Survival. Pictured l. to r.: Cheri Gaulke, Anne Gauldin, Sue Maberry. (Photo: Joyce Dallal)

213        Marvel Cox. Guardian Angel. 1979. Painting.

218        Rosie Thompson. Oracle –6. 1984. Mixed media (straw, bones, ribbons, paint, rocks, nylon, cement fragments, bamboo). 42″ x 16″ x 12″. (Photo: Richard Faughn)

# INDEX

## A

# D

# J  K

# L

# M

# N

# Q R

# S

# T

# U V

# W